Expect Us

Oxford Studies in Digital Politics

Series Editor: Andrew Chadwick, Royal Holloway, University of London

Expect Us

ONLINE COMMUNITIES AND POLITICAL MOBILIZATION

JESSICA L. BEYER

OXFORD
UNIVERSITY PRESS

Oxford University Press is a department of the University of Oxford.
It furthers the University's objective of excellence in research, scholarship,
and education by publishing worldwide.

Oxford   New York
Auckland   Cape Town   Dar es Salaam   Hong Kong   Karachi
Kuala Lumpur   Madrid   Melbourne   Mexico City   Nairobi
New Delhi   Shanghai   Taipei   Toronto

With offices in
Argentina   Austria   Brazil   Chile   Czech Republic   France   Greece
Guatemala   Hungary   Italy   Japan   Poland   Portugal   Singapore
South Korea   Switzerland   Thailand   Turkey   Ukraine   Vietnam

Oxford is a registered trademark of Oxford University Press
in the UK and certain other countries.

Published in the United States of America by
Oxford University Press
198 Madison Avenue, New York, NY 10016

Library of Congress Cataloging-in-Publication Data

Beyer, Jessica Lucia.
Expect us : online communities and political mobilization / Jessica L. Beyer.
   pages cm
Includes bibliographical references and index.
ISBN 978-0-19-933076-8 (pbk. : alk. paper) — ISBN 978-0-19-933075-1 (hardcover :
alk. paper)   1. Online social networks—Political aspects.   2. Social media—Political
aspects.   3. Political participation—Technological innovations.   4. Communication in
politics—Technological innovations.   5. Young adults—Political activity.   6. Youth—Political
activity.   I. Title.
HM742.B49 2014
302.30285—dc23
2013051016

9 8 7 6 5 4 3 2 1
Printed in the United States of America
on acid-free paper

For my mother, Catharine Hoffman Beyer, who taught me how to write.

Contents

List of Figures

List of Tables

Acknowledgments

When I was working on the final revisions of *Expect Us*, Anonymous organized its biggest "in real life" protest yet—the Million Mask March. Unlike the 2008 protests that I document in this book, which were largely located in industrialized, Western countries, the Million Mask March occurred in hundreds of cities across the globe, including protests in the so-called Global South. While the total number of protesters in each location is still unclear at the time of this writing, photos circulated and verified on Twitter showed protests from London to Washington, D.C., from Bangkok to Sao Paulo.

If someone had told me in 2007 that I would be watching such protests in 2013, I would not have believed it. When I began the research for *Expect Us* in 2007, Anonymous was not a political actor; the Guy Fawkes mask was not yet ubiquitous in protests around the world; The Pirate Bay's administrators had not yet lost in court; and the Pirate Parties had yet to begin winning votes. I was sure that what was happening in social spaces online mattered for politics, but I had no real-world evidence. Thus, setting forward on the research path that led to *Expect Us* was something of an act of faith, and it is not a path I could have walked without a large community of scholars, colleagues, friends, and family.

I would not have been able to pursue this topic or complete the thesis that served as an early draft of this manuscript without my doctoral dissertation committee at the University of Washington: Joel Migdal, Phil Howard, Gina Neff, and Michael McCann. Joel Migdal has known me for nearly two decades and his intellectual integrity, gifted teaching, loving mentorship, and faith in my abilities have changed my life. Phil Howard and Gina Neff are walking, breathing role models for any aspiring academic. They have each been generous with time, encouragement, advice, and they have graciously mobilized their considerable networks on my behalf. Michael McCann has been a constant source of thoughtful comments and support. Together and separately, these four wonderful people have guided me and advocated for me with humor and kindness. I am grateful beyond measure to have them in my life.

In addition to my committee members, Catharine Hoffman Beyer, Arda İbikoğlu, Fenwick McKelvey, Iza Hussin, Laura Osburn, Nathan Lee, Richard Beyer, Emily Beyer, and Jeremy Pritchard read and reread crucial portions of the manuscript. Each offered support while I researched and wrote, listened to ideas, asked pointed questions, and each gave me the gift of their faith in my work when my own confidence faltered. Fenwick McKelvey receives all the credit for the book title. Arda's advice to me early on in the process is one that I still return to in every research project: "What is the question that is in your heart? That is the question you need to answer."

While writing *Expect Us* I was also privileged to work closely with other people who helped me in my thinking and work. Sara Curran has been a mentor, a colleague, a friend, and a constant source of support. Jennifer Earl's work has been an inspiration, and working with her has been a great collaborative experience. Ellis Goldberg's intellectual fire, honesty, and fierce collegiality have been a model for me in all of my interactions. Don Hellmann has offered unwavering support, stories, and care-filled advice. Stephanie Hofmann was my first moment of true intellectual partnership. Kim Johnson-Bogart, a dear friend, has been a source of support and inspiration for how to live with intellectual adventure and expansiveness. Christine Ingebritsen gave me my first moment of understanding what was possible for female scholars; she has been my longtime advocate and introduction to those "colder states to the north" that (as she predicted!) always find their way into my research. David Notkin, who is so deeply missed, became an unexpected rock of support—offering me the gift of his insight, his time, and his friendship. Each of these people shaped my thinking in important ways, and if you read closely, you can hear each of their voices in this manuscript.

Many others offered a wide range of support, help at key moments, and comments at critical junctures in the writing and research process: Hala Annabi, Lance Bennett, Mary Callahan, Jim Caporaso, Manuel Castells, Rachel Cichowski, Kate Crawford, Robin Datta, Karen Fisher, Kirsten Foot, Deen Freelon, Steve Herbert, Muzammil Hussain, Elisabeth Jones, Natascha Karlova, Dave Karpf, Beth Kier, Tuna Kuyucu, Jon Mercer, Andrés Monroy-Hernández, Karine Nahon, Heather Pool, Tilde Rosmer, Shawn Walker, and Susan Whiting.

In addition, I am grateful for my students over the years. They have made me a better speaker, a better writer, and a nicer person.

I was able to complete the manuscript of my book because I received invaluable support from the Center for Global Studies while serving as a postdoc in the Henry M. Jackson School for International Studies at the University of Washington. I am grateful to Sara Curran, Don Hellmann, Reşat Kasaba, and Tamara Leonard for this opportunity.

I am also grateful for the helpful editorial team at Oxford University Press including the anonymous reviewers whose tough but kind and constructive comments helped me revise the manuscript. Andy Chadwick and Angela Chnapko at Oxford were both helpful and encouraging, offering useful writing advice and other guidance, and I feel lucky to have worked with them.

It is important to note that portions of the book draw upon or are taken from an article I wrote for the *Journal of Computer Mediated Communication* titled "The Emergence of a Freedom of Information Movement? Anonymous, WikiLeaks, the Pirate Party, and Iceland." Pieces of this article appear in the introduction, the chapter about The Pirate Bay, and the conclusion.

I also owe a huge debt of gratitude to all of the people across all of the online spaces that I watched. They entertained and delighted me throughout my research. I now have an unexpected array of dear friends from the online world that inspired this text as well, including all of Smashing, in particular AJ, Adam, Josh, Joe, David, all three Matts, Dan, Lake, Erin, Chris, Ann, and Yalçin. Also, I thank Bill, and everyone in the IC, particularly Steve, Stuart, Robbie, Jacquie, Rene, Matt, Shadow, and Johannes.

This project was sustained by my extended family and friends, some of whom were recruited to read pieces of the book manuscript and did so with good cheer. Many are mentioned above, but support and insights also came from Dave Lee, Susan Lee, Jonathan Lee, Tristan Lee, Maddi Lee, Adrienne Allen, Marty Shorb, Gabe Bogart, Anja Richter, Doug Judge, Kelly O'Conner, Mickey Grooters, Larry Grooters, Don Schlientz, Dorothy Schlientz, Art Hoffman, Lucia Hoffman, Phyllis Beyer, Kit Woods, John McFarland, Chandler Clifton, Devin McLachlan, Maryam Zahra McLachlan, Suhail McLachlan, Joe Piha, Cheryl Piha, Stephanie Gianarelli, Joan Graham, Gayla Shoemake, Stephen Pritchard, Wendy Pritchard, Ben Pritchard, Jonathan Pritchard, Rebecca Palmer, Craig Palmer, Ryan Palmer, Emma Palmer, Hilary Limont, Paul Limont, Bethany Stevick, Susan Hanley, Janie Beyer, Jessamy Whitsitt, Adam Gallant, Chris Niesing, Adam Pierce, Jillian Witt, Betsy Oliphant, Wendy Peters Moschetti, Morgan Moschetti, Russ Hugo, Kelly Whetstone, and Deborah Woolley.

Finally, my family has always been what makes everything possible: Catharine Hoffman Beyer, Richard Beyer, and Emily Beyer. My mother, who told me that mentioning her by name in my acknowledgments was "too dorky," read every single word of this manuscript through every iteration and revision. She read it so many times that she can probably recite it from memory.

And then there's Jeremy Pritchard, the best thing I ever found online or off, who reminds me of how lucky I am every day.

Expect Us

1

Online Communities and Political Mobilization

> Ha. You guys can complain all you want about the INTERNET HATE
> MACHINE becoming an activist group or political pressure group, but
> THERE'S NOTHING YOU CAN DO ABOUT IT.
> —Anonymous, February 13, 2008

In December 2010, the whistle-blowing website WikiLeaks went offline. In the days that followed, the US government successfully pressured corporations to stop providing infrastructural support to WikiLeaks. As WikiLeaks struggled to stay online, Anonymous hacktivist[1] groups mobilized on behalf of the site in the name of freedom of information. Anonymous groups' mobilization included successful distributed denial-of-service (DDoS)[2] attacks on the corporate websites perceived to be complicit with the US government—such as MasterCard and PayPal—as well as an informational campaign that some called the "first infowar." Simultaneously, various Pirate Parties, whose births and fortunes had been closely linked to the infamous file-sharing website The Pirate Bay, also entered into this conflict. Pirate Parties offered domain names, server space, and mirrored the WikiLeaks site, thereby ensuring that the content remained online.

As part of this action on behalf of WikiLeaks, these international groups of protesters used abstract rights rhetoric to articulate grievances combined with concrete action, such as hosting proxies, disseminating information, mirroring controversial content, and attacking the cyber and informational infrastructures of corporate and government websites. For the first time, the name "Anonymous" appeared simultaneously across major news sources internationally, as these actors appeared to behave in line with Sidney Tarrow's (1998, p. 2) definition of a social movement: "sequences of contentious politics that are based on underlying social networks and resonant

1

collective action frames, and which develop the capacity to maintain sustained challenges against powerful opponents." Even though their transformation into political actors had begun long before December 2010, the appearance of these groups of activists took many by surprise because their origins were highly populated online communities occupying *nonpolitical* websites.

Internet activists' work in support of WikiLeaks was a relatively new kind of activism that revealed an online political mobilization that is growing in force, frequency, and ferocity. However, this type of political activism is not the extent of the political behavior online. While explaining the emergence of entities such as Anonymous as political actors is important, it is also important to highlight the political "nonevents" that occur within online communities as well. Posting boards, file-sharing websites, video games, and other social spaces are often disregarded as potential fountain points of political activism because the interactions within them do not fit easily into conceptions of civil discourse and they remain unconnected to online political forums, blogs, or groups associated with building civil society. Further, in the most populated social spaces, a large portion of participants are often under the age of 30 and, therefore, are the age group scholars have considered the least politically engaged (e.g., Levine & Lopez, 2002). However, the drama surrounding WikiLeaks was the subject of heated political discussions across online social spaces, evidence for arguments that political conversation is the norm in every social space online (e.g., Munson & Resnick, 2011; Munson, 2012; Wojcieszak & Mutz, 2009).

As communication technology becomes more ubiquitous and the boundaries between our offline and online selves erode, online conversations, negotiations, and connections have become key to understanding politics. In social sites I observed, young people argued vehemently about politics without knowing each other's names. They taught each other about religion, diet, new music, art, and hacking. They opened windows for each other into dramatically different lifestyles, belief systems, and countries because of the friendships and fights they had online. They came out to each other and shared the photos of their new babies. They sent each other holiday gifts, shared their joys and despairs, and found lifelong friends. They changed their minds and did not change their minds; they were kind and cruel; and they even fell in love.

The mobilization on behalf of WikiLeaks is just one of the instances that show that politics are being transformed in these unexpected, darker, and more anonymous corners of the Internet. To explore this world of online communities, *Expect Us* focuses on communities occupying four of the online social spaces that millions of individuals entered, spent time in, and exited moment by moment between late 2007 to mid-2011. The communities are Anonymous, a community that emerged from the popular image-board system 4chan.org, with more than 3.2 million users in 2008 (and about nine million in 2011); The Pirate Bay, one of the world's most popular file-sharing websites with more than 25 million users; World of Warcraft, a popular massively multiplayer online role-playing game (MMORPG) with about 11.5 million players; and the posting boards attached to IGN.com, which had about one million registered users. As I discuss in the section on methodology (appendix), these communities were different in form, but like many online communities, none appeared likely candidates for political mobilization when I began my research.

In all four of these online communities, members engaged deeply with political issues in a range of ways. However, members of two of the communities moved beyond heated speech and began mobilizing politically—Anonymous and The Pirate Bay. Neither had been an obvious candidate for wide-scale political mobilization. It may be odd for those of us who have closely watched both Anonymous and The Pirate Bay become powerful political actors to imagine, but if anything, six years ago both seemed less likely to generate political mobilization than did other online communities, such as IGN.com's posting boards or World of Warcraft, where political discussions happen daily, and online and offline relationships are often connected. In contrast, although The Pirate Bay was founded and supported by many dedicated and hardworking activists who were outspoken opponents of conventional intellectual property rights, the majority of users appeared to be on the site for a purely commercial transaction—trading music files for music files. In addition, although Anonymous members had mobilized prior to the anti-Scientology protests, their mass mobilizations had been more about entertainment and breaking things online than about politics. Why then, if political behavior occurred in all four communities did some of these sites foster political mobilization among their participants while the others did not?

Drawing on ethnographic studies of the four communities, *Expect Us* shows that social spaces online are important sites for understanding politics. With that in mind, the book's central argument is that key structural features of the birthplaces of each online community shaped the type of political behavior that each manifested. I argue that higher levels of anonymity had a positive relationship with political mobilization and that anonymity within online communities is shaped by formal site rule systems and the availability of small-group or one-on-one interaction. This argument is counterintuitive in that we would expect small-group interaction and low levels of anonymity to foster group behavior. However, I demonstrate that the likelihood of political mobilization rises when a site provides high levels of anonymity, low levels of formal regulation, and minimal access to small-group interaction. The nature of the communities themselves—their cohesiveness, values, and emergent norms of behavior—then appears to influence whether there is a conflict between the dominant norms in the online community and offline legal and behavioral norms. Although this kind of online/offline normative conflict is by no means a perfect "recipe" for predicting political mobilization, in the cases I observed, it certainly appeared to set the stage for cohesive political action by an online community.

As is the case in any thick description of cultural contexts, I do not mean to ignore the myriad of other factors that influenced community shape, values, and collective action. In each case study other important factors emerge, such as the distinct cultural attributes of each community. However, these distinct cultural attributes are deeply linked to structure. For example, others have argued, as I do here and elsewhere, that the structural restrictions of 4chan.org that caused users to post anonymously turned anonymity into a cultural value (e.g., Beyer, 2011b; Knuttila, 2011; Coleman, 2012c; Sauter, 2012; and Simcoe, 2012). In the same way, I discuss the distinctive characteristics of each community as related to politics in *Expect Us* because those characteristics influenced outcomes. For example, in the case of World of Warcraft, the vast geographical space that a user must navigate while in the game and the game's demand that players create small groups to tackle challenges had a significant effect on whether WoW players mobilized politically. In contrast, in the case of The Pirate Bay the administrators of the site played a key leadership role in articulating a political agenda for users of the site who may not have otherwise framed their file-sharing as a political action.

However, even when buried in the details about a single case, I always returned to questions of how people were known in the community, the elements of the community space that enabled people to be known, how these characteristics relating to anonymity shaped the community itself, and, in turn, how they shaped the ways the community related to the rest of the world, online and off. In light of my findings about the presence of political conversations in all online communities, I argue that when examining online communities and asking questions about political engagement, it is these structural factors—anonymity, regulation, and spatial divisions—that researchers should first identify.[3]

Anonymity

Anonymity is credited with playing a central causal role in creating a multiplicity of outcomes within online communities—most of them negative. Although some political theorists, such as Przeworski (2010), have discussed the relationship between anonymity and democratic equality, prominent scholars of civil society such as Putnam (2000, p. 177) point to a decline in social capital occurring in places such as the United States due to the anonymizing impact of the Internet. In addition, although anonymity seemed to play a clear causal role in facilitating the political mobilization arising from 4chan.org and The Pirate Bay, journalists, in particular, have given anonymity causal power for so many divergent outcomes it is unclear what outcomes anonymity actually fosters. This indeterminacy largely stems from treating anonymity as a discrete characteristic of online space, when instead, as a structural characteristic or affordance of online space, it is inherently conditioned by other structural elements. A close look at anonymity online illustrates that it is not dichotomous, but rather it is conditional, changing in relation to other factors around it.

In discussions of online communities (and the Internet in general), anonymity is often discussed as a cause of negative behaviors such as hate speech or the posting of disturbing imagery (e.g., Chesney et al., 2009, p. 533; Herring et al., 2002, p. 371; or Zhuo, 2010). In response to this preconception, websites have been moving to policies that require users to use their "real names" when posting. The name requirement is often grounded in the problematic belief that "real" identities are a necessary condition to create civil interaction in online communities. Thus, the move to such policies is because anonymous sites are considered to be spaces where negative interaction will flourish (particularly when combined with low levels of moderation). Under this conceptualization, such spaces are considered to be rife with trolling,[4] social norms violations, and permissive of a range of content that would be defined as normatively "bad."

Many of the discussions of negative behaviors online argue explicitly or implicitly that the affordances of online space create an opportunity structure that allows bad behavior to flourish. In such cases, the idea of anonymity is dichotomized into "anonymous" and "not anonymous" (see Carey & Burkell, 2007). These anonymous spaces are usually spoken about as being lawless, filled with offensive content, and offering a place for dangerous individuals to flourish. For example, Suler (2004, p. 321) discusses the effects of anonymity in terms of an online "toxic disinhibition effect," which allows individuals to say and do things online that they would not otherwise do in the "real world." For Suler, "dissociative anonymity" is one of the central causes of this behavior online (p. 322). This idea was expressed humorously in the often cited Penny Arcade comic (2004) titled the "Internet Fuckwad Theory," which posited that Normal Person + Anonymity + Audience = Total Fuckwad. In this vein, the anonymity of the Internet also is spoken about as fostering online communities that are viewed negatively, such as pro-anorexia communities, known as "pro-ana" communities.[5]

Such a dichotomous understanding is problematic because there is substantive evidence from a range of researchers that online anonymity does not just create normatively negative behavior, but it also enables normatively positive behavior. Scholars have discovered that conversation in anonymized spaces can be far more open than conversations in the offline world because the veil of anonymity allows people to ask questions that they might not be willing to ask offline or when using their legal names. For example, women living outside Muslim countries writing to fatwa-issuing websites often ask personal questions related to their bodily health, questions that they might otherwise be afraid to ask offline (Beyer & Hussin, 2012).

Others have found that anonymized spaces also foster creativity and collaborative cultures. In 2011, Christopher Poole, the founder of 4chan.org, argued that 4chan.org's anonymity fostered a fiercely creative and collaborative culture. He stated that in such an environment a good idea, such as the lolcats (originally "Caturday"), must be adopted by community members because it is a good idea. Once adopted by community members, divorced from a single creator, the entire community can work on modifying, adapting, and formulating the idea. Poole asserted that such an environment would not occur in a space that was less anonymous because individuals' post counts and other identifying elements create hierarchies and status based on each user's reputation in the community. He claimed that in such spaces, reception of creative material is conditioned on an individual's social power and the power of cliques; furthermore, the idea would have ownership, making it more difficult to build upon the content. I observed this exact process in my comparison between 4chan.org and IGN.com, as have scholars such as Knuttila (2011) and Simcoe (2012), who both have focused on 4chan.org's culture.

Tied to the creative collaboration that can arise from anonymized spaces, scholars have found that they foster identity play. Some have found that this type of identity play allows individuals to explore personas, identities, orientations, and aspects of their personalities in places made safe by anonymity (e.g., Bell, 2010; DiMarco, 2003; or Simpson, 2005). Young people living in unsympathetic communities or with judgmental parents may find safe spaces online to explore their sexuality.[6] Transgender people may be able to use in-game avatars in spaces such as World of Warcraft to explore their gender identities without the same potential censoring and danger that exists offline (e.g., Allen, 2013). Identity play also encompasses the less nefarious sides of trolling, those trolls who engage in activities akin to performance art, as Bergstrom (2011) has shown looking at Reddit, or, as Coleman (2012d) has argued, those who take on the role of the trickster.

Anonymity does produce negative outcomes, particularly for marginalized and minority groups such as women (e.g., Herring, 1999; Herring et al., 2002). However, to say that anonymity solely creates negative interaction is to ignore that people regularly say and do inflammatory things online under their "real names" or under persistent online identities, as scholars such as Phillips (2013) and I (Beyer, 2011a) have noted. In fact, the greater the levels of approval from a given community, the more likely people are to feel free to express opinions and ideas that might be considered negative in other contexts. These online and offline normative contexts must also be taken into account when examining behavior that an outsider may consider to be normatively "bad." For example, on Facebook, an individual may express racist, homophobic, or misogynist opinions without censor and even with encouragement. Thus, these negative behaviors and the disproportionate impact they may have on already marginalized groups are not solely about anonymity, but also about broader cultural values and other structural features of an online space—such as anonymity.

While the popular press usually divides anonymity into dichotomous terms, scholars are more likely to divide anonymity into trichotomous terms, breaking it instead into a three-part categorization of "anonymous," "pseudo-anonymous"—those online spaces where individuals have unique aliased identities that are not their legal identities—and "not anonymous," which often means users post under their legal names. While this breakdown approximates the realities within online communities more accurately than a dichotomous conception of anonymity does, the categories of anonymous and pseudo-anonymous are still problematic because each encompasses a range of possible ways to be known in online spaces. To be fair, many mention anonymity as a contextualizing or facilitating factor within a particular online community rather than giving it a central causal role. For example, anonymity as an attractive feature of websites is mentioned within writing about pro-ana communities. Anonymity considered in this respect is not necessarily a causal factor, but rather as something that attracted individuals to the spaces and allows them to speak about a societally disproved topic with some freedom. That said, I found in World of Warcraft and IGN that persistent identities in an online community, even when aliases are used to mask legal identities, can have long-term implications for the community because individuals tend to protect their aliased identities in relation to community and offline norms.

Thus, anonymity alone is indeterminate as a cause of either positive or negative outcomes in online communities. As anonymity emerged from my research as important to understanding political outcomes, I realized that while anonymity did seem to be creating outcomes, it was not a concept for which one could create fixed ideal types. As I outline in the appendix, instead of such fixed categories, in the cases I explored anonymity appeared to be shaped by other aspects of an online space:

- The required use of legal names
- The required use of user names
- The use of static names
- The use of static names encouraged by sunk costs in a name, such as community "points" of some kind
- The use of indentifiers in the space, such as post counts, avatars, guilds, customizable features (Donath, 1998)
- The presence of searchable archives
- The use of IP tracking by site owners/administrators

For example, as I will discuss in chapter 5, IGN.com requires users to have a user name to interact with others. In addition, the site includes archives, where anyone can look up all the posts made by a particular user, and an extensive avatar system that includes icons, post counts, and registration date, among other factors. In contrast, as mentioned previously, 4chan. org is so anonymous that anonymity became a central community value. Users do not need to have user names to post in the space. The site has no archives, no post tracking, and no fixed avatars. However, although 4chan. org is anonymous, its administrators track users' IP addresses, making users far more "known" to site administrators than a user name would. In World of Warcraft, identifiers such as guilds are part of the game's design, but Blizzard Entertainment leaves guild regulation to the players. Guilds are created, policed, and maintained by users who are often using tools outside the game itself. In addition, in any space, even those that are completely anonymous, any individual at any time can reveal "real life" information about him- or herself—much as individuals do in the offline world.

Among the many ways that anonymity can matter when considering a particular outcome, the way that anonymity matters in *Expect Us* concerns

Table 1.1 **Causes of Political Mobilization in Online Communities**

	Mobilizers		Nonmobilizers	
	Anonymous	*Pirate Bay*	*World of Warcraft*	*IGN.com*
Level of anonymity	High	High	Low	Low
Level of formal regulation	Low	Low	Medium	High
(Level of informal regulation)	(High)	(High)	(High)	(High)
Opportunities for small-group interaction	Low	Low	High	Medium
Conflict between online and offline social and legal norms	Yes	Yes	No	No

the way it becomes a cultural attribute and the way in which individuals protect identity. In the case of this study, anonymity is important because in spaces in which users have identities over time, they will protect those online identities. Individuals will protect any online identity—even "aliases," such as user names or avatars. This protectiveness means that individuals will curtail inflammatory speech and avoid behavior that could draw censure from other users in such spaces.

Additionally, having an identity allows users to form interpersonal relationships, and, as I will discuss in chapters 4 and 5, interpersonal relationships seem to thwart political organizing in online spaces. Furthermore, in places where users have identities, hierarchies of individuals and groups can emerge. Such hierarchies allow some users to set and enforce rules that shape the behavior of other users, as is also discussed in the next section on regulation.

Table 1.1 provides a basic summary of the relationship of the four cases in this study to the three critical aspects of the technological space online, as well as tracking the level of conflict between online and offline norms in the four cases. As the table shows, the level of anonymity is high in both cases where political mobilization occurred—Anonymous and The Pirate Bay. In contrast, it is low in communities where political mobilization did not occur.

Regulation

In the four cases in *Expect Us*, the level of formal regulation on a website shaped anonymity profoundly and was instrumental in creating political outcomes. As table 1.1 shows, the level of formal regulation is medium to high in both cases that do not show evidence of political mobilization—WoW and IGN.com. However, formal regulation is extremely low in the two cases where political mobilization occurred—The Pirate Bay and Anonymous. Regulation is important because in spaces with high formal regulation, site "police" will often discourage behaviors that could turn into political action, including behaviors that conflict with offline norms and laws.

Like the discussion of anonymity, a discussion of formal rules within online communities must specify clearly what the concept of "formal rules" is before assigning the presence or lack of such rules a causal role. Much of our understanding of social systems rests on Hobbes's concept of a state of nature, which presupposes that any social space without a powerful, ordering actor is one in which abusive actors will exercise their power over the weak. Conversations about what institutional structures facilitate positive societal outcomes are common in political science and sociology and have a long lineage as attempts to understand the ways that institutions shape society and the relationship between state and society (e.g., Goldstein, 1993; Hall, 1986; Huntington, 1968; Migdal, 1988; Powell & DiMaggio, 1991; among many others). When dealing with nonoptimal outcomes, such as deviance or violence, scholars disagree about whether rules reflect societal norms or create deviants. However, in spite of this disagreement, scholars agree that there will always be those who are not captured by rule systems (e.g., Durkheim, 1893; Elias, 2000).

In contrast, in relation to the Internet, a vein of techno-utopianism implicitly and explicitly argues that controlling deviance online is a matter of engineering, rather than deviance being an inherent component of any human collectivity. In such a view, a site full of jerks is the natural outcome of bad site design. For example, Dash (2011) wrote a widely read blog post entitled, "If your website is full of assholes, it's your fault," which outlines the ways in which an online community can be kept civil through the use of measures such as constant moderation, community policies, and accountable identities. The idea that good community behavior is simply a matter of a robust moderation system is one that is often cited across the popular press as well as academic studies (e.g., Preece, 2001; Preece & Maloney-Krichmar, 2003; Wise, Hamman, & Thorson, 2006).

However, while a robust moderation system can minimize some negative behavior, much like anonymity, the difference between highly regulated sites and sites with minimal regulation is less a dichotomy than a continuum of rules that interact with other structural features. As outlined in the appendix, to understand the level of regulation in each of my four cases I focused on many aspects of regulation. These included the following:

- The number of official rules, types of Terms of Service/Use, End User Licensing, and other types of regulation
- The presence of open-ended rules that allow moderators to sanction users who have not violated a specific rule
- The level of presence of regulatory authorities in the space, such as moderators
- Searchable archives that allow regulators to sanction behavior after the fact
- Regulated speech, with offensive words/phrases forbidden
- Regulated conversation, with conversation topics forbidden
- Image regulation

Tied to these aspects of "formal" rules are community-level considerations, such as whether the community polices itself and whether informal rules in the community differ from the formal site rules. While the level of formal regulation appeared to be more influential in shaping anonymity within an online community, it is also worth mentioning that in every community informal norms had a profound impact on the behavior of participants. In nearly every case in *Expect Us*, some of the important community values and informal norms of behavior emerged as a consequence of the structure of the web space.

It could be said that anonymity and lack of formal regulation go hand in hand (co-vary) to such an extent that there is no need to make them analytically distinct concepts. However, although formal regulation and anonymity often go hand in hand in practice, this relationship is not required in theory. The use of IP address tracking by administrators means that site managers could create very extensive rule systems that were executed on the basis of those addresses, and the site itself could limit the view of such addresses to only moderators. Alternatively, some websites are pseudo-anonymous and require the use of a user name to post but have a very low level of regulation, such as Reddit, which has produced political mobilization, most notably in response to the Stop Online Piracy Act (SOPA) and the Protect IP Act (PIPA).

Spatial Divisions

The four online communities in this study represent widely divergent types of online communication spaces, and in every case the division of the interaction space had an impact on the nature of the community. The division of space can serve to create greater cohesion among community members, divide the community into factions, and allow community members to differentiate between new and older users. My findings suggest that spaces that do not allow for small-group interaction are more likely to produce political mobilization. As table 1.1 shows, the availability of opportunities for small-group interaction is low for both sites where political mobilization occurred. In contrast it was medium to high for both sites where there was political conversation but no mobilization. This appeared to be the case even though in every community participants were drawing on an array of "off-site" tools and online spaces to facilitate conversation and mobilization, such as Anonymous activists' use of the IRC,[7] World of Warcraft players' use of voice software such as Ventrilo, and IGN users' frequenting of other posting boards and instant messaging programs, such as MSN Messenger.

I found that in spaces where speech is controlled and individuals are allowed to break into small groups, users will find other people who share their belief systems. In chapter 4, I examine why WoW players have not mobilized politically. I argue that WoW players find enclaves of other players whose beliefs about appropriate speech, fairness, and scarce resource divisions are consistent with their own beliefs. These groups tend to crosscut traditional cleavages (with the possible exception of guilds with age requirements or GLBTQ friendly guilds),[8] with no grouping patterns emerging other than beliefs and time availability for group activities. For example, in the North American realms, Canadians are not forming Canada-only groups, and even language-specific guilds are rare. The ability to be known and the availability of small-group communication mean that differentiation between beliefs can become very finely grained. For example, one group may prohibit the negative use of the word "gay" while another may not, and this difference would be considered a strong distinguishing mark between the two groups.

In contrast to these subtle divisions, in spaces in which levels of anonymity are high, regulations low, and opportunities for small-group interaction minimal, belief is much more coarsely identified than in the nuanced and diverse gradations found in WoW. For example, a belief in the concept of "freedom of information" has become dominant across users in Anonymous and The Pirate Bay. What precisely "freedom of information" means can vary, but at the foundation of the concept is the idea that "information wants to be free"—an old hacker ideology that argues against any restriction on the transmission of information. In online communities, the idea of freedom of information tends to encompass a range of freedoms, but it has at its foundation the argument that communication in any form should not be restricted. It usually encompasses an idea that accurate public information can be made widely available without fear of censure or punishment. It often also includes an implicit argument for greater government and corporate transparency and, in some cases, includes an argument for the dramatic revision or removal of current intellectual property regimes.

While the most crucial spatial division to political behavior is whether the online space facilitates small-group interaction or not, other aspects of spatial division also appeared to be important in ways that are usually related to anonymity. For example, in cases where the communication interface is difficult to use, the difficult interface appears to serve as an entry barrier to new users; such barriers can lead to greater group cohesion. Additionally, when users do not have to be present for important community events in order to know about them, group cohesion is lower than when they do need to be continually present. In the former case, anyone can "pretend" to be a community member. As the spatial divisions are widely varied, I discuss them in greater detail in each case chapter.

Normative Conflict

Factors such as anonymity, regulation, and spatial divisions lead to the development of distinct communities, each with its own norms, beliefs, and behavior expectations. As illustrated in table 1.1, when community norms develop in such a way that online norms conflict with offline norms and legal realities, there is a greater likelihood of political mobilization than when such conflicts are not present.

Speaking in generalities about normative conflict, both behavioral and legal, is difficult because of the diversity of offline contexts occupied by community participants in all four communities I studied. Community members stand inside their own social, political, and legal contexts, even as they interact in the many cross-national spaces of the Internet. Therefore, it would be inaccurate to say anything but that the online world can be conceived as millions of online worlds that overlap and connect in unexpected ways. These vast continents of conversation, file-sharing, gameplaying, picture rating, and innumerable other activities, are divided in a multitude of ways, including language, demographics, layers of state control, custom, and infrastructure. However, the online communities in this book are all largely populated by individuals living in liberal democratic countries, which are either made up of English speakers or speakers who have extensive English language education. The common language means that behavioral challenges will be understood, and the similar legal, political, and economic traditions mean that legal challenges will be understood as well. The implication is that there are similar enough elements across offline contexts that online norms will pose similar but varied challenges to offline norms across these societal contexts.

Scholars such as Papacharissi (2005) and Baym (2002, p. 42) have convincingly argued that distinctions between the online and offline—"real life" in contrast with what happens online—are not analytically useful. Scholars such as Phillips (2012b) have pointed out that the online and offline spaces are not only wrapped up in each other but reflect each other. For example, Phillips (2012b) and Bakioglu (2009) both argue that trolls are mirroring "offline" culture and media and should not be exotified as a solely online phenomenon.

However, while the online is deeply connected to the offline, as I noted previously, each community is a distinct cultural space with its own set of values and norms. 4chan.org's cultural influence online illustrates these divisions. The online world in which Anonymous carries cultural power is not occupied by everyone who is online. For example, individuals familiar with or people who are a part of Anonymous would be aware of concepts such as "Rule 34." (Rule 34 is "If it exists, there is porn of it.") Users who have heard of Anonymous but who are not direct participants in the Anonymous communities may not know about Rule 34, but they may be aware of Anonymous-produced memes such as lolcats[9] or Rickrolling.[10] Meanwhile, users whose online worlds do not intersect with Anonymous in any way may have never heard of any of these phenomena.

The cases I examine here do not necessarily share a culture, but the communities intersect and overlap in a multitude of ways and have a common cultural context. Over the course of my observation, I discovered that members in each of the four online communities were aware of the existence of the other communities. Anonymous and 4chan.org were repeatedly mentioned on IGN.com, as was WoW. There was limited mention of The Pirate Bay, perhaps because it was frustrated by the IGN.com site rule preventing discussion of piracy. In 2009, a quick survey found many WoW players had named their characters after some of the most common Anonymous "inside" jokes, and WoW general channels were full of Anonymous phrasing and allusions to Anonymous jokes long before Anonymous culture became ubiquitous online. The easiest to spot was the classic 4chan.org sentence structure—"bad player is bad" or "obvious player is obvious." Finally, Anonymous has mobilized on behalf of The Pirate Bay, and many WoW characters are named after The Pirate Bay or some term related to The Pirate Bay.

Figure 1.1   Andrés Monroy-Hernández's Word Cloud of Five Million 4chan Posts.
Copyright 2011 by Andrés Monroy-Hernández. Reprinted with Permission.

Therefore, while the distinction between the online and offline world
may be blurred, it is important to identify both the boundaries of each community and to pay attention to where they intersect, in order to define the
online world under study. Once the online world is defined, it is possible to
observe the norms at work in each community and note where those norms
overlap. Recording the boundaries of each online world clarifies the online
norms enacted in the sites so that conflict between those norms and those of
the offline "worlds" becomes visible.

Prior to the use of DDoS attacks and other illegal "hacking" strategies,
Anonymous's central conflict with offline norms was a conflict with norms
of appropriate behavior and speech. For example, figure 1.1 is a word cloud[11]
of five million 4chan.org posts created by Andrés Monroy-Hernández as
part of a study on anonymity and ephemerality on 4chan.org's general topic
board (Bernstein et al., 2011). While norms of appropriateness, of course,
vary depending on individuals, communities, and societies, many of the
words in the word cloud would be inappropriate in most English-speaking
public settings. In addition, such words are often accompanied by imagery
that many people would find offensive, such as explicit pornography.

Similarly, to exist, The Pirate Bay also challenges offline norms. The
Pirate Bay is not challenging norms of appropriate behavior necessarily, but
rather the site's purpose conflicts with many states' legal definitions of intellectual property. Tied to the Pirate Bay's challenge to offline legal norms,
its users, through their actions (file-sharing) are committing political acts

(McKelvey, 2008). Merely by participating in these communities, users have engaged in a continual challenge to legal norms and state authority.

In contrast, very little about what people do while using the IGN posting boards or playing WoW is a challenge to "real life" rules or laws. On the IGN posting boards, the moderators aggressively police behavior so it is in relative harmony with outside legal and social norms. In threads about 4chan.org, IGN users will often indicate that they like the "milder" nature of discourse on IGN than that found on Anonymous. For example, in response to a thread about the infamous /b/ board on 4chan.org, a user stated about IGN's no-topic board the "Vesti," "I'm fine with the Vesti. I'd rather avoid a site filled to the brim with child pornography and gore."

Similarly, the WoW community is more heavily regulated by the users, themselves, than by WoW moderators—although there is also moderator regulation—and users regulate each other in relation to beliefs about appropriate behavior that have clear analogous doubles offline. Additionally, WoW moderators are most likely to step in aggressively when users violate mainstream legal or social norms in public forums. For example, on the official WoW forums, Blizzard aggressively regulates public speech by creating a "ban list" of words that the interface prevents users from posting. Predictable words such as "fuck" are banned and other "drama causing" words are also banned, such as "Nazi." Words seem to migrate on and off the banned list, such as "lesbian" and "gay" being banned for a while and then unbanned, while "dyke" remained unbanned.[12] "Rape" and "grape" have long been on the list. There are reports (unconfirmed) that the ban list is different on the European forums than the North American / Oceanic forums. However, the aggressive nature of Blizzard policy means that anything that may offend is usually moderated—including discussions about politics.

To understand why these differences between online community norms and offline norms create conflict and lead to political mobilization a look to the boundaries between spaces is important, as boundaries are often zones of conflict over legal and behavioral norms. Migdal (2008, p. 6) has argued that boundaries are not only the geographic lines marking out the state; the social world, too, is made up of many overlapping boundaries. Each boundary delineates the edges of where the ways of "doing things" change and unlike the boundaries of the state, social boundaries do not appear on maps. According to Migdal (2008, p. 6), these mental maps "incorporate elements of the meaning people attach to spatial configurations, the loyalties they hold, the emotions and passions that groupings evoke, and their cognitive ideas about how the world is constructed." The boundaries marked by checkpoints and mental maps can line up with state boundaries, but, more frequently, they are the edges of other geographies.

The online world has created a new set of boundaries that overlap with traditional state boundaries. As Migdal has argued, when competing boundaries appear, individuals must decide which border logic to follow, and such decisions can cause the conflict that leads to social change. In online spaces, people suddenly come into contact with normative and legal universes different from those they experienced previously. For example, young people believe that parking in a fire zone is more morally wrong than sharing music online (Solutions Research Group, 2006)—a belief their offline communities might not share—and suddenly they find online communities that share this value. They talk to Swedes who say, "Look our copyright laws are not like the United States' laws, so it is okay to share music online." Or, in the actual words of one of The Pirate Bay's administrators (anakata, 2004):

> As you may or may not be aware, Sweden is not a state in the United States of America. Sweden is a country in northern Europe. Unless you figured it out by now, US law does not apply here. For your information, no Swedish law is being violated.

Therefore, using Migdal's conception of overlapping boundaries, the online space then intersects and crosses the borders of the offline space in each case. Groups within each online space may put forth an alternative law in their challenges to offline legal realities, or they may remain firmly inside a given legal context depending on aspects such as anonymity. When there is a conflict along the imagined boundary between the online space and the many states represented in the space, the online community mobilizes, with each individual mobilizing or not in relation to her own state.

In the online spaces I studied, overlapping boundaries are not only the boundaries between online behavior and state law. They also are found in individual beliefs and normative practice. Migdal puts forth the idea that when an alternate code to state law appears, for example through a challenge to the law, the challengers present a spatial logic different from the borders of the state (2008, p. 13).[13] Migdal also argues that "collective lawbreaking" should not just be considered as deviance from the norm, but rather, as a group offering an alternative law.[14] In the act of lawbreaking, groups are proposing that another set of boundaries takes precedence over that of a given state's boundaries (2008, p. 14). In the case of this study, the predominantly English-speaking populations in the websites may not have common legal institutions within their countries, or even common national narratives, but they do share similar narratives about individual liberal freedoms. As Robert Cover (1983) argues, the normative universe does not need a state to exist.

Thus, although online spaces are cross-national, certain ideas can become shared symbols. Freedom of information becomes a rallying point, and users invoke their "rights," such as the right to privacy and freedom of speech in relation to the concept of freedom of information. In the four cases I studied, invocations of the right to privacy and of free speech were focal points for the two sites that politically mobilized and were recurring ideas and topics of conversation on the two that did not. Even though the rights that users from different national contexts invoked may not have identical meanings, in the mobilization I observed, rights became something of a shared resource. The idea of rights as a shared resource is in line with the findings of many law and society scholars, such as McCann (1994), who focuses on the role of legal consciousness in mobilization and builds upon Scheingold's (1974) conceptions of the myth of law and the politics of law.

In communities such as Anonymous, the separate normative universes of participants share enough common elements that a single rights-based rhetoric can serve as a mobilizing point for cross-national communities. Anonymous websites show high levels of disagreement about partisan politics. For example, during the 2011 Wisconsin protests over Republican attempts to remove public employee collective bargaining rights some Anonymous users wanted to mobilize in support of the public employees who were protesting in Madison. There were high levels of disagreement among Anonymous users about whether Anonymous should be involved, and ultimately there was a brief DDoS attack on the Koch brothers, who were backers of the Republican governor, but no further action. The disagreement over taking action was not primarily about the partisan issues involved; rather, it focused on whether Anonymous should take a partisan stance when all Anonymous members could not agree on any partisan political platform.

In contrast, there is little evidence of disagreement among Anonymous users about the concept of freedom of information. All citizens of Western liberal democracies have some concept of freedom of information enshrined in legal codes and national myth, and Anonymous users are unified in their support of the concept, as they should be; the birth of Anonymous and its entire existence relies on freedom of speech. These mobilizing ideas can then be considered "boundary objects"—or objects that have a local meaning but also have meaning across many communities (Star & Griesmer, 1989, p. 387). Thus, in spite of the national differences in the Western groups that populate anonymous English-speaking online spaces such as The Pirate Bay, the concept of freedom of information is homogenized—or already shares enough commonality to retain, as Star and Griesmer argue, (1989, p. 387), "its integrity across time, space, and local contingencies." Therefore, community members may inhabit many social, legal, and political contexts, but in the intersection between them, common beliefs and language, become dominant. In line with Migdal, these new online zones then are encompassed by their own boundaries dividing the online space from the offline context.

Chapter Outline

The chapters of *Expect Us* show that we can take political conversation and interactions as givens in any online social space. The argument that social sites are important to politics may be less controversial than it was when I began my research; as many scholars have found that nonpolitical social networking sites have facilitated protest (e.g., Howard and Hussain, 2011; Tufekci and Wilson, 2012; or Theocharis, 2013). Even before the Arab Spring or Iran's 2009 so-called Twitter Revolution, Zuckerman (2007, 2008) argued as part of his "Cute Cat Theory" that "Web 2.0" meant there were tools that made it easier for normal people to share photos of their cats, simultaneously creating technology that is useful to activists.

However, using comparative ethnography, I unpack *why* one community will organically mobilize politically and another will not, rather than treating all online spaces as equal or as simply facilitating offline movements. *Expect Us* enters into and informs the conversation about the politically significant behavior occurring in unexpected places online and about politics that have been changed forever by the affordances of online technology (e.g., Bennett, 2008; Earl & Schussman, 2008; Earl & Kimport, 2011; Coleman, 2012; McKelvey, 2012; Postigo, 2012; and Sauter, 2013). The pro-WikiLeaks mobilization in December 2010 illustrates this contribution. Although this mobilization occurred at the tail end of my observational research in these four communities, it is a single instance that effectively illustrates a "day in the life" of each community as each responded to a major international political event.

As stated previously, when WikiLeaks was under attack in late 2010, Anonymous activists were some of the first to respond. Chapter 2 addresses the question of why Anonymous members first mobilized in 2008 and includes information about how this community became politically active. I argue that Anonymous became involved in political activism because the technological spaces of 4chan.org and other Anonymous posting board systems—particularly their extreme anonymity, lack of regulation, and shocking content—created a highly cohesive online community with a history of collective online activities of questionable legality and morality. The history of organized community activities granted Anonymous members a sense of capability that empowered them to take on the Church of Scientology in 2008.

As chapter 2 discusses, Anonymous activists, who came from 4chan. org, an online community with more than nine million users in 2011—and first covered in the press as an "Internet Hate Machine"[15]—began online protests on behalf of WikiLeaks. In the online spaces where Anonymous organizes and decides who will be targeted, users framed the WikiLeaks issue as an "infowar," saying they would be fighting censorship on behalf of freedom of information. For example, one online flyer stated:

Julian Assange deifies everything we hold dear. He despises and fights censorship constantly, is possibly the most successful international troll of all time, and doesn't afraid of fucking anything[16] (not even the US government). . . . Therefore, Anonymous has a chance to kick back for Julian. We have a chance to fight the oppressive future which looms ahead. We have a chance to fight in the first infowar ever fought.

In a YouTube video viewed nearly 900,000 times, Anonymous stated (LetterfromAnon 2010):

When we all have access to information, we are strong. When we are strong, we possess the power to do the impossible—to make a difference, to better our world. This is why the government is moving on WikiLeaks. This is what they fear. They fear our power when we unite. Please, do not forget this. The intention of Anonymous is to protect free flow of information of all types from the control of any individual, corporation, or government entity. We will do this until our last dying breath. We do this not only for ourselves, but for the citizens of the world. We are people campaigning at this very moment for your freedom of information exchange, freedom of expression, and free use of the Internet.

And, protest they did—bringing down MasterCard's and Visa's service temporarily and slowing PayPal, corporations that had removed service from WikiLeaks in response to pressure from the US government, which had reacted strongly to the release of the secret diplomatic cables (Cohen, 2010). Anonymous also revealed documents stating that at least one US security firm had proposed plans to attack WikiLeaks on behalf of the US government.[17] Anonymous's protest on behalf of WikiLeaks captured the attention of the international press, which began covering the group. The news stories tended to treat Anonymous as a single anarchic group, but Anonymous is, in fact, an entity comprised of many subgroups occupying hundreds of online community spaces that are sometimes warring with each other, as was captured when, in the same video cited above, Anonymous also stated:

> Please do not despise us, as we are not the Anonymous that you may be familiar with. Anonymous' past is not our present. May we remind you that Anonymous is a dynamic entity.

In the past, Anonymous was better known online for inter-website wars and MySpace hackings. Historically, its framing of itself was nihilistic; for example, in a YouTube video viewed over a million times, Anonymous claimed (AnonymousHateMachine, 2007; dearfoxnews, 2007):

> We are the face of chaos and the harbingers of judgment. We laugh in the face of tragedy, we mock those who are in pain. We ruin the lives of others simply because we can. A man takes his aggression out on a cat, we laugh. Hundreds die in a plane crash, we laugh. The nation mourns over a school shooting, we laugh. We are the embodiment of humanity with no remorse, no caring, no love, no sense of morality.

Some members put it more simply: "Anonymous: Because no one of us is as cruel as all of us."[18] Chapter 2 of this study discusses the transformation of Anonymous from an "Internet Hate Machine," only caring about entertainment, to a collection of activist groups.

However, in its protest on behalf of WikiLeaks, "new" Anonymous drew on an array of mobilization strategies and actions developed by "old" Anonymous while site users were engaging in acts of online vandalism and banal cruelty.[19] The strategies included use of IRC networks, wikis, websites, imageboards, YouTube, social networking sites, and other tools[20]—to mobilize, choose targets, and disseminate information to Anonymous members who wanted to help. However, "new" Anonymous was correct in noting that its pro-WikiLeaks manifestation was different. The WikiLeaks protests represented an increasingly empowered, sophisticated, and growing conglomerate of Anonymous activist groups born online that were and are now drawing on the opportunities presented by the Internet to create a cross-national and highly effective activist force, a change that has now also been documented by scholars and journalists (notably, Coleman, 2011 and 2012c; Norton, 2011a, 2011b, 2012a, 2012b; and Olsen, 2012).

Anonymous was not the only set of actors from online communities who mobilized on behalf of WikiLeaks in late 2010. By mid-December, the only reason WikiLeaks was still online was because of the work of Internet activists. WikiLeaks ended up on a domain registered to the Swiss Pirate Party and mirrored[21] by the international network of Pirate Parties. After the Swiss Pirate Party donated its domain name to WikiLeaks, individuals and groups affiliated with the Pirate Party acted to support WikiLeaks, and the number of WikiLeaks' site copies began multiplying. In one week, one thousand mirrors appeared (Beschizza, 2010), and, as of March 2010, there were 2,552 mirrors of the site.[22]

As I discuss in chapter 3, the international Pirate Parties' rises are closely tied to The Pirate Bay and activists who, long before WikiLeaks, had mobilized on behalf of a file-sharing site, The Pirate Bay—a site with more than 25 million users. The Pirate Bay became the focal point for anti-intellectual property activists and people concerned with privacy online. Although the site was begun by activists, the site's legal troubles in Sweden have made it a rallying point in online and offline activism. Its popularity also greatly facilitated and influenced the rise of an international network of Pirate Parties in countries all over the world. In chapter 3, I argue that in the case of The Pirate Bay, the technological space appears to be anonymous, unregulated, and based on commercial exchange, but it allows users to engage in a set of behaviors that puts them in direct conflict with legal norms and various authorities, including the United States and influential corporations. Additionally, the leadership of The Pirate Bay stands as the jetty in the legal sea of copyright issues, taking the legal attacks of the recording industry on behalf of its users, which furthers the site's function as a political platform (McKelvey, 2008).

In another multi-million-person online community boasting about 11.5 million users—Blizzard Entertainment's World of Warcraft (WoW)—the North America / Oceanic forums were conspicuously silent on the issues of WikiLeaks and Julian Assange.[23] As I discuss in chapter 4, over 11.5 million people in the world have played WoW, cooperating to fight dragons in real time using text and voice software in cross-nationally populated fantasy landscapes. Players constantly engage in debates about norms of fairness, appropriate public speech, and resource distribution, and frequently WoW relationships "cross over" into the "real world." However, little political mobilization arises from WoW. I find that political organization and protest in WoW are "foiled" for a number of reasons. Central among these reasons is that the need to negotiate the in-game space creates smaller groups with boundaries that are not based on cleavages normally observed outside the game, such as nationalities, ethnicities, sex, race, or age. Instead, the boundaries of these smaller groups are created by shared value systems. Once people exist in these "bubbles" of shared values, they are less likely to engage in political activism.

Thus, in spite of the idealistic rhetoric often employed by individuals and groups mobilizing politically on behalf of "freedom of information" and the Internet,[24] the opportunities for fast, low-cost mobilization online did not entice everyone to protest. In December, buried in a thread complaining about Amazon's customer service, someone posted the following:

> Amazon lost my business forever when they dropped their hosting of wikileaks.org. As has been said, if they are so opposed to free speech and the dissemination of verifiable factual information, they should stop selling books and start burning them instead.[25]

A moderator on the WoW forums deleted the post, but not before several other posters quoted it. There was a smattering of discussion about this statement in the thread; however, the bulk of the thread's conversation was about Amazon's customer service. Most of the other WikiLeaks references on the WoW forums at this time were tongue-in-cheek responses to other topics. For example, in response to a thread speculating about a Blizzard Entertainment policy, someone stated, "Unless WikiLeaks or Blizzard publishes it, don't make assumptions." In another thread, someone asked the question of what would happen if there were a WikiLeaks in the fantasy landscape in the game that was publishing the letters of in-game kings and queens. On the European realm group general forums, there were also very few (although more than on the North American / Oceanic forums) threads discussing the issue of WikiLeaks. In one of the longer discussions (~200 replies), a user began his response with, "This thread doesn't belong on World of Warcraft General Discussion forum."[26]

However, while the general discussion areas in World of Warcraft may have been relatively free of WikiLeaks conversation, the player base was certainly aware of the issues. Out of 238 realms in the North American realm group, 97 realms had a character named Assange playing on the realm (only one character per realm is allowed to have any given name), and of the 109 realms in the European realm group, 99 realms had a character named Assange.[27] Ninety-five realms in the North American group and 94 in the European group also had characters named WikiLeaks, and 37 North American and 23 European realms had characters named "Wikileak."[28] Many other characters were named after Anonymous-originated jokes.

In contrast with the relative silence among the WoW community, in another highly populated online community with more than a million registered users—IGN.com—users approached the news of WikiLeaks' woes much differently than did users of The Pirate Bay or Anonymous. Chapter 5 describes IGN.com's posting boards. The board systems attached to IGN.com are not anonymous and are highly regulated. People on IGN.com engage in conversations about every subject possible. Thus, they also end up vigorously debating everything—politics, religion, food, bathroom habits, race issues, video game quality, and which actresses are hotter, among other topics. In spite of the constant debate and the fact that people in the space splinter into small groups and form long-lasting relationships, the space has not produced any real political mobilization. The lack of anonymity on IGN.com means that people form smaller groups within the larger group. Large-group cohesion is further weakened by an extremely accessible board format that allows for private conversation between users and minimizes a need for a strict lexicon or knowledge of community history to indicate belonging. These factors, tied to a high level of regulation of speech and behavior on IGN.com, undermine collective group mobilization. However, even though there is no political mobilization, there is extensive debate about politics and some indication that these conversations influence user beliefs.

In contrast with Anonymous, instead of engaging in activism IGN.com users argued vigorously and passionately about whether WikiLeaks was morally right and whether Julian Assange was evil. They debated whether the rape charges against Assange were real or a CIA plot, speculated over what else WikiLeaks might be able to release (e.g., "WIKILEAK: USA PLANNED 9/11 ATTACKS"), and disagreed about what the US government should do in response to WikiLeaks' release of classified documents. For example, in one thread the debate began with the following, and then changed into an argument about the role of secrecy in governing, WikiLeaks' role in politics, and whether Assange was guilty of rape charges:

USER 1:   I love how all the internet nerds have such a huge boner for a RAPIST.

USER 2:   wikileaks exposed a bit of truth for the first time in decades.

USER 1:   So you support Assange's right to rape?

USER 2:   I believe in someone being innocent until proven guilty, you fascist moron.

Users of IGN.com created joke threads about the issue and the attention it was receiving, such as "SCENARIO: You wake up as Julian Assange, what do you do?" or "If Assange was a dog would he be a marmaluke?" They argued so much that users began to complain about the number of conversations (threads) having to do with WikiLeaks and Assange.[29] These arguments were mixed with threads that appeared to be apolitical, such as "Who is hotter—Sophia Vergara or Katie Perry?" or "I have a snow day tomorrow." The ferocious arguments about WikiLeaks were just another political argumentative tempest in the teapot that is IGN, as I describe in chapter 5.

In chapter 6, I conclude by addressing two central implications of my findings. First, nonpolitical websites and online communities are essential to understanding civic engagement. Because of their importance, understanding the implications of privately owned online spaces and the choices of website owners and administrators in shaping online community spaces is crucial. Second, it is unclear what the future holds for Internet activists such as the activist Anonymous groups or the Pirate Parties. However, there is some indication that groups such as these are part of an emergent social movement focused on freedom of information.

2

Anonymous

Carnival to Mobilization

We used to joke about Anonymous being a hivemind and stuff. It was all for fun.
And now these retards are taking it serious and think that we're some sort of
political pressure group.
—Anonymous, February 13, 2008

On February 10, 2008, protests involving 5,000–8,000 people occurred
at local Church of Scientology branches in 108 cities across 17 countries at
precisely 11:00 a.m. in all locations.[1] Protesters in every location displayed
signs with the same imagery, passed out the same flyers, wore similar cloth-
ing, and, when interviewed, framed their protest platforms in a common language. Protesters also followed local rules of protest, such as filing notices
with police in advance, and, in the United States, showed awareness of the
restrictions of freedom of speech on private property. The protests were
peaceful, and no one was arrested. When asked, the protesters identified
themselves as "Anonymous," the self-given name of participants in a chain
of sprawling online communities.

Prior to 2008, very little on the Anonymous posting board systems
would have led people to predict these worldwide political protests. Instead,
Anonymous populated posting boards revealed strongly shared values such
as the belief that nothing was sacred and that participants should not care
about anything "serious." In addition, members of the community expressed
apathy about and disconnection from moral norms. Furthermore, the community's posting boards were not connected to any online political forums,
blogs, or groups associated with building civil society. Before its coordinated
action against the Church of Scientology, conducted in the name of freedom
of information and human rights, Anonymous's coordinated community

actions had been more about entertainment than advocacy. However, with the Church of Scientology protests, Anonymous—or the subsections of Anonymous that have remained involved in activism—has increasingly framed its aims in the language of human rights and freedom of information. Some subsections of Anonymous have also begun to resemble more conventional social movements, which petition the state for change while trying to convince other segments of society of their viewpoint.

Additionally, since the 2008 beginning of the Church of Scientology protests, the Anonymous community has divided into three perspectives on the issue of political activism: rejection of any kind of political activism, advocacy of political activism that only uses legal methods of dissent, and advocacy of political activism that combines hacktivism with legal strategies. The two groups that advocate for political activism now profess an overarching belief in freedom of information and in user control of the Internet. They have mobilized in support of the Iranian protesters, against copyright and intellectual property regimes, and against Internet censorship.

No part of the Anonymous community's involvement in political activism makes sense in light of its birthplace. Why then, in 2008 did we see this anonymous, online, cross-national group that claimed to be only interested in pursuing entertainment suddenly involve itself in "real life" large-scale protest and political activism?

Anonymous became involved in political activism because the extreme anonymity, lack of regulation, and shocking content of its birthplace created a highly cohesive online community with a history of shared online activities of questionable legality and morality. Its own history of organized community activities granted Anonymous a sense of its own capability that empowered it to take on the Church of Scientology.

What Is Anonymous?

When I began my research in late 2007, Anonymous was known on the Internet for its online activities, which were largely focused on destruction and mischief, sometimes with a side motivation of freedom of information. Anonymous, both the individual members and the overall group, was born on 4chan.org, an imageboard system that began with a loose focus on discussion of anime, manga, and related popular culture topics.[2] Imageboards are a type of posting board that requires participants to post an image to make a thread. In August 2008, 4chan.org was accessed by 3.2 million unique visitors. In contrast, in August 2013, 4chan was accessed by 22.5 million unique visitors (Poole, 2013).

In 2008, unlike most posting boards, none of the Anonymous board systems required users to supply personal information before posting; therefore, all posts were authored by "Anonymous." While Anonymous continues to be primarily identified with 4chan.org, subsections of the Anonymous community created and populated other posting board systems online—often with similar names (e.g., 7chan.org). In every case, each board system is made up of many posting boards, each with its own specific topics, such as art, photography, or electronics. Although the board systems included forums on many topics, historically, it is from the "no topic" board, or /b/ board, on 4chan. org that the greatest numbers of collective activities have arisen. As other scholars have explored, 4chan.org is a powerful producer of cultural content online and is known for its shocking content, such as explicit pornography and offensive language (e.g., Bernstein et al., 2011; Bakioglu, 2009; Bakioglu, 2011; Knuttila, 2011; Norton, 2011a; Phillips, 2012b; to some extent, Phillips, 2011; Auerbach, 2012; and Simcoe, 2012). In this chapter I have included quotations in order to give readers a feeling for conversation in the community, although outsiders may find the language of the community to be shocking and difficult to understand, as I discuss later in this chapter.[3]

Prior to 2008, the name Anonymous referred to people using any of these Anonymous-affiliated boards, but most frequently it was used to refer to someone who frequented 4chan.org's general topic board, /b/. For example, in 2007, a longtime 4chan.org user said to me, "Basically Anonymous (how the users all singularly personify themselves) are very much 'the face of the Internet.' There's so much cultural imperialism going on from that place, with so much of Internet culture being exported from it."

After Anonymous members' mobilization against the Church of Scientology and the subsequent development of an Anonymous activist identity, the name "Anonymous" not only referred to individuals who had been a part of the pre-Anonymous communities but also to people who were part of the newer Anonymous activist identity, and this latter group includes individuals who never used 4chan.org or any other of the original posting board systems. Thus, Anonymous now may refer to the collection of the Anonymous communities, groups, and individuals, or it may just refer to a single subsection. Anonymous multimedia materials also often argue that Anonymous is an idea rather than a person or a group.

In 2012 as in 2008, the posting board systems and other online spaces that could be considered part of the Anonymous community, not to mention the co-option of the name "Anonymous," have become so numerous that it is difficult to measure the size of the community. However, 4chan. org has become one of the most trafficked posting board systems online, recently receiving its one billionth post (Poole, 2012a). Even in 2008, when Anonymous mobilized against the Church of Scientology, 4chan.org was a very high-traffic posting board system. As I outline in the appendix, I began my research on the /b/board on 4chan.org but subsequently followed the mobilizing Anonymous members as they moved across other online spaces.

In 2008, Anonymous had no internal structure, no clear boundaries between groups, and no leadership or identifiable hierarchy. There were experts among Anonymous who designed tools, educated other Anonymous users, hosted websites, hosted IRC servers, created press releases and other publicity materials, and drew on their knowledge to provide services to the community. However, these roles would not map onto a leadership hierarchy in which identifiable actors were making decisions alone, ordering others to follow them, or in any way "commanding" Anonymous. Instead, then as now, when users "worked together" on an activity, one or perhaps a few members suggested a "target," and this suggestion would either be ignored or debated by the community. If the target and purpose of the action—for example, anticensorship—struck enough people as important or entertaining, those people then activated using a rote set of actions and tactics. If target and purpose did not resonate with enough people, nothing happened. Norton (2012b) calls Anonymous a "classic do-ocracy" because of the nature of the mobilization process. It is possible for different Anonymous communities, Anonymous activists, and Anonymous-affiliated activists to disagree with each other and, in the past, wage war.

Community Values: Lulz and Freedom of Information

The rise of organized political action from the community occupying the Anonymous boards is surprising not only because of the nonpolitical nature of the boards, but also because of the value system of the community. Before the Scientology protests, two of the most prominent driving principles in Anonymous communities boards were the nihilistic pursuit of entertainment, referred to as "lulz," and the idea that "knowledge is free," an idea grounded in an older hacker ideology. These two principles, in particular the "lulz," can be seen operating in most organized Anonymous activities prior to the struggle with the Church of Scientology.

The pursuit of "lulz" is the pursuit of entertainment for entertainment's sake. The term "lulz" is a reference to a common Internet abbreviation, "lol," which is shorthand for "laugh out loud." In the pursuit of "lulz," board users have used their Internet savvy to cause mischief online. These acts can be both callous and creative, but over time they have given the community a reputation as a site of vigilante justice on the Internet. Prior to 2008, the Anonymous community rejected this characterization. Anonymous community members were constantly reminding people that their motivation was entertainment, not justice. For example, early in 2008, individuals arriving at the board dedicated to "invasions" (/i/) within an Anonymous board system (711chan.org) were greeted with a reminder that was similar across Anonymous boards: "We are not your personal army, we will not raid your ex or some random person without a lulzy motivation." In February 2008, following beginning of the anti–Church of Scientology mobilization, the message later changed to say:

> WE ARE AN INTERNETZ HAET MACHINE, NOT SOME FUCKING MERCENARY GROUP THAT JUST ATTACKS SHIT YOU DISAGREE WITH AND THAT WILL HAVE NO LULZ-POTENTIAL. PEOPLE YOU WANT TO EXALT YOUR REVENGE ON AND THAT MADE YOU BAWWWWWWWWW. WE DONT CARE. GO CRY SOME MORE, EMOKID. PEOPLE YOU WANT TO EXALT ANY SHIT ON, THAT PROVIDE NO FUCKING LULZ FOR ANYONE, EXCEPT FOR YOU, YOU FAG: SUCH AS YOUR RETARDED TEACHER, YOUR MAMA, YOUR 5-YEAR-OLD BROTHER BECAUSE HE DIDNT WANT TO SUCK YOUR COCK ETC. LULZ AND RAIDWORTHY TARGETS: -CHATROOMS, WEBSITES, WEBCAM CHATS, FAGGY FAGS WHO ARE EVIDENTLY FAGGING MY INTERWUBZ UP WITH THEIR BULLSHIT AND RETARDEDNESS SO THAT IT IS VISIBLE FOR ANYONE, SOCIAL NETWORKING SITES, GAMES, GAMESITES, BDSM-FAGS, ISLAMISTS, CHRISTUNS, BUDDHISTS, VEGANS, BEEFEATERS, RETARDED PEOPLE, ANYTHING, AS LONG AS IT IS TRULY FUCKING FUNNY AND NOT JUST BASED ON YOUR VERY OWN DISLIKE.
>
> reposted. and yes, this scientology raids fucking suck. this needs sticky. everyone who participated in them should be ashamed of themselves.

As I will discuss, the statement reflects the tension between the Anonymous members who participated in the anti–Church of Scientology mobilization and those who did not think that Anonymous should be involved in such political action.

A good example of the pursuit of entertainment taking precedence over all other motivations is the case of Trey Burba. In late 2007, a young man named Trey Burba posted on 4chan.org's general topic board that he intended to set off two pipe bombs and shoot many of his fellow students at his Pflugerville, Texas, high school; he also posted a picture of the pipe bombs. Many community members were skeptical that he would actually attack his school. However, a member discovered that, because Burba had uploaded the photo straight from a digital camera, the name of the "owner" of the camera was in a data cache attached to the photo. Members then used the name attached to the camera to "dox"[4] Burba—finding his home phone number and address. In doing so they discovered the camera's owner, Burba's father, had a website, and on his website was a photograph of his high school age son, Trey Burba. Once Anonymous members had this information they called local police and reported the thread to the FBI's Internet watch website. They also called the high school and Burba's parents. Trey Burba was subsequently arrested, although he claimed the whole thing had been an elaborate prank.

While this story seems to suggest that users were employing a concept of right and wrong that is broadly shared in society, a close look at the discussion surrounding the topic shows a more complex picture of the community norms. Throughout the threads dealing with the issue, user response to the original post was mixed, and a debate raged about whether 4chan.org should have gotten involved in the issue at all. Five major types of responses emerged. First, some people claimed that the community should have supported Burba in killing his classmates because that would be entertaining. Second, some people claimed that although it might have been entertaining if Burba had killed people, it was *more* entertaining to get Burba in trouble, as illustrated in the quotation below from November 9, 2007.

> fucks sake, what is this "LOL YOR A FAG FER REPRTING HIM" and "OH NOES ANON REPORTING ANON WUT IS GOIN ON WE R LEGION" shit? we are not some happy club that having membership to means we look out for you. there is no organised underground anonymite clan of leet hackers. we dont care for each other, you dont care for me and i sure as fuck dont care for you. you miss the point of being a /b/tard—there IS no point in being a /b/

tard. its certainly nothing to be proud of. the kid was never gonna do anything anyway, and its funnier if hes v& and we find out about it. anon did it for the lulz, and i applaud the anons who called.[5]

Third, some people argued that the board systems had already received enough negative attention from the media and that reporting Burba was the right thing to do to protect the community. Fourth, some Anonymous members argued that Burba deserved to be targeted, because he had comported himself in a way contrary to the norms of the community, as can be seen in the following response:

> Thank you anons for reporting this. Not because it could have potentially saves lives or some shit like that, but because this stupid fag was lame and was just trying to get attention and an attention whore is an attention whore, no matter what method is used. I'm glad he got V&

Fifth, some Anonymous comments indicated that members were glad Burba had been caught because what he was planning was wrong. The people claiming he was proposing to do something morally wrong were a minority in the threads. For example, in the same thread, a user stated:

> You guys are fucking idiots if you think /b/ is about killing people. Let this be a warning to you Chofagwannabes.[6]

While there were five distinct types of responses, the majority of the people on the board argued from the perspective that reporting Burba was the right thing to do because it was more entertaining to see him get caught than to watch him kill people.

Prior to 2008, events such as the Trey Burba reporting, which could be considered online vigilantism, were mostly scattered and overwhelmed by the number of more cruel attacks such as MySpace hacking. The general reason Anonymous members gave for any attack—cohesive or scattered—was that it was solely for the community's entertainment, a response they still give. As figure 2.1 illustrates, a common, tongue-in-cheek refrain has been, "Anonymous: because none of us are as cruel as all of us."

While articulated less clearly than the ethic of pursuing "lulz," prior to 2008 users also frequently referred to a freedom-of-knowledge ethic, although without much discussion as to what this value meant. The most common reference to this ethic is found in Anonymous media and art, in

Figure 2.1   Because None of Us Are As Cruel As All of Us.

Figure 2.2   Project Chanology Card.

which the phrase "knowledge is free" is used as a mantra as can be seen in figure 2.2, which is a card from the anti–Church of Scientology actions.

The "knowledge is free" ethic harmonizes with an older "hacker" ethical structure, most clearly outlined by Levy in 1984. Levy argues that "hackers" have a clear ethical code that has several components. First, Levy argues that a value of the hacker community is that "information wants to be free." The Anonymous communities often used the catchphrase "knowledge is free," tied to the group activities of the community. Second, Levy argues that hackers believe in promoting decentralization because of a fundamental mistrust of authority. He argues that this means the hacker community is strongly individualistic, anarchistic, and libertarian. In addition, Coleman (2012b, p. 3) also discusses the hacker ethic, arguing that collectively hackers are committed to "productive freedom." As part of this, Coleman argues that hackers "reformulate key liberal ideals such as access, free speech, transparency, equal opportunity, publicity, and meritocracy." Coleman notes that while Levy's account of hackers still holds true, it is important to examine hackers as embedded in a larger milieu of liberal culture. She asserts that there is no single "hacker" ethic, but rather the hacker ethic is "distinct yet connected moral genres."

Indeed, prior to 2008, Anonymous appeared to be a skeleton sketch of Levy's original argument combined with a more nihilistic, "Fight Club–esque" philosophy. The lulz was a self-aware ironic perspective that suggested that even when an attack was being waged in the name of freedom of information, it was still meaningless. Since the transformation of Anonymous in 2008, the idea that everything is meaningless is no longer apparent among many Anonymous projects.

Prior to 2008, the best example of this ethic has been the community's attack on eBaum's World. eBaum's World is an "extreme Internet content" website that attempts to archive all of the creative material being produced online—most often photos, videos, and audio. In the early days of eBaum's World, the owner reportedly "farmed" other websites for content, watermarked content borrowed from other sources, and then hosted it on eBaum's World without credit to the original creators. This was highly controversial because it gave eBaum's World intellectual ownership over content that the site owners had not created themselves. The Anonymous community, along with other online sources of Internet memes and popular materials, has engaged in more than one concerted attack on eBaum's World in response to what they argue is Eric Baum's "stealing" of material. In these attacks on eBaum's World, both the pursuit of lulz and the idea that information should be free are apparent.

Carnival to Mobilization

In early 2008 a shift happened in the way in which Anonymous engaged with the outside world. Anonymous members decided to fight the Church of Scientology in the name of freedom of information and for their own entertainment. The move against the Church, which resulted in thousands of Anonymous members protesting in "real life" across the globe, was Anonymous's first step into self-conscious political protest.

Prior to 2008, Anonymous group activities tended to fall into two distinct types: large-scale raids and smaller, less organized destructive acts. Large-scale raids were highly organized activities that employed a large subset of the community in destroying an online target through methods such as DDoS attacks. For example, in 2006, Anonymous engaged in a DDoS attack on white nationalist radio show personality Hal Turner's website.[7] The tactics of large-scale raids tended to be common across raids. In fact, in 2008, among the Anonymous board systems were boards that taught people how to engage in DDoS attacks and other tactics in untraceable ways. Huge raids, such as those waged on eBaum's World and initially on the Church of Scientology, became an important part of the shared cultural history of the community.

Smaller, less organized actions usually involved single users or small groups engaging in destructive acts and then posting the results on the boards for the community's entertainment. For example, in the past, groups of Anonymous members would hack MySpace accounts. On one occasion, a user found a naked picture of a high school student who had forgotten to make her Photobucket private, accidentally giving the public the ability to view her photos. The Anonymous member posted the photos on the board and members of the Anonymous community "doxed" her—tracking down her MySpace account, which they hacked, stripped of content, and filled with her naked pictures. Using her MySpace account, other Anonymous members found her home address, phone number, email address, and high school. They then called her house repeatedly and emailed the naked pictures to everyone in her address book, as well as to the entire faculty of her high school. For a time, the practice of MySpace hackings was common enough that FOX News covered Anonymous, calling them "hackers on steroids treating the web like a real life video game" and an "Internet hate machine."[8] The term "Internet hate machine" was humorously co-opted by Anonymous to describe itself.

Not all small-scale efforts were characterized by banal cruelty. In another smaller scale action, Anonymous helped to find and arrest a pedophile named Chris Forcand. After some community members encountered Forcand in a chat room, Anonymous tracked down his name and address, mailed some of his chats to his church, and reported him to the Toronto police. He was subsequently arrested.

Operating within the genre of large-scale raids, in January 2008, Anonymous began a coordinated attack on the Church of Scientology in response to the Church's reaction to a video of Tom Cruise that was leaked to the Internet. The video of Tom Cruise extolled the virtues of Scientology and appeared on various video-sharing websites. The Church claimed that the video, which was not particularly flattering to Mr. Cruise, was part of a Church-produced video and was, therefore, the copyrighted property of the Church. Its lawyers sent letters to all of the sites hosting the video threatening to sue if it were not removed. Some sites, such as Gawker.com, said that the video was newsworthy, left it online in spite of threats from Scientology lawyers, and made the threatening letters public. Others, such as YouTube.com, took the video down. In the wake of YouTube removing the video, an Anonymous user started a thread proposing an attack on the Church of Scientology.

In response to that user, Anonymous mobilized. Anonymous began with a series of DDoS attacks on the Church's websites, posting step-by-step instructions online about how to engage in an untraceable attack. Anonymous also began to prank-call Scientology Centers and send endless faxes of black sheets of paper. These actions were international, occurring all across the Western world. Although spokespeople for the Church claimed that none of the Church's websites ever went down, according to Jose Nazirio, a senior analyst at a company that specializes in Internet attacks, the scale of the attack was large. In his words, "It's not just one or two guys hanging out in the university dorms doing this" (McMillan, 2008). His assessment backs up Anonymous's claims that the group successfully took down several of the Church's websites. Whether claims of victory were inflated or not, the Church did move its websites to new servers run by a company specializing in resisting DDoS attacks.[9] In addition, in this first wave of attacks, Anonymous combined its DDoS attacks with a hacking effort to gain access to and release online Church material that only Church members were allowed to view.

Once the attacks began, members of the Anonymous community began framing the protests in relationship to the actions of the Church itself rather than in relation to the removal of the Tom Cruise video from the Internet. They discussed reported abuses of the Church and argued that Anonymous could be a force for good. As I will discuss in chapter 3, just as the Pirate Bay administrators created a framework that defined user actions as activism, Anonymous activists reframed their organization—the number of people involved, the lack of leaders, the chaotic nature of the boards—as virtues. In their framing, they moved the focus from much of what characterized the community in the first place—specifically, the malicious attacks on individuals and the nihilistic rejection of common morality—in favor of descriptions of Anonymous as something of a vigilante superhero fighting on behalf of the weak for what was right.

Following the initial successful DDoS action, Anonymous released a YouTube video declaring a full-scale attack on the Church of Scientology (Church of Scientology, 2008c). The video was characterized by a robotic voice, a landscape visual, and some of the catchphrases of Anonymous, such as "We are legion. We do not forgive. We do not forget. Expect us." In a very short time the video had been viewed over a million times.

In response to the actions of Anonymous, Mike Bunker, a long time anti–Church of Scientology activist, made a YouTube video, in which he implored Anonymous members to be careful not to expose themselves to legal action from the Church. He stated that using illegal tactics made Anonymous look bad (xenutv1, 2008). He said that Anonymous's destructive actions were similar to those of the Church. He suggested that the best way to hurt the Church was to try to get rid of its tax-exempt status. He briefly outlined how one would go about doing this and provided a link to a site about the Church and the IRS. There was discussion of his comments within community spaces, and some Anonymous members agreed with him.

On January 28 a new video appeared on YouTube (Church of Scientology, 2008a). The video, posted by the same Anonymous user, employed the same visual feel, robotic voice, and phrasing of the first video. However, in this second video, a much clearer message was articulated. Additionally, although videos up to this point had included the phrase "knowledge is free," this video included a more clearly moralistic tone than the previous videos. For example, the speaker says, "Anonymous is a collective of individuals united by an awareness that someone must do the right thing, that someone must bring light to the darkness, that someone must open the eyes of a public that has slumbered for far too long." A search of YouTube using the key words "Anonymous" and "Scientology" on February 15, 2008, found 3,550 videos made in the previous month. Although applying the term "official" to any Anonymous video would be rejected by the community, the first two of these videos can probably be considered the most "official."

Along with the change in the way the motivations of the Anonymous community were framed, Anonymous members invited others to engage in real-life protests outside Scientology centers worldwide. Flyers advertising this protest illustrate this call to action, and samples are included in figure 2.3.

As Anonymous engaged in the anti–Church of Scientology action, it drew on a range of online tools and began to move its organizing across online spaces. For example, it moved the planning of the attack to invasion boards,[10] such as the one on 711chan.org, that were not a part of the high-trafficked 4chan.org boards.[11] The 711chan.org site contained less "mainstream" content. The site contained a board that gave step-by-step instructions explaining

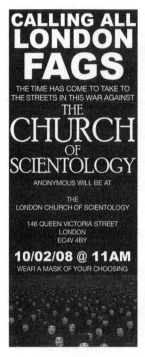

Figure 2.3   Various Raid Flyers.

how to hack things (/h4ck/); the board meant for planning "invasions" (/i/), such as hacking MySpace pages; and a board that contained animated content depicting children in sexual situations (/loli/).[12]

By the time the second video was posted, invasion boards were becoming inundated with individuals wanting to participate in the anti–Church of Scientology action. 711chan.org had to split off another board focused only on the Scientology project (/xenu/), because the project was becoming so large that it was overwhelming the normal invasion board. Anonymous members also used other Anonymous online locations such as partyvan.info to organize and disseminate information such as lists of Church addresses and links to legal information regarding protester rights in various locations.[13]

As these new organizing boards appeared, a third widely viewed video was released that outlined a code of conduct for the coming February 10 protests (Church of Scientology, 2008b). The code of conduct advised Anonymous protesters to register their protests with local police, to stand behind a natural barrier across from the Churches they were protesting to ensure they remained on public property, and to film the protests. According to the Anonymous video, filming would document the protests for Anonymous, and it would assist protesters in case they were arrested. The video also suggested that Anonymous not use the language of the community when talking to outsiders because outsiders would not understand it.[14] In addition, the video advised protesters to wear good shoes, bring water, and never arrive at protest sites alone. This video, along with others, was translated into other languages such as Spanish. Often accompanying the translated video or other videos about the event were links to legal rights for protesters, who were encouraged to be aware of the rights that were and were not protected in their areas (disposableacc, 2008). For example, next to the video entitled "britfags confirmed for brawl" the video creator (Legio9000Brittanica, 2008) linked to a list of British protesters' rights from a May Day protest page (Legal Defense and Monitoring Group, 2001).

As the numbers of interested participants swelled, new boards— notably Enturbulation.org—appeared outside the known and, until then, used Anonymous spaces such as 711chan.org and the partyvan. info, to help coordinate what had become known as "Project Chanology." The more highly trafficked Enturbulation.org was more "general public" friendly than the earlier spaces, which were seeped in Anonymous culture.[15] Enturbulation.org included no illegal behavior, a measure that ruled out DDoS attacks,[16] and no derogatory or racist language.[17] These rules stood in stark contrast to the rules on the /xenu/ board, which were as follows:

No CP.
No WHEN I WAS.
No faggotry.[18]

It also stood in stark contrast to the language used within the Anonymous community, which frequently drew on derogatory language. Other websites started appearing to coordinate action, including localized posting boards meant to organize each city, such as www.lulzinseattle.com. These forums provided Anonymous members with language to use when speaking to the press, text for signs and flyers, and advice outlining how to dress and cover their faces without violating local laws.

As the Enturbulation.org rules indicate, among the Anonymous members involved in Project Chanology, awareness of public perception began to increase, and discussions about how to handle the influx of new users wanting to participate in the anti-Scientology action began. For example, in early March 2008 a user posted on the 711chan.org/xenu/forum the following:

> I would like to remind everyone that we are now dealing with the fucking public. banning random people from IRC, the chans, and anywhere fucking else is not helping our cause. You can go back to being assholes when this is over, but we have lost hundreds of people because someone thought that lulz was more important than the only reason we even have the opportunity for lulz.

The language of the poster still is couched in terms of "the lulz" as the primary motivation for the Scientology action, an indication of the changing framing of the Anonymous actions as well as a foreshadowing of a debate that would heat up over what was appropriate "Anonymous" behavior. In response, another poster stated:

> We cannot deal with every 13yo who stumbles in here and asks "can i be anon now LOL where's our secret site where we stage our raids LOLOL, will you also read my blog?" While we should be mindful on other forums, and we are mindful, too, /xenu/ is deep anon territory, only anons allowed. Why? Because only anon will be able to operate in this environment. Everyone else should go to enturbulation.

The worry about how to deal with new Anonymous users brought forth a new public face of Anonymous that was dramatically different from its previous face even in places that would have previously been considered "deep anon territory" such as partyvan.info. As stated, the language framing action in moral terms increased, but participants also increasingly drew on legal information and terminology to frame their activism. For example, the Project Chanology page on the partyvan.info website also included legal guidelines for protesters, quotations from the Universal Declaration of Human Rights, and quotations from Supreme Court cases about the First Amendment. The authors end the page saying:

> The concepts expressed on this site are protected by the basic human right to freedom of speech, as guaranteed by the First Amendment of the Constitution of the United States, reaffirmed by the U.S. Supreme Court as applying to Internet content on June 26, 1997.

This site contains copyrighted material the use of which has not always been specifically authorized by the copyright owner. We are making such material available in an effort to advance understanding of environmental, political, human rights, economic, democratic, scientific, and social justice issues, etc. We believe this constitutes "fair use" of any such copyrighted material as provided for in section 107 of the US Copyright Law. In accordance with Title 17 U.S.C. Section 107, the material on this site is distributed without profit to those who have expressed a prior interest in receiving the included information for research and educational purposes.

In spite of some users' belief that sites such as Enturbulation.org were a more appropriate point of first contact for novices interested in becoming involved in Project Chanology, many of the sites where the project was being discussed were public websites viewable by the broader public. As such, these public websites also served as landing points for individuals interested in the anti-Scientology protests. Throughout the first heady days of Project Chanology in particular, they served as a public forum for discussion of tactics, ideas, and planning. Individuals who found such sites were encouraged to log into the IRC as well. While the IRC was and is central to how Anonymous mobilized, it was into these public spaces that new people unfamiliar with what Auerbach (2012) calls "A-Culture" arrived, as well as Anonymous members who had not been involved in previous raids.

Against this online backdrop and after extensive online discussion, on February 10, 2008, Anonymous hit the streets across the globe at 11:00 a.m. local time. No "official" news source counted total attendance across all protests, but a number was compiled by people present at each protest location. Estimates place the number between 5,000 and 8,000 people in 108 cities across 17 countries. No one was arrested at any of these protests, because the protesters carefully followed laws of public assembly. Protesters also spoke in a common rhetoric across locations and conveyed a unified message on signs and fliers. Anonymous members were warned to cover their faces out of fear of Scientology retaliation, and a large number of them also wore Guy Fawkes masks matching those featured in the movie *V for Vendetta* (see Sauter, 2012 for more on the use and history of the mask).

The protest in February 2008 was followed by monthly protests organized in a similar manner. In March 2008, on Scientology founder L. Ron Hubbard's birthday, 6,700–9,000 people in cities across the world protested again, many of them handing out cupcakes to passers-by. In April 2008,

4,600–5,600 people protested again at Church of Scientology buildings. Although the number of people in the streets decreased over time, every month for a long time after February 2008 there were protests, many of them thematic. For example, in June 2008 all the protesters dressed as pirates.

Although the impact of Anonymous's protests is contested, the protesters claimed the following outcomes (WhyWeProtest, 2009a):

- Scientology is under investigation worldwide including action in Australia, Belgium, France, and Kazakhstan.
- Many Scientology documents that Church members previously had to pay to see are now available for free online.
- Other Scientology leaked documents reveal the unstated aims and strategies of the Church.
- Protests garnered large amounts of media coverage that lead to questions about the Church itself.
- Several Scientology organizations closed.
- Church employees working illegally in the UK were reported to authorities (WhyWeProtest, 2008).
- Information about the poor behavior of Scientology was disseminated to the general public.
- Courts in many countries rejected litigation from Scientology.
- Public opinion toward the Church changed.
- Anonymous became the face of a movement against Scientology. For example, Anonymous was invited to attend a German government organized conference about the dangers of Scientology.

In contrast, the Church of Scientology claimed that the protesters were engaging in hate speech and hate crimes and that they had little or no impact on the organization.

Although Anonymous's original ethic was that everything was meaningless except the pursuit of entertainment, a healthy percentage of community members appeared willing to become involved in a struggle with the Church of Scientology. As the anti-Scientology campaign began, it was both framed in terms of entertainment and in terms of normative claims about right versus wrong. Debates such as the one over whether to stop Trey Burba from blowing up his school made it appear that the majority of Anonymous members did not care about anything but the lulz. In contrast, the numbers of people willing to be involved in anti-Scientology protests that were framed in moralistic terms indicate that in the Burba case some people may have been driven by a desire to stop him before he harmed others—even though these same people may have been using the language of the community to frame their objective of stopping Burba as the pursuit of a lulzy outcome.

Following the February 10, 2008 protest, a large and divisive debate appeared across Anonymous boards about whether Anonymous should be involved in "real life" action. As a result, three clear orientations toward political activism appeared within Anonymous. The boundaries between the three groups are unclear, although each has its own online presence. The first orientation was the mass of users still participating in the general boards and continuing to engage in small-scale destruction, such as the MySpace hacking, and smaller-scale altruistic acts, such as tracking down animal abusers. These users rejected engaging in political activism. They called the activist Anonymous "moralfags" on the various boards that made up the Anonymous community, and as Project Chanology gathered steam they argued that protesters were acting contrary to Anonymous beliefs. Soon after, discussing Scientology action was forbidden on many of the Anonymous boards and supporters were encouraged to use dedicated Project Chanology boards to discuss the campaign.

After this initial split between Anonymous members who wanted to be involved in normatively driven online activism and those arguing that Anonymous should not be involved in any political activism, there was a second split among the people engaged in anti-Scientology activities. The first faction chose to pursue only legal means of protest against the Church. This meant that previous Anonymous strategies such as DDoS attacks were no longer acceptable tactics. By mid-2008, Anonymous affiliated with online locations such as Why We Protest downplayed entertainment as a motivation for their actions and highlighted their role as Internet activists working in support of freedom of information. When speaking of their past, they began to mention the "good" activities of Anonymous rather than activities such as the MySpace hacking. For example, the "Why We Protest" website stated:

> Anonymous is a cultural phenomenon which began on internet image boards. Many such boards require no registration for posting, and every poster remains anonymous. This format of communication is inherently noisy and chaotic. However, the unprecedented openness made possible by such boards has nurtured the appearance of a unique and persistent culture.
>
> . . . Anonymous has left its mark on society more than once. Previous Anonymous projects have resulted in the closing of the white-supremacist radio show produced by Hal Turner, and the

criminal prosecution of Canadian pedophile Chris Forcand. Anonymous has been called a "Cyber Vigilante Group" by The Toronto Sun and Global News, though in reality we are much more than that.

We are Anonymous. You can be Anonymous, too. Together, we can shape society.

However, in August 2008 a third major faction appeared along with it a video (Church of Scientology, 2008d), which argued that Anonymous had strayed from its true nature. Still invoking the idea that Anonymous was working on behalf of freedom of information, it argued that it needed to return to its original values:

Today when we look back upon our efforts, we see that those who answered that call now outnumber those that remain who came from the motherland.

. . . This has resulted in Project Chanology becoming polluted by people who are judgmental of our ideology, and serve the wills of special interest groups concerned for their own survival, and not the survival of Anonymous. . . . We thought that perhaps, a new war needed new tactics. This has had unintended consequences. Those who remain in the trenches to protect our ideals have reached an impasse.

. . . We ask those who have left Project Chanology to return and reclaim it. Bring back the lulz, bring back the hate machine, and do not let some rather forceful detractors sway you.

The time for making allies at the expense of our ideals is over.

. . . Do not consider this a new call to arms. Consider this a call to reclaim what is ours.

. . . We will ensure that Anonymous retains what is ours. Anonymous will reclaim Project Chanology once and for all.

This third Anonymous faction returned to many of the original tactics of the community, in particular the use of DDoS attacks. Additionally, the group attempted to marry the idealistic pursuit of freedom of information with bringing back "the lulz" and the "Internet hate machine." It is this faction that has been the most effective at capturing media attention.

It is difficult to tell how much overlap there is in the three separate Anonymous orientations. There are indications that some members of each faction interact with other groups, but posts and images on the various boards indicate that the largest overlap is between the faction that uses "traditional" Anonymous tactics and those who say they have given up activist activities. It is now more appropriate to speak in terms of Anonymous groups rather than a single Anonymous entity.

Over time, both activist Anonymous groups have expanded their pursuits. Anonymous activists have now been involved in a wide range of activities supporting protesters in the Middle East, working as part of the Occupy Movement, working in support of actors such as WikiLeaks, and broadly supporting freedom of information worldwide.[19] For example, following the 2009 Iranian elections, as beleaguered Iranian protesters faced a severe government crackdown, Why We Protest Anonymous created a dedicated board separate from its Scientology project titled "Iran: Why We Protest," and Anonymous groups who were using "traditional" tactics such as DDoS tactics also supported the Iranian protesters with a project named "Project Greenwave." As with the Scientology projects, the largest difference between the two appeared to be the tactics each was willing to engage in on behalf of its objectives. Anonymous groups also continued projects in support of The Pirate Bay specifically, and anticopyright in general; projects against government censorship and surveillance of the Internet; and a project to create an Anonymous country.

The name Anonymous also became a mobilization tool for other online activist campaigns, such as projects against the Australian government's plan to filter the Internet and mobilization on behalf of WikiLeaks. In the case of action against the Australian government, in 2009, the group pushing for organized action against the Australian government advertised its activities across all the Anonymous posting boards hoping to garner support and participants. The Why We Protest stance on the two organized hacktivist campaigns that Australian Anonymous members organized was to criticize their choice of online illegal attacks instead of offline legal strategies.

In addition, Anonymous has become a well-known umbrella for many divergent groups that all share a common interest in freedom of information and anticensorship use. Protesters wearing the *V for Vendetta* Guy Fawkes mask now participate in nearly every major protest around the world and often are the people whose photos appear in news stories about protest. Scholars such as Coleman (2012a) have asserted that Anonymous has become the face of contemporary civil unrest. Thus, in a very short time Anonymous moved from one of the darkest corners of the Internet to become this public face of political activism. If the Church of Scientology protest was the moment that Anonymous stepped out onto the global political stage, why did it engage in such a breathtaking transformation?

Explaining Anonymous's Political Mobilization

Given the nature of Anonymous, whose central activity prior to the anti-Scientology movement was pursuing entertainment, it seems highly unlikely that this community would put thousands of coordinated protesters in the streets of many countries, convey a cohesive message, and demonstrate a sophisticated understanding of local law. Furthermore, it seems odd that the politically active wings of Anonymous would consequently frame its actions in increasingly normative terms.

The anti-Scientology protests arose from these posting boards because the nature of the technological space had a significant effect on the shape of the community that occupied the space. In the case of Anonymous, the birthplace of the community, 4chan.org, is a highly interactive conversational space structured with complete anonymity, a relative lack of moderation, a confusing and difficult-to-navigate interface, shocking content, and incomplete archiving of threads and recording of important community events.[20] Because the community is anonymous and only loosely moderated, members were able to organize collective online activities—such as DDoS attacks—that would not have been permitted in other places online, creating a template for political action.

As I argue here and in my other cases, the level of anonymity, the level of formal regulation, and the spatial divisions within an online space play a key role in creating the type of community that occupies it. In the case of Anonymous, these factors created a community that was more likely to end up politically mobilizing than the communities created by other spaces.

Anonymity

The completely anonymous nature of the Anonymous community means that participants must assert their membership status by extreme adherence to community practices and norms, while replacing individual identity markers with community symbols. Most online posting boards force each user to register and create a distinct online identity before using the space. Users' identities are then attached to every interaction in that space. Because of the identifying features, people protect their online reputations, often by self-regulating the content they post. Also, registration systems in most online communities create status hierarchies with user status in each community attached to identity. Markers such as registration dates and post counts become important because they reveal how long an individual has been a community member.

Because the Anonymous boards remove these two features—distinct identity and ability to identify community members—users assert their membership status in different ways. To signal that they are community members, users must use an extremely dense lexicon; show familiarity with community jokes and stories (signaling knowledge in a very particular way); articulate community values both directly and in the ways in which they frame conversations; and adhere to community norms of anonymity in all interactions, even when telling personal stories (e.g., "my math teacher is so stupid..."). Because of these norms of behavior, although the space is technically "anonymous," outsiders are easily spotted.

Individual identity markers are then replaced with group identifiers, as can be seen in community-produced videos and art. Additionally, over time, how Anonymous represents itself to outsiders has grown increasingly cohesive. As illustrated in the description of the anti-Scientology mobilization, Anonymous videos are marked with disembodied robotic voices, moving landscapes, the Guy Fawkes *V for Vendetta* mask, and catchphrases.

Anonymous members' inability to rely on externally given markers—most notably, user names, post counts, registration dates, and personal relationships—means that the community is paradoxically both less cohesive and more cohesive than other communities. It is less cohesive because unless they predated Anonymous membership, many of the off-board ties between people that characterize other online communities do not exist for Anonymous members. Because discovering and using an individual's real name is considered the height of trolling accomplishment, users who are not careful to remain anonymous open themselves to punishment, such as phone calls to friends and relatives or the dissemination of embarrassing photos to people they know. Therefore, users do not engage with the community in the same way they often do with other online communities, for example, taking interaction into their "real" lives.

The anonymity also makes the online community more cohesive. Because being a distinct flower in the field of anonymous daisies only leads to punishment, users have to adhere to a very strict code of behavior and ritualized language, which means they are always monitoring their own discourse patterns. Having a shared discourse and pattern of behaviors in a completely anonymous environment creates something like a secret society. Shared discourse and behaviors also create a high level of group trust that lays the groundwork for political action—in spite of the barriers to revealing personal information. For example, the conversations on the posting boards indicate that when members were presented with evidence of Church of Scientology abuses, they accepted that evidence with a presupposition that fellow board members were telling the truth.

The strength of the shared discourse can be seen in offline examples. When I was first studying 4chan.org and giving public talks about my research on Anonymous, people would sometimes speak to me using very specific phrasing to signal their Anonymous status to me in way that would not be obvious to other listeners. 4chan.org's continued increase in popularity, the strength of its cultural influence online, and the prominence of Anonymous activists has changed the way members identify themselves. The first indication of this change was when I heard a friend of mine who had never visited an Anonymous community space use a sentence structure that originated in the Anonymous community. However, at the time of Anonymous groups' mobilization in 2008, it was still the case that community members could identify each other through markers, such as word choice and knowledge of community jokes.

Regulation

In the Anonymous community, anonymity works hand in hand with the regulation structure to shape the community. Initially unmoderated, over time some of the Anonymous boards have been blocked by Internet providers because their anonymous nature has facilitated unsavory content. In 2008, the boards had some level of moderation, most of which focused on improper posting by people who did not understand the norms of the community and on the removal of all child pornography. Over time the amount of moderation has increased on some of the community spaces, most notably on 4chan.org.[21] Even with changing rules, in 2012 the boards still remained largely unregulated by the standards of most board systems. They were even less regulated in 2008. For example, in 2008, the first rule for the general topic board on one of the central board systems other than 4chan.org was, "ZOMG NONE!!!"[22]—meaning, there were no rules other than a ban on child pornography and improper posting.

Also, due in large part to the anonymity, there is a great deal of "shock" posting on Anonymous boards, which involves widely circulated shock-images.[23] In 2008, rather than remaining outside of these exchanges, the moderators were often the perpetrators, posting these images them-selves. Sometimes, particularly on boards outside 4chan.org, moderators would set shock images as the wallpaper of the posting boards. The lack of moderation on Anonymous board systems raises another informal barrier to group membership in that new users have to navigate language and images that may be shocking and offensive to them.

In addition, language that is not tolerated by moderators in most online spaces, such as use of racial and homophobic slurs and misogynist language, is not only permitted on the Anonymous boards but is a part of the group's highly structured discourse pattern. For example, "oldfags" are longtime board users; "newfags" are new users who do not abide by the norms of the community; "scifags" are representatives of the Church of Scientology; "britfags" are British board members; and so on.

Thus, the combination of anonymity and the fact that users have to navi-gate an unregulated and visually "dangerous" space increases group cohesion. Users have the feeling that they belong to a highly cohesive group, and at the same time the group members are unknown to each other and are unregulated.

Spatial Divisions

As part of the anonymity in Anonymous spaces, there are no places for one-on-one or small-group interaction. To have personal conversations and form any kind of long-lasting personal relationships, users must leave Anonymous spaces for other online tools—such as the IRC. As described later, in cases where small-group interaction is available in the community space, such as IGN or WoW, it appears that these personal relationships interfere with a highly cohesive group identity and group mobilization. However, in cases such as Anonymous, there appears to be power in the lack of smaller subgroups within the broader community. In these cases, as dis-cussed in relation to anonymity, the lack of small-subgroup interaction com-bined with anonymity helps create a cohesive larger community.[24]

Structural Factors: Board Accessibility and Content Ephemerality

Two other important structural factors influenced the development of the Anonymous community and contributed to Anonymous becoming a politi-cal force: accessibility and ephemerality. Most posting board systems are difficult for novice users to navigate. However, posting board systems tend to share some structural features in common, making it easier for new users to move between them. In contrast, the Anonymous board systems do not resemble most others. They are simple image-based bulletin boards. As the popularity of sites such as 4chan.org have increased exponentially, over time interaction guides have occasionally appeared on some of the Anonymous systems. However, these guides were not always present. Even with a guide, people seeking to navigate and interact with the boards find themselves on a learning curve that is much steeper than those of other posting board systems. This means that the system itself is a barrier to participation, as non-community members can be easily identified by their inability to post properly. Thus, the Anonymous community members have had to overcome this initial barrier in order to even begin to participate in the community, which is the first step to creating some group cohesion.

In addition, most technological spaces typically include a system for archiving community interaction. Many boards preserve threads for long periods of time, sometimes even years. However, even on the least trafficked Anonymous boards a thread may not be accessible for longer than a few hours before it disappears because the Anonymous boards include no system for archiving conversations. This is another barrier to outsiders because part of identifying as an Anonymous community member is participation in, or knowledge of, some of the common group activities on the boards.

Some community content is archived, but only in places external to Anonymous boards. Community members can petition to put a thread into an archive (maintained by a volunteer community member) if it is a record of an important community event. In order to be archive-worthy, many members must consider the event to be so significant that it must be maintained. In addition, a wiki site records the history of the community— Encyclopedia Dramatica. However, the site uses the lexicon of the community, as well as the humor and references, and, therefore, its contents are not transparent to outsiders. In addition, in line with Anonymous humor, it can be inaccurate and misleading. Once a person has become a member of the community, however, the wiki becomes understandable. The two central archiving sources foster the sense of community in that they create a shared memory, but it is not a complete record.

Historical Factors: Past Patterns as Templates

In addition to the two structural factors of board accessibility and content ephemerality, the ability to draw on past patterns as templates for future action also contributed to the transformation of Anonymous into political actors. As discussed previously, the technological nature of the community created a cohesive environment that fostered the community's long history of online mischief. Each successful raid expanded the community's sense of its own capability, and, the ritualized nature brought them closer together and made each member complicit in the fringe nature of the community. Also, because the group was responsible for quite a few of the more popular Internet "memes"—as mentioned in chapter 1, the most well known being the lolcat/Caturday phenomenon—there was a sense that the group had broad influence. The initial Anonymous threads asking for mobilization against Scientology revealed this sense of the community's capability. While some Anonymous members argued that action against the Church would fail, others spoke of being willing to try because of the success of past actions.

The protests against the Church of Scientology followed almost ritualized online raiding protocol with the addition of "real life" community action. Thus, when Anonymous members began the project against the Church of Scientology, they made choices that were highly structured by past behaviors. The initial DDoS and hacking attacks on the Church of Scientology repeated past large-scale raid patterns, and based on their online success the group planned the "real life" protests on February 10. However, Anonymous threads and other websites reporting on protests after February 10 suggested that many people were surprised at the number of protesters. Thus, following the template of previous collective behaviors led Anonymous into new territory.

After the first and second protests, the number of sites documenting the protests multiplied, as did art and other artifacts associated with the anti-Scientology campaign. Anonymous members made Flickr albums of protest photographs, created video montages, and engaged in other reporting across many websites. Furthermore, local media covered the February 10 protests, and after the March 15 protests *The Economist* and other media covered all the protests together. The wide coverage created the sense that Anonymous was far more powerful and capable than it had imagined. Also, because of the coverage, a large number of new users arrived in the space wanting to join the community, making 4chan.org one of the most trafficked posting board systems online.

Normative Conflict

Even taking into account the distinctive nature of the many online worlds and the many offline social and legal contexts, it is possible to say that Anonymous has come into conflict with offline behavioral and legal norms.

In the case of Anonymous, users regularly violate social norms of acceptable behavior with their speech and with the images they post. Anonymous members have taken special care and pride in leaving no norm of appropriateness or morality untouched. In community-associated places such as Encyclopedia Dramatica, Anonymous members have sometimes included instructions for how to anger individuals in groups that Anonymous users may not be familiar with, helping users to know what that group may find offensive. For example, in 2011, the Encyclopedia Dramatica article about the "United States of Australia" also included a section on "How to Troll." It stated:

(1) Confuse them for Germans;

(2) Say the Gallipoli campaign was less important to WWI than a dry fart in a trench;

(3) Invite them to see an Australian film;

(4) Say that Bart vs. Australia was the best travelogue you've ever watched;

(5) Interrupt them when they start talking by saying "a dingo ate your baby";

(6) Start every conversation with "Thank God for the USA";

(7) Apply your own culture's racial stereotypes to televisions shows and advertisement;

(8) Ask them, "Why are the Lebanese so poorly treated in your country?";

(9) Tell them any Australian detention centre is worse than Guantanamo Bay;

(10) Tell them the Bali bombing was a forced meme;

(11) Tell them their version of football is gay;

(12) Purposely confuse their flag with the New Zealand flag;

(13) If you hear them talk, tell them they sound British;

(14) Remind them they are the spawn of convict buttrape (disregard that, that's their greatest source of pride).

The Argentina entry included the following tips:

- The Falklands are not called "Malvinas," and they never have been, nor ever will be, Argie.
- Point out that their neighbor, Uruguay, pwned them in the very first World Cup, and that Luis Suarez > Lionel Messi.

In another example, the entry for "Germany" just included a giant flashing swastika, with no text.

As the examples in the section entitled "What Is Anonymous?" illustrate, prior to 2008, by participating in any of the Anonymous communities, members actively engaged in behaviors that were aligned against dominant cultural practices and were explicitly transgressive. The shared transgressions reinforced the sense of group identity as well as underscored an "us versus them" mentality in relation to authority. However, with the mobilization against the Church of Scientology, Anonymous also began to challenge legal norms.

As the rhetoric changed, illegal tactics, such as DDoS attacks, were reframed as acts of civil disobedience. Scholars such as Earl and Schussman (2008) have claimed that petition and protest online are the "predictable outgrowth of the convergence" between our internalization of protest tropes and the opportunities presented by digital technology. Anonymous groups have increasingly drawn upon the language of social movements to frame their actions against the state and in the name of freedom of information. However, this framing would not have happened without the initial conflict and mismatch between online and offline norms.

Conclusion

The case of the Anonymous communities in combination with the cases of The Pirate Bay, IGN.com, and World of Warcraft indicate that higher levels of anonymity and lower levels of moderation in online spaces make it more likely that the community will engage in on- and offline political activism. Prior to 2008, a user arriving on any of the boards that make up the Anonymous constellation of board systems was greeted with a technological space that shaped the community in key ways. Unlike the identity creation requirement on most other posting board systems, it was very difficult to create a distinct online identity on any of the Anonymous board systems. In addition, the level of content moderation has been fairly low and, in the past, was nearly nonexistent. The ability to engage in one-on-one or small-group interaction was frustrated by the community space.

Furthermore, the archiving of threads and other information about the history of the community was, and continues to be, incomplete and spread across sites external to the posting board systems themselves. The community shape that resulted was a semisecret society of users who used highly ritualized language and set ways of referencing important community history to identify their status as community members in the anonymous space. Additionally, identifying with the space meant identifying as a consumer of often shocking content. These factors produced a high level of cohesion among Anonymous members that was not present in other types of online communities.

Preexisting engagement in successful behaviors that offline society defined as morally questionable or illegal strengthened in-group ties and granted a sense of power. Once this sense of capability was created, it empowered the group to take further action. For example, it is likely that following the first anti-Scientology protests, the Anonymous community's surprise at its capacity for political action helped to create the subsequent activism of Anonymous groups working on behalf of other political causes, such as engaging in actions in support of the Iranian protesters and against censorship.

3

The Pirate Bay

Contribution to Mobilization

As you may or may not be aware, Sweden is not a state in the United States of
America. Sweden is a country in northern Europe. Unless you figured it out by
now, US law does not apply here. For your information, no Swedish law is being
violated. . . . It is the opinion of us and our lawyers that you are morons.
—Response to a legal threat from Dreamworks posted on
The Pirate Bay, 2004

During the 2009 Swedish trial against the four men considered responsible for The Pirate Bay—one of the world's largest file-sharing websites—Professor Emeritus Roger Wallis testified for the defense, stating that there was no proven link between record company sales and online file-sharing. At the end of Wallis's testimony the judge asked if he wanted compensation for his travel expenses, and Wallis responded that although he did not need compensation, the court was welcome to send flowers to his wife as compensation for spending the day without him. By 9:00 p.m. that night, his wife had received around $4,400 worth of flowers—sent from people all over the world (Julander, 2009).

The coordination behind the flower campaign began in Internet Relay Chat (IRC) channels as soon as the professor stepped off the stand, and it drew on an international network of supporters closely watching the trial. The trial also was accompanied in Sweden by protests organized by the Swedish Pirate Party. The Pirate Party, formed as the Swedish government began to mobilize against The Pirate Bay, has become a large youth organization in Sweden—with branches all over the world and seats in the European Parliament. However, this pro-piracy/anti-copyright movement is deeply connected to a highly anonymous website only meant to facilitate the exchange of music, movie, and television show files. Why would an anonymous group of people, engaged in what appears to be a transaction-based relationship (i.e., file-sharing) using The Pirate Bay, mobilize politically and develop into an internationally supported political movement?

As was true in the case of Anonymous, the political mobilization that occurred on The Pirate Bay was fostered by the high level of anonymity, low level of regulation, and lack of opportunities for small-group interaction on the site. However, in contrast to the case of Anonymous, the structure of The Pirate Bay meant that the site administrators could use The Pirate Bay as a political platform from which to define the act of file-sharing as a political act.

What Is The Pirate Bay?

The Pirate Bay, established in 2003 by activists, has been one of the world's largest and most well-known file-sharing websites in the world. The site was originally founded and hosted in Sweden. For much of its existence, The Pirate Bay was an open tracker search engine specifically geared to allow individuals to find and download files anonymously through the BitTorrenting protocol. BitTorrenting is a way to transfer a file quickly to one person by drawing pieces of the file from many individuals simultaneously and then building the complete file, much like a puzzle. In November 2009, The Pirate Bay removed its centralized tracker, but continued listing available torrents, relying on a Distributed Hash Table system (DHT). DHT is essentially a system in which the users themselves make up the system, but without a centralized location. All modern clients join the decentralized peer-to-peer network by default, so if a new user gains access to the files of a single user in the network, the new user will then be exposed to the entire network of users. The shift to the new system meant that The Pirate Bay hosts no files at all but, rather, just provides a list. The Pirate Bay claims this is the future of file-sharing and also that this practice shifts legal responsibility from The Pirate Bay to the individual file-sharers.

In spite of the controversy surrounding The Pirate Bay and legal threats from a range of powerful actors, The Pirate Bay has been operating with increasing success since 2003. Its success has been due in part to differences between Swedish and US law, as well as to the not-yet-harmonized European Union and nation-state copyright laws. However, The Pirate Bay's success is also due to the persistence of its site administrators. Corporations interested in maintaining the copyright status quo—most visibly the Recording Industry Association of America (RIAA), which has national branches in many countries; the International Federation of the Phonographic Industry (IFPI); the Motion Picture Association of America (MPAA); and large corporations such as Warner Brothers—assert that Pirate Bay's "matchmaking" is a violation of copyright law and the equivalent of stealing. In contrast, although The Pirate Bay long hosted a torrent tracker (allowing people to find individuals who were willing to share their files), the administrators have stated that they do not store any copyrighted or illegal material on the website. In addition, the administrators have maintained that they do not profit in any way from the website, saying that, instead, the site barely breaks even through the use of advertising (Ernesto, 2007b).

Who runs The Pirate Bay is not clear. For much of the Pirate Bay's existence people have considered three of the four men who have faced legal charges to be the site administrators. They are Peter Sunde Kolmisoppi (Pirate Bay user name: brokep), Hans Fredrik Lennart Neij (Pirate Bay user name: TiAMO), and Per Gottfrid Svartholm Warg (Pirate Bay user name: anakata). These three men were also affiliated with the Swedish anti-copyright organization Piratbyrån (The Piracy Bureau), which originally established the Pirate Bay site in line with the idea of "kopimi" or "copy me" claiming that The Pirate Bay was a long standing piece of performance art.[1] Philosophically kopimi is grounded in the idea that the world is made up of copies, and as such, everything should be available to be copied. Kopimism is now a registered church in Sweden (Romig, 2012). Piratbyrån claimed that it gave the site away in 2004 and that the site is run by Hans Fredrik Lennart Neij and Per Gottfrid Svartholm Warg.[2] However, Neij, Svartholm, and Sunde claim that they gave the site away in 2006 and do not know who currently owns it. Since 2006 it has been run by a non-profit organization registered in the Seychelles. Sunde retired from the site in September 2009, and Neij and Svartholm do not seem to be involved in the operations of the site any longer. However, whether they are involved in the site or not, the Sunde, Neij, and Svartholm have been the individuals held legally responsible for the site.

The Pirate Bay rose to notoriety after a 2006 raid of the website's servers in Stockholm, conducted allegedly after the US government threatened the Swedish government with trade sanctions.[3] The Pirate Bay administrators claimed that the publicity following the raid increased the number of users dramatically (The Pirate Bay, 2008). In January 2008, Swedish prosecutors filed charges of "promoting other peoples' infringements of copyright laws" against three site administrators and Carl Lundström, a businessman who gave the site server space and bandwidth early in its life. The trial began in April 2009 and the four men were found guilty. They have since exhausted all appeal processes and now collectively owe 46 million Swedish kronor (around 7 million US dollars) and each face between four months to a year in jail.

Contribution to Mobilization

Although The Pirate Bay has stood at the center of an activist movement, the website seemed an unlikely catalyst for a political movement. Much like most file-sharing sites, The Pirate Bay is a nominally regulated and highly anonymous space created to facilitate file transactions between users without affording them any substantive space to engage in any conversation. Thus, the central mechanism of interaction between the majority of Pirate Bay users has been impersonal file-sharing transactions involving lists of files and an exchange of goods.

Along these lines, corporations have characterized file-sharing sites as places offering a service that is in competition with their own corporate business models. Generally, they frame the practice of illegal file-sharing as another economic endeavor, albeit an illegal one. For example, the RIAA stated (2010a), "We do know that the pirate marketplace currently far dwarfs the legal marketplace" and "We know the best way to deter piracy is to offer fans compelling legal alternatives." They also frame online file-sharers as businesses, for example stating (2010b), "Music theft can take various forms: individuals who illegally upload or download music online, online companies who build businesses based on theft and encourage users to break the law, or criminals manufacturing mass numbers of counterfeit CDs for sale on street corners, in flea markets or at retail stores." Because of such characterizations, the recording industry has frequently framed file-sharing in instrumental terms—e.g., file-sharers are after free stuff.

However, in spite of the highly anonymous and unregulated nature of The Pirate Bay, the lack of places for interpersonal contact, and the argument that file-sharing sites such as The Pirate Bay are companies, the file-sharing community has not behaved as a collection of utility maximizing individuals engaged in impersonal transactions. Instead, file-sharers have supported file-sharing sites financially and rhetorically. They have used online "hacktivism" and offline protest on behalf of The Pirate Bay. They have participated in political parties bearing the "Pirate" label that have now won elections in several European countries. User mobilization on behalf of The Pirate Bay indicates that people see the administrators as rallying points to

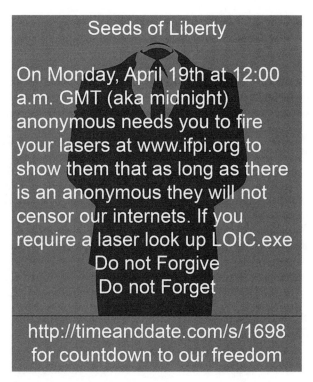

Figure 3.1　Flyer Advertising Online Activism.

express pre-existing beliefs about file-sharing as well as leaders who deserve support from the community.

Pirate Bay users have mobilized online on behalf of the Pirate Bay's leadership every time the site's administrators have appeared in court or have been subject to legal sanctions, such as the 2006 raid of the website's infrastructure. Usually this mobilization has taken the form of DDoS attacks on the websites of the "other side" of the debate. For example, after the 2006 raid on The Pirate Bay, the Swedish police site was taken down for several hours by a DDoS attack. In April 2009 it is estimated that 700–1000 people engaged in a DDoS attack on the IFPI website forcing it to shut the site down (BBC, 2006; Leyden, 2009). The Pirate Bay administrators always ask that these attacks not occur, as such attacks erode administrators' argument that they are law abiding, but site users make sure they occur nonetheless. During the trial in 2009, Anonymous users from 888chan organized "Project Baylout," which was focused on distributed denial of service attacks on websites involved in the prosecution, with much of their effort focused on the IFPI. Figure 3.1 is a flyer from that action.

Additionally, the thousands of dollars' worth of flowers sent to Professor Wallis's wife as a thank you for his pro-Pirate Bay testimony was also organized and conducted online—largely using the same tactics used to organize DDoS attacks. Those tactics included flash organizing in IRC channels, distribution of information using posting boards, and use of the Internet to then execute the plan, in this case, finding and distributing information about florists near Wallis's house.

Furthermore, site supporters did not restrict their activism to online pursuits, but rather, they matched most major legal decisions against The Pirate Bay with protests in Sweden. After the 2006 raid on Pirate Bay there were protests in Stockholm and Gothenburg totaling around 1,100 people. In response to the guilty verdict in 2009, the Swedish Pirate Party and other groups organized protests in the streets of Stockholm and other cities that drew crowds of over 1,000 people a day (Swedes Demonstrate, 2009).

Support for The Pirate Bay is also apparent in the surprising success of the Pirate Party—a political party whose fortunes have risen along with the prominence of the Pirate Bay administrators. The Pirate Party, while not directly affiliated with The Pirate Bay or Piratbyrån, was founded on January 1, 2006 because of concerns over the effect of copyright and patent law on the privacy of individuals, as well as because of a general concern over current intellectual property regimes.

The issue of privacy versus the ability of the recording and film industry to make money seems to have become important with voters in many countries. The Pirate Party claims as a part of its three point platform that copyright and patents should be eliminated and that privacy must be respected. For example, the party claims that the purpose of copyright laws was to promote the creation and spread of culture, but that these laws no longer fulfill this purpose. The party says that the Internet could become "the greatest public library ever created" if the monopoly on copyright were broken. Additionally, spokespeople for the Pirate Party assert that pharmaceutical patents kill people in the Global South every day, that patents are morally repulsive, and that they should be outlawed. Finally, the party states that the post-9/11 rush to increase the levels of surveillance and control over the European population must stop (Swedish Pirate Party, 2009).

Although the party's membership was growing steadily prior to May 2006, the police raid on The Pirate Bay in May caused its membership to double overnight, bringing total membership to around 3,600 members (Swedish Pirate Party, 2009). In April 2009, after the guilty verdict in the Pirate Bay trial, the party gained 3,000 members in seven hours, and, within a week, it had 40,000 members, a 167 percent increase over the 15,000 members in the party before the guilty verdict (Swedish Pirate Party, 2009). Thus, the Swedish Pirate Party suddenly became the fourth largest Swedish political party and the party with the largest youth membership as well as the largest youth organization in Sweden. The Pirate Bay's legal woes coincided with changes in Swedish and European laws regarding surveillance and intellectual property, creating a perfect moment for vocal activists such as those associated with the Pirate Party and the Pirate Bay administrators. In 2009, the Swedish Pirate Party also won two seats in the European Parliament and is now represented by Christian Engström and Amelia Andersdotter at the European level.[4] It is worth mentioning that Erlingsson and Persson (2011) found that support for the Pirate Party was not due to overall dissatisfaction with the Swedish electoral system, or "protest voting" but, rather, that voters believed in the Party's main platform.

Additionally, The Pirate Bay, Piratbyrån, and the Swedish Pirate Party are credited with shifting other Swedish political parties' stances on the issue of file-sharing as well. Immediately prior to the 2006 elections the Green Party changed its earlier position on copyright reform. Also, the Moderate Party and the Left Party changed their platforms, with their candidates publicly saying that they did not think file-sharing should be illegal. As one official of the Moderate Party, subsequently the Prime Minister, Fredrik Reinfeldt, stated, "We cannot hunt an entire youth generation" (Kudinoff, 2006).

This phenomenon is not restricted to Sweden. There are now Pirate Parties in more than 40 countries.[5] In Oct 2009, the German Pirate Party managed to gain two percent of the vote in parliamentary elections, amounting to around 845,000 votes (Swedish Pirate Party, 2009). Several prominent political figures in German politics have joined the Pirate Party, such as Herbert Rusche, one of the founding members of the German Green Party (Bild.de, 2009). The German Pirate Party also received 1.9 percent of the vote in the 2009 Saxony state election and has won seats in local elections in Münster and Aachen. In the 2009 elections, around 13 percent of first time German male voters voted for the Pirate Party (Allen, 2009). As of July 2012, the German Pirate Party has seen 209 members elected to office at various government levels, with 45 of these being seats held at the state level (German Pirate Party, 2012; Ernesto, 2011).[6]

Further, the Czech Pirate Party won a seat in the national parliament in 2012 (Jones, 2012) and the Icelandic Pirate Party won three seats in the Icelandic Parliament in 2013 (Steadman, 2013). In Spain the Cataluñian Pirate Party won two municipal seats in 2011 (Belmonte, 2011); in Switzerland a Pirate Party representative won a city council election in

2010, and in 2012 a Pirate Party representative became mayor of Eichberg (Nordenfur, 2012); in 2013 a newly established Croatia Pirate Party won two Samobor city district seats (De Voegt, 2013); and in 2012 the Austrian Pirate Party won a municipal seat (Falkvinge, 2012).

The mixed and small-scale successes of Pirate Parties in elections have led some to declare that Pirate Parties are a passing fad or that their initial surprising successes were a flash in the pan (e.g., articles such as Meiritz, 2012). However, as the recent Icelandic and Czech elections indicate, it is still too early to know the long term impact of these parties, particularly in proportional representation systems if concerns over state surveillance and individual privacy increase, as they have with recent revelations about surveillance in the United States. Thus, one of the Pirate Bay's basic claims seems to have gained ground politically: that the technology underlying file-sharing is so dispersed that the recording and film industries will have to use increasingly intrusive surveillance measures to enforce copyright laws. The Pirate Bay administrators and now the various Pirate Parties are effectively verbalizing the concern over loss of privacy and dissatisfaction with current intellectual property regimes.

Explaining Political Mobilization around The Pirate Bay

The Pirate Bay is characterized by extremely high levels of anonymity and low levels of formal regulation—which, combined with a lack of a central community conversational space, means that the bulk of user interaction is around the transmission of files, something that involves no real personal contact between people. Although The Pirate Bay is an anonymous and relatively unregulated space with few opportunities for small-group interaction, the broader community of file-sharers has cohesion because the very act of engaging in file-sharing is an act of trust. Further, as file-sharing websites have been closed, file-sharers have moved from website to website as a group.

Anonymity

Anonymity on The Pirate Bay is a pragmatic policy choice that protects users in the case of legal action being taken against the site, and it is part of the Pirate Bay administrators' articulated belief system about the importance of anonymity online. Thus, an ethic of anonymity is also a part of the Pirate Bay's membership structure. It is possible to use the site without ever registering, and the site does not keep track of anyone, even registered users. The Pirate Bay tracks use in three separate ways. First, it tracks the number of registered users—which, as of 11:02 am PST on December 9, 2009, was 4,014,364.[7] Second, it tracks the number of "peers"—people sharing files. When I was conducting research, the number of peers tended to stay around 25 million; in August 2013 users numbered more than 40 million. Occasionally, the site will publish how many requests the site's tracker receives per second, and in January 2007, it was 12,000 requests a second (The Pirate Bay, 2007b).

Additionally, as part of the site administrators' ethic of anonymity, administrators do not keep records of individuals using the site, including not keeping track of user IP addresses. When they were in negotiations to sell The Pirate Bay to another owner, Global Gaming Factory, in July of 2009, the Pirate Bay administrators began building a user deletion tool for the site and reassured users by writing (The Pirate Bay, 2009b and 2009c), "We also want to point out that we have no logs of anything, no personal data will be transferred in the eventual sale (since no personal data is kept). So no need to be worried for safety. We always care for that."

Regulation

In addition to being an anonymous space, the site is only loosely regulated, focusing only on modest enforcement of torrent quality standards (the shared files). Only registered users can upload content—and registered users gain rank through a reputation system.[8] However, most regulation is self-regulation by the users, who are expected to pay attention to the number of comments attached to a given download and to how many people are sharing it.[9] Users will post negative comments on poor quality uploads and will not share uploads that do not meet quality standards.

The Pirate Bay's stance has been that only explicitly illegal content, such as child pornography, is removed from the site. Other than that, users are responsible for moderating themselves. As Peter Sunde stated in an interview in January 2007, "It is important to point out that we don't delete controversial stuff, only stuff that is described incorrectly." He also stated, in response to a question about how he would feel if he were indirectly involved in the spread of child porn due to the site's moderation policy, "We do not censor anything. Again, it is the responsibility of the user" (Jones, 2007). Echoing Sunde in response to a question about Pirate Bay's responsibility to fight viruses, Svartholm stated, "Our users have to do their own thinking.

We are doing what we can, but the Pirate Bay is only the medium." He also said in a later interview in response to a question about child pornography, "We can't do investigations of our own. And if the police say we should remove a torrent we will" (Jones, 2007).

Spatial Divisions

The site also lacks any major space for users to interact and form any kind of bond or interpersonal relationship. Users on The Pirate Bay have no opportunities to interact, other than the short comments attached to individual uploads or through the comment feature attached to the site's blog. On the blog, people tend not to interact with each other but, rather, only respond to the blog post itself. While The Pirate Bay, like most file-sharing sites, has an attached forum where users can post questions and interact, the number of registered users who engage in any kind of posting, either on The Pirate Bay or on the affiliated posting board, are a fraction of the total number of users. For example, on December 8, 2009 at 1:52 p.m. PST, there were 107,840 registered members of the forum (with "registered members" meaning they can post on the forum), 4,011,820 registered users on The Pirate Bay (meaning they can post in comments on the site), and 25,386,207 people sharing music using the site's tracker.

In spite of its transactional and anonymous nature, file-sharing is entirely dependent on the collaboration of many people engaging in an act of trust. Users exchanging files are vulnerable to viruses and Trojans, as well as legal trouble, but in spite of these very real threats, file-sharers continue to trust the network and their peers—risking much to share their files.[10] Additionally, the very nature of a space that is self-regulated places users into close contact in a way that a highly regulated space does not. In highly regulated online spaces—such as IGN and World of Warcraft—not only is the range of behavior options significantly limited, but also the sense of group identity is much weaker. In more highly regulated and less anonymous spaces, smaller groups tend to form within the larger group, sometimes facilitated by technological design, such as guilds in World of Warcraft. Although informal enforcement of group norms in highly regulated spaces occurs, in anonymous and less regulated spaces, membership can only be indicated by adherence to social norms, speech patterns, and ritualized behaviors. Therefore, although The Pirate Bay is an anonymous space with little regulation, both the anonymity of the space and the lack of regulation help to create a more cohesive community, which is then mobilized by the Pirate Bay leadership in line with individual and community beliefs.

Other Factors: The Impact of The Pirate Bay Leadership

Anonymity, lack of regulation, and the spatial division of The Pirate Bay fostered political mobilization, but to understand fully why The Pirate Bay became the center point of political mobilization against current intellectual property regimes, it is necessary to take into account the role of the Pirate Bay leadership in articulating a political platform. The central role of the Pirate Bay leadership is related to the nature of the file-sharing community.

Unlike the other cases addressed in this book, the community attached to The Pirate Bay is not "geographically bound" because its users are not tied to one foundational online space. The Pirate Bay's anonymous nature and lack of regulation reflect the values of the broader file-sharing community, rather than the structure of the online space shaping community values and culture as it does in the case of Anonymous. File-sharers move across file-sharing websites, often using more than one and migrating to the next trustworthy website as sites are shut down. Thus, file-sharers have a common experience that binds them together, forming them into a kind of community that is not dissimilar to the music fandom communities that Baym (2007) describes. However, file-sharers are a political community. As McKelvey argues (2008), the very act of sharing a file is a political one, immediately involving the sharer in a political struggle over copyright, even if his intent is only to acquire a music album for free. The person sharing a file is breaking the law in most Western countries and, in doing so, is vulnerable to the other people on the site because he could be traced to the action.

Thus, when the Pirate Bay administrators began to use the site as a political platform, serving as a lightning rod for the ire of the recording industry, the community of file-sharers responded. Because of the administrators' efforts, while there have been many prominent file-sharing sites online, none has garnered the same amount of attention or rallied as much support as The Pirate Bay. Individuals tied to The Pirate Bay have supported it financially, rhetorically, through online and offline activism, and, as mentioned previously, through the support of Pirate Parties. The Pirate Bay has become a central figure in the "anti-copyright" movement in large part because of the administrators of the site.

As other file-sharing sites disappeared one by one, the Pirate Bay administrators became increasingly more vocal about their political platform, articulating their actions as a political stance and characterizing themselves as spokespeople and defenders of a movement. The Pirate Bay has remained online throughout the disappearance of places such as Mininova (Netherlands, 2009, which removed all illegal torrents in response to legal challenges), TorrentSpy (United States, 2008, which cited a hostile legal climate), Demonoid (Canada, 2007, which cited a hostile legal climate, then came back a year later), OiNK's Pink Palace (UK, 2007, which was raided by police), Razorback2 (Belgium, 2006, part of the eDonkey2000 network, which was taken down in a raid), Suprnova (Slovenia, 2004, which closed after legal threats), LokiTorrent (United States, 2005, which shut down after legal challenges), eDonkey2000 (United States, 2005, which shut down after legal threats—although the network is still active), and ShareReactor (Switzerland, 2004, which shut down after a police raid but was brought back in 2008 with help from The Pirate Bay). In fact, for many years, the page title for every Pirate Bay page read, "The Pirate Bay—The world's most resilient BitTorrent site." As of August 2013 it said, "The galaxy's most resilient BitTorrent site."

However, as the list of sites that have shut down shows, while most of these major sites were either removed by legal challenges or threats, The Pirate Bay continued not only to challenge the antipiracy interests, but to do so seemingly without fear—all the while articulating a coherent rationale for sharing files. According to the administrators' rhetoric, file-sharing was not an act motivated by people wanting the movies or music they could obtain by file-sharing, but, rather, file-sharing was a fight against evil corporations that were stealing from artists. It was a statement of protest against surveillance and for privacy; it was active support for the idea that information should be free. Meanwhile, the site disappearances forced the file-sharing community to move from site to site. File-sharers were unhappy to be uprooted, and in response they contributed money and rhetorical support to the various site administrators for their legal battles. For example, the administrator of OiNK's Pink Palace recently revealed that $300,000 was anonymously donated to him by his users to pay his legal fees, and the owner of LokiTorrents received $40,000 in anonymous donations from users to fight the Recording Industry Association of America (RIAA) in court (Ernesto, 2010a).

Until The Pirate Bay, no other website's administrators were as vocal or "in your face" in challenging the recording industry.[11] The Pirate Bay's approach to the recording and film industry and any legal threat was in sharp contrast to that of most other file-sharing sites—most of whom agreed to remove files, or links to files, that violated copyright law. As illustrated previously, rather than disappearing in response to legal threats, The Pirate Bay posted the legal threats against the site online, along with its own abusive responses. For example, in 2006, after police seized all of Pirate Bay's servers, Pirate Bay administrators brought the site back up within three days with a new logo that showed the Pirate Bay ship shooting and destroying a Hollywood sign. As the site regained its pre-equipment seizure functionality, the logo showing The Pirate Bay's ship destroying the Hollywood sign was replaced with another logo showing The Pirate Bay's ship as a phoenix rising.

The changing logos reflected an overall strategy by The Pirate Bay of responding offensively, rather than simply defensively, to the attacks on its site by antipiracy groups—a strategy that quickly earned the administrators widespread admiration in the file-sharing community and a large following. That strategy included a change in the basic technological organization of the site, the practice of filing countersuits against "pro-copyright" groups, the provision of support for other file-sharing sites in legal trouble, and the habit of engaging in theatrical protest behaviors. As Svartholm said (King, 2006), "I see the TPB [The Pirate Bay] as sort of organized civil disobedience to force a change of the current copyright laws and the general copyright climate."

The Pirate Bay also remained a leader of the pro-file-sharing community because it anticipated attacks on the site and worked to make the site as resilient to takedown as possible, protecting both the servers the site was dependent upon as well as the leadership of the site. The inability of the recording industry to make the site disappear, as it had so many other sites, also increased The Pirate Bay's visibility and role as a leader. For example, to protect the servers, after the police seized its equipment in 2006, the Pirate Bay administrators claimed they distributed the site infrastructure, so that if one part of the site were compromised by law enforcement, The Pirate Bay could reroute traffic. Administrators said that while it had taken three days to bring the site back up after the 2006 seizure, the next time it would only take three minutes. When asked about the site at a conference, Peter Sunde stated that no one of the administrators knew where all the servers were—and that he only knew where one was located (Jardin, 2009). In line with this claim, there is an unsubstantiated rumor that the site was experiencing difficulty during the men's 2009 trial until one of the Pirate Bay employees brought the site back online within minutes from his laptop in the courtroom. Whether this story is true or not, the mythology surrounding The Pirate Bay is that it is indestructible.

Additionally, to protect the administrators of the site, after the 2006 incident Pirate Bay administrators claimed they gave the site to a company in the Seychelles and that they did not know who actually owned it anymore, adding that they "just worked there." As Peter Sunde said in an interview, "We saw to it back in 2006 that we would not have the ability to make some money from The Pirate Bay, so we set up a system where we gave away The Pirate Bay but could still have some impact on it." He additionally said, "We like distributed things. We set up a system where The Pirate Bay itself was distributed so you can't tell where the nodes are, and we've kind of done the same type of thing with the ownership of The Pirate Bay" (Jardin, 2009). The ownership structure of The Pirate Bay has allowed the administrators to claim in court that they have no responsibility over the site. Meanwhile, much to the frustration of the recording and film industry, no one has ever been able to concretely verify their claims or who actually now owns the site. Again, the difficulty this introduces into prosecuting the Pirate Bay administrators also adds to the reputation of the site and opens prosecutors to credibility-damaging accusations of attempting to persecute the administrators even though they are not the owners.[12]

Another key strategy that has established The Pirate Bay as a leader capable of influencing site users to engage in activism is that the administrators have also operated proactively in response to legal threats from the recording and film industry. Previously, most file-sharing sites operated until they were threatened with legal action, and then responded to the legal threat. However, The Pirate Bay has proactively pursued legal strategies against the recording and film industry. For example, in 2007, The Pirate Bay reported MediaDefenders—one of the organizations that investigates file-sharing copyright violations for the recording and film industry—to the police, as well as the organizations that hired MediaDefenders, for infrastructural sabotage, denial-of-service attacks, and hacking and spamming (The Pirate Bay, 2007a). The Pirate Bay also contended—based on subpoenaed emails—that MediaDefenders hired private investigators to spy on them. In another example in 2008, Peter Sunde filed a lawsuit for defamation against Tim Kuik of the Dutch pro-copyright organization BREIN for his claims that Pirate Bay administrators were engaged in illegal activities such as denial-of-service attacks (The Pirate Bay 2009a).

The Pirate Bay administrators have also cultivated a leadership role by proactively aiding other file-sharing entities having legal trouble—most notably resurrecting prominent sites that had disappeared due to legal woes. For example, in 2008, after the former administrator of Suprnova gave The Pirate

Bay the domain name, The Pirate Bay brought Suprnova back online. When asked why it had done so, Peter Sunde said (as quoted in Ernesto 2007c), "We talked it over and decided it was something people would have use for, it would help the torrent community and it would also signal that if you shut one down it will get back up again." They also resurrected ShareReactor and had planned to rebirth OiNK as BoiNK after it was shut down.

The Pirate Bay's larger-than-life leadership role has been reinforced by engaging in "theatrical" activist performances, all of which contain the central message that administrators are not intimidated by the recording industry. For example, in 2007, the International Federation of the Phonographic Industry (IFPI) let its domain registration lapse for ifpi.com. The Pirate Bay claimed that an anonymous donor then gave it the IFPI domain, which administrators then turned into the "International Federation of Pirates Interests" site. Two months later, the IFPI was given the name back after the United Nation's World Intellectual Property Organization decided that The Pirate Bay was using the name in bad faith (Ernesto, 2007a). Another example of Pirate Bay theatrics occurred after a court decision in Denmark ordering an ISP (Tele2) to block its users from using The Pirate Bay. The Pirate Bay administrators created a Danish site named after an IFPI spokesman—a Mr. Jesper Bay—that instructed Danish users on techniques to circumvent the ban.[13]

The Pirate Bay administrators (along with associated organizations such as Piratbyrån) not only serve a leadership role by communicating their message, protecting their site from takedown, and attempting to help other file-sharing sites, but they have engaged in generative activism—reinforcing their leadership role by beginning a multitude of projects and programs in support of their stated political platform. For example, a selected list of the site's associated projects in 2010 included the following:

- Open Internet: "Open Internet has been created to fight on the side of the citizens, be a support in legal processes and create opinion when the foundations of the Internet are threatened. A struggle for that the Internet should continue to be the fantastic tool for human communication that it is." Open Internet received around $12,101 in donations.[14]
- T-shirt sales: the proceeds of which went to Piratbyrån, the anticopyright think tank.[15]
- Slopsbox: A disposable email account meant to increase anonymity online.[16]
- BayWords: An anonymous blogging site—"A court in the US had decided that Google had to give out the identity of an anonymous

blogger. This is very, very, very wrong. We need our freedom of speech, and included in that is the right to be anonymous! This is a democratic right and we will not allow that to be infringed upon. Baywords is now back again, and we're not taking any details on the users. As long as it's legal to write, we won't close down your blog. We will not give out any information, IPs or anything else—that data is deleted when no longer needed."[17]

- BayImg: "bayimg.com is a place where you can host all your images. We do not censor them. We believe in freedom of speech, it's of utter importance to us. As long as your pictures are legal they will be hosted here."[18]

- Pastebay: An anonymous, uncensored, or regulated web application that allows users to paste in text and save it.[19]

- IPREDator: In the wake of the Swedish government's adoption of the European Union's IPRED legislation, which allowed ISPs to be compelled to give up user information (much like the United States' Digital Millennium Copyright Act), The Pirate Bay launched this service, costing five euros per month service, that would anonymize a user's IP address.[20] The Pirate Bay's effort was extremely popular, reportedly signing up 100,000 people at its launch. Much like other projects, the administrators of IPREDator do not track user behavior or keep any records. In January 2009 the service opened to the public.

- Sealand—a self-proclaimed "island nation." In order to escape the increasingly restrictive movement of copyright law Pirate Bay moved to purchase this country on a World War II sea fort in the North Sea.[21] To raise the reported $500 million to buy Sealand, the administrators asked their users for donations. In about a month, users had donated around $20,000. However, the rate of donations and the amount meant that they were not going to be able to raise enough money. Also, the owner of Sealand refused to sell to The Pirate Bay. Initially, the administrators looked into buying another island, but they never pursued the plan.[22]

Thus, the Pirate Bay administrators have successfully sought a leadership role in the file-sharing community. They have been able to pursue this role largely because they serve as a lightning rod for the aggression of the recording industry, all the while articulating a cohesive political message. As in the other cases in my book, the structure of The Pirate Bay—as well as other BitTorrenting sites—helped create the type of community that coalesced around the site. Even though the administrators have since lost in court,

they, along with The Pirate Bay name and site, have continued to be synonymous with file-sharing and attempts to reform intellectual property regimes.

Normative Conflict

File-sharers tend to migrate across file-sharing sites—often using more than
one at the same time. As noted earlier, when sites are closed, file-sharers
move to the next trustworthy source for sharing files. By the time The Pirate
Bay's use began to rise, file-sharers had already witnessed and weathered the
closing of many prominent file-sharing sites. Thus, file-sharers arrived on
The Pirate Bay site with experience not only in file-sharing, but also having
formed some belief systems vis-à-vis the state's attempts to end file-sharing.
The Pirate Bay administrators then articulated this conflict between everyday online practice and offline legal norms in political terms.

Although recording industry leaders claim that piracy is a business
model serving a consumer need, the anticopyright groups surrounding
The Pirate Bay do not frame their actions in terms of corporate culture. The
Pirate Bay administrators tended to frame the debate around file-sharing as
profit-driven corporations versus a new collective, contributory, and generative culture. For example, in a speech before the Chaos Communication
Congress 22C3 in Berlin, in December 2005, Rasmus Fleischer, a founding
member of Piratbyrån, said, "Like in a contemporary epic: with the creation
at our fingertips we are now pounding the old mass medial aura and we are in
a state of transgressing the hierarchical consumer-producer society." Peter
Sunde has framed the conflict in plainer terms. When asked during the trial
against The Pirate Bay why he continued to be involved in the site, Sunde
stated, "It is the process of democratization and the things around the trial
that keeps me to carry on, the ideas of freedom of speech within it. And simply to take away the power from single corporations who dictate what people
should take part in. I'm a devoted supporter of the participant culture and
wish everyone to take part in things" (TheOddOne2, 2009). The Pirate Bay
administrators frame the issue of file-sharing as one of participant culture
versus corporate culture and the act of sharing as a political act, not an act
motivated by greed or convenience but something of value.

Regardless of whether file-sharers believe that they are part of a cultural
shift, their online behavior and their responses to surveys indicate that they
are a part of a shift in belief system about legal norms of ownership. Since the
mid-nineties the network of recording and film industry corporations, the

legal firms and interest groups that focus on copyright violations, and the lobbyists of both groups have pursued an aggressive and proactive campaign to end the practice of illegal file-sharing online—something they articulate as being a mortal fight for the survival of their industry. However, in spite of their efforts, they appear to have failed to convince file-sharers that their behavior is tantamount to stealing.

Depoorter and Vanneste (2005) argue that there is now a significant mismatch between the legal structure surrounding copyright and what people under the age of 28 believe about copyright. Studies indicate that young people do not believe that file-sharing is wrong in spite of state legal action to protect copyright. And, the sheer number of file-sharers suggests that conceptions of ownership have changed. Studies show that most 16–28 year olds who engage in illegal downloading are aware it is illegal, but only 16 percent actually consider their actions to be wrong (Delgado, 2004). In 2003, CBS conducted a poll that found that people between the ages of 18 and 29 were three times more likely than those over the age of 30 to say file-sharing was always permissible no matter the circumstances (Cosgrove-Mather, 2003). A 2006 study, conducted by Canadian research organization Solutions Research Group, found that 32 million Americans aged 12 and older had downloaded a full-length movie illegally, and 20 million of those were regular downloaders. Additionally, the research group found that only 40 percent of the people polled believed that downloading a copyrighted movie from the Internet was a very serious offense—and offered as a point of comparison that 59 percent of Americans believe that parking in a fire lane is a very serious offense (Solutions Research Group, 2006). Research has also found that half of 14–24 year olds would happily share all their music online, and that 96 percent of all British youth between 18 and 24 practiced illegal copying in some form (Sabbagh, 2008). A 2004 study of student attitudes about peer-to-peer file-sharing found that the majority of respondents did not believe that file-sharing was unethical. Seventy-one percent of the respondents additionally stated that they did not believe that sharing files was the same as shoplifting (Moore & Corzine McMullan, 2004). A Swedish group found that 75 percent of those surveyed believed it was "okay" to download files (Ewing, 2006). And Depoorter and Vanneste (2005) found that young people's beliefs about the ethics of file-sharing were not at all swayed by pressure from parents or other authority figures. Thus, the recording and film industries are failing to convince people that there is anything unethical about sharing their files.

While the ethics of file-sharing may be contested, what is difficult to contest is the "vote with their feet" effect of the massive numbers of people using the Internet to share files. Although it is difficult to estimate how many people are involved in online file-sharing, some sources attempt to approximate the number. For example, the Pirate Bay administrators claim that, when the site went down due to a police raid in 2006, Internet traffic in Sweden dropped by one-third.[23] A 2004 study found that around 70 million people had shared files online (Delgado, 2004). And there are some indications of file-sharing traffic in overall traffic drops when a major file-sharing site disappears. For example, when the Swedish IPRED law came into effect on April 1, 2009—a law that would force ISPs to give up users' names— Swedish Internet traffic dropped by 30 percent, although it recovered a few days later.

Studies also are finding that people are not afraid of increasingly strict legislation to stop file-sharing. For example, a 2008 study of Swedish youth found that 72 percent of respondents answered no to the question, "Do you think that new laws that expand the possibilities to identify and convict file-sharers will stop you or others from file-sharing?" (Svensson & Larsson, 2009). In the same study, in response to the question, "Do you think that since illegal file-sharing is illegal one should never download or upload copyrighted content on the internet?" 76 percent of respondents answered "no" (Svensson & Larsson, 2009, p. 57). In 2011, Lund University's Cybernorms Research Group conducted a survey of The Pirate Bay's users with The Pirate Bay's help. Over 75,000 people took the survey and the results are now available on TheSurveyBay.com. One of the questions asked was, "How do you see the future of file-sharing?" In response, 61.8 percent chose "File-sharing will develop in ways that neither law nor market can control" (Svensson, Larsson, & de Kaminski, 2014).

In 2008, *Wired* magazine conducted a survey of peer-to-peer traffic studies to attempt to ascertain the amount of file-sharing occurring in the face of the recording and film industry's claims that file-sharing was decreasing in response to the legal strategies the industries were employing. One traffic optimization firm, Ellacoya, claimed that in June 2007 peer-to-peer traffic in North America was about 37 percent of total Internet traffic; however, the study's methodology was not transparent. Another firm, the Cooperative Association for Internet Data Analysis, ran tests in 2003 and 2004 using an Internet backbone link in California. It found that peer-to-peer traffic was increasing but that it was extremely hard to track peer-to-peer bits as the technology was changing to make tracking more difficult. However, in spite of all of these data, a *Wired* review of peer-to-peer traffic studies concluded that not enough data had been collected and that none of the studies was very reliable (Singel, 2008). *Torrent Freak* also surveyed different studies about Internet traffic and similarly concluded that it was difficult to tell how much of the traffic was file-sharing. However, the site concluded that the often-cited figure that peer-to-peer file-sharing traffic was about 30 percent of all Internet traffic was likely close to the truth (Ernesto, 2006).

In addition, the success of the Pirate Party indicates that users also have responded to the Pirate Bay administrators' claims that file-sharing is part of the natural march of technology and that the recording and film industries are pushing their drive for profit over individual privacy rights. The Pirate Bay administrators and the Pirate Party argue that, because of the nature of the Internet, the only way for industry to stop file-sharing is to violate individual privacy. User posts in response to stories about new laws aimed at prosecuting file-sharers indicate that people are worried about their privacy.

Finally, users not only appear to believe that file-sharing is not wrong and that their privacy is more important than the recording industry's profit, but there is some evidence that they also are responding to the Pirate Bay administrators' framing The Pirate Bay's legal woes as an issue of US legal bullying. In addition to framing file-sharing as a privacy issue, Pirate Bay administrators and others are framing prosecution of file-sharing as the United States pushing its own legal system on other countries through threats, bullying, and undemocratically created international treaties. US actions over time indicate that the US film and recording industries are pushing for international agreements that harmonize domestic copyright laws with US-style copyright law and enforcement. This move is a change from past efforts to create minimum standards of copyright protection.

Thus, the community of file-sharers whose political beliefs were articulated by the Pirate Bay leadership has come into direct conflict with offline legal norms. Changing beliefs about the ethics of file-sharing as well as the large number of people engaged in file-sharing indicate that a normative shift has occurred in attitudes about file-sharing, a shift that The Pirate Bay has helped create. The young people's beliefs that file-sharing is not morally wrong means that there is a mismatch between legal norms and what the state argues is morally correct. This type of mismatch creates the perfect situation for political mobilization. However, the nature of US law and its two-party political system, which makes third parties such as the Pirate Party largely irrelevant, creates an interesting dynamic where the challenge to copyright law as it stands will largely come from other nation-states standing up to US pressure. This means that places such as Sweden now face a dual set of pressures—one from the international system and one from the demographic that will inherit political power—the young people who do not believe that file-sharing is wrong, who do not want to compromise their privacy to protect copyright, and who are angry about US pressure.

Conclusion

As in the other cases, The Pirate Bay's political impact arises from a combination of its distinct technological space and a conflict between online and offline legal norms. In the case of The Pirate Bay, while the technological space is anonymous, unregulated, and based on commercial exchange, the ongoing process of exchanging files also requires trust and the imagination of a broader community of sharers. Additionally, the leadership of The Pirate Bay takes the legal attacks of the recording industry on behalf of its users and to further their political platform. The Pirate Bay administrators do this, in part, by articulating a political platform that is in line with three central user beliefs about file-sharing: that it is not wrong, that the state is sacrificing individual privacy rights to protect industry profit, and that the United States is attempting to use its hegemony to change national laws.

4

World of Warcraft

Cooperation without Mobilization

The first time I ran Gnomer, the cloth helm that shoots lightning dropped, and
I rolled need. The mage in the group went nuts. It was the first time I ever ran
a dungeon with a group and killed bosses; I didn't know what I did was wrong.
I just saw. . . it was better than. . . whatever I was wearing at the time. The mage
won the roll and proceeded to call me a ninja. I explained that I didn't know
what that meant. I think that's when the group actually took pity on me.
—WoW player discussing learning the player-generated
rules of the game

Although neither website began as explicitly political spaces, in the cases of
The Pirate Bay and Anonymous, users engaged in behavior easily identifiable as "political." They organized, protested, and voted offline in support of
clearly articulated political platforms. In contrast, users of World of Warcraft
(WoW) seem to lack a community-defined set of attached offline political
behaviors or engagement. Unlike the political action that moved offline in
the cases of Anonymous and The Pirate Bay, in WoW, no large-scale group
movement has occurred offline. Rather, we see the development of primarily
individual-level social relationships. Further, while one case of an in-game
protest in 2005 regarding an in-game issue has been widely cited[1] and some
level of debate about political events is ongoing in shared conversational
spaces, the WoW community is rarely, if ever, activating around any political issue.

Additionally, unlike the cases of Anonymous and The Pirate Bay, the
ties between WoW players' online socializing and offline relationships have
been noted by the popular press and scholars. Nick Yee's widely cited studies
show that 70 percent of WoW players are playing with someone they know "in
real life" (IRL); most say that they have become good friends with someone

they have met in the game; and most say that these in-game friendships are of the same quality as "IRL" friendships (Yee, 2007a). These findings suggest that WoW seems better suited than a space such as the Anonymous forums to offer a platform for finding others with common political interests, particularly because of the connection between in-game social relationships and social relationships outside the game. In spite of that connection, players rarely protest game-related issues even in-game, let alone mobilize offline in any meaningful political way. When players gather en masse outside the game, it is usually for annual gaming conventions. In-game, players are more likely to gather for a naked gnome race than for a political protest.

Considering the strong ties between WoW players, why is there not more political mobilization by the WoW community? Beyond the fact that WoW is an online social space full of young people, it seems unlike Anonymous and The Pirate Bay in every sense. It is not anonymous; it is regulated; and the in-game existence is deeply connected to offline lives. However, WoW shares more in common with these spaces than may be immediately apparent. While players never engage in the type of large political mobilization seen among Anonymous and Pirate Bay users, the requirements of the game embed players in an extremely politicized universe, in most cases for over 20 hours a week (Yee, 2005c; Schramm, 2009). Players—particularly young male players—constantly debate norms of fairness, the distribution of scarce resources, and appropriate speech in public while playing WoW.

As I argue in the cases of Anonymous, The Pirate Bay, and IGN, my findings indicate that the demands of the game, the lack of anonymity, and the need for self-regulation create smaller groups in the game with boundaries that are not based on cleavages normally observed outside the game, such as nationalities, ethnicities, sex, race, or age. Rather, these cleavages are based on shared value systems such as what constitutes appropriate public speech and resource distribution. The fact that players are known to each other and must divide into small groups to accomplish in-game tasks frustrates the creation of an overall cohesive group identity and filters political action into individual-level negotiation.

What Is World of Warcraft (WoW)?

Created by Blizzard Entertainment, WoW is one of the most successful games in the "massively multiplayer online role-playing game" (MMORPG) genre. An MMORPG is a type of video game played on a computer in which a large numbers of players interact within a virtual world. To interact with the world each player controls a fictional character with a set of powers and abilities.

MMORPGs come from early multiplayer games known as Multi-User Dungeons (MUDs), many of which were text-based real-time computer games (Mortensen, 2006). Many credit the role-playing, turn-based imagination game Dungeons and Dragons for significantly influencing the form of role-playing video games (e.g., Schiesel, 2008).

In WoW, players gather in the game to navigate individually and collectively a fantasy landscape; to battle game-generated evil creatures (mobs), such as giant spiders; to work together to defeat powerful game-generated opponents, such as dragons (bosses); and to fight the characters of other players (rather than game-generated characters) in duels in which one player is "killed." Players move across a vast geography that contains many cities, continents, mountain ranges, roads, bodies of water, plains, and open areas. Players interact with the geography much as people interact with actual geographic space. Travel time over the landscape is dependent on distances. Routes across the landscape vary in their safety and ease of travel. For example, players can choose to run along roads, ride a horse through fields and forests avoiding the road, or use "public" transportation in the form of flying taxis. The game's universe draws upon common Western fantasy and mythological tropes, and interactions between players and the game are structured by game-generated lore and game-granted tasks.

In the fantasy landscape, players also interact with each other in real time. The most common form of interaction is the use of "chat" channels that function like chat rooms. Users type text to "speak" to each other and what users say scrolls through the screen depending on the speed of a conversation and the number of participants. It is also not uncommon for players to use third-party voice software such as Ventrilo (Vent) to speak to each other.

The game does not force players into a linear playing path, such as a game like Super Mario Brothers, which has a start point and an end point. Rather, a player can choose what she would like to do at any given moment. Additionally, players also often use an in-game provided tool to form guilds—somewhat permanent groups that have their own names, guild tabards, and rule systems.

The World of Warcraft is designed to be as much like a "world" as possible. For example, there is an active economy—which is now being studied and modeled by economists[2]—whose central location is an auction house. The WoW economy also spills its bounds, with an extensive offline economy connected to selling virtual items in the game.

In large part because WoW is its own universe, there are innumerable online resources meant to help players navigate the in-game universe. These resources cover a wide range of topics, including ways to customize characters, strategies for in-game tasks, commentary on game features and Blizzard design choices, extensive mathematical modeling of best choices for characters in terms of character customization, and analysis of in-game connections to offline legality and politics (Corneliussen & Walker Rettberg, 2008). One blogger has even published a book outlining strategies for effective group leadership (Andrews, 2010b). As will be discussed later, players appear to find and navigate this web of resources through word-of-mouth tips given by other players.

As in all MMORPGs, the virtual world exists and changes outside the experience or control of each individual, and it does so constantly. In other words, the in-game world is changing even when an individual does not have the game on and is not playing—sometimes because of the actions of other players and sometimes because of the program itself. This means that there is no pause button on the game, and so, when a player turns off the game, much like going to sleep, in-game life continues without her involvement.

The "cartoons" (or "toons," the in-game name for characters) are generated when individuals begin playing WoW. A new player is greeted with a character creation screen. On that screen, he creates an "avatar." When creating a character, individuals choose what faction they will join—the Alliance or the Horde. Alliance and Horde are hostile factions that are at war with each other and as such, players on each side cannot speak, trade, or join groups with each other. New players also chose the type of character their avatars will be—healers, warriors, magicians, and others—and the sex of the character. New players are able to customize their characters' appearances by choosing hair color, facial features, and skin color.[3] Further, each faction includes variety of races that players can play.[4]

Additionally, the WoW community is divided into realms (also commonly referred to as servers). Realms come in three different types: Player versus Environment (PvE), Player versus Player (PvP), and Role-Playing (RP) realms that can be either PvE or PvP. On PvE realms (also commonly called "normal" realms), players only fight "non-player characters" (NPCs). That means that they fight characters generated by the WoW computer program but not other real players like themselves (unless they choose to enter a PvP environment such as a battleground that includes other players).

On Player versus Player realms, players fight nonplayer characters, as well as characters, like themselves, who are real players from the opposing faction (e.g., the Alliance or the Horde). This means that players (and nonplayer characters) can be "killed" at any time unless they are in a sanctuary area where combat is prohibited, such as a major city.

Role-Playing realms have two subcategories: Role Playing-Player versus Environment and Role Playing-Player versus Player. In the former, players only fight nonplayer characters; in the latter, players fight other players like themselves, as well as nonplayer characters generated by the game. On Role-Playing realms, players develop a story for the characters they are playing and, in theory, stay in that character at all times.

Realm divisions also split along linguistic lines. In May 2010, WoW included around 241 "North American" realms and 263 European realms. The North American realms also included three Latin American realms and 12 Oceania realms. The European realms were divided by language, including 109 British English realms, 37 French realms, 87 German realms, 11 Spanish realms, and 19 Russian realms. People with US versions of the game cannot play on the European realms and vice versa. People who do not fall into a clear language category can choose their servers.

In addition to these divisions, in 2010 realms were divided into Battlegroups.[5] Battlegroups interacted with each other in the Battlegrounds—areas where players kill each other in organized games, such as a "Capture the Flag" type game. Battlegroups also interacted with each other in the cross-realm dungeon tool, a random grouping tool that put people together from other realms in dungeons.[6] Over the course of my research, the groups formed by the cross-realm dungeon tool became central locations for the debate of norms in the game. In 2010, there were 13 Battlegroups in the North American group, with the majority of the Oceania realms collected in one Battlegroup and all of the Latin American servers collected in another single Battlegroup. The European realms included 27 Battlegroups—ten British English, five French, eight German, two Spanish, and two Russian. The Battlegroups created places of interaction between realms, which often became places of struggle around norms of behavior.

In the game, people control single characters and are able to play the game alone or in groups with the largest rewards and greatest prestige being awarded to group-based work. Players tend to focus on different types of play, with some primarily choosing solitary or casual playing and others choosing group-driven playing. Surveys estimate that the average WoW player spends 17–23 hours per week playing the game, making the game as time consuming as a part-time job (Yee, 2005c; Schramm, 2009).

Millions of people participate in this "part time job." In November 2008, WoW had 11.5 million subscribers, making it the largest MMORPG ever by several scales of size (Blizzard Entertainment, 2008) and eclipsing other MMORPGs in terms of its number of players. In 2008, Woodcock estimated that WoW had 62.2 percent of the total MMORPG market share. As of 2010, in terms of population the next closest game was Lineage with three million players, most of them in South Korea. Generally, most MMORPGs have had fewer than one million users at their peaks. WoW's success has been credited to Blizzard's creation of an extremely accessible MMORPG that appeals to a wider audience—specifically, to women, children, and new MMORPG players—than past MMORPGs did. Even so, in 2005, Nick Yee found that around 84 percent of WoW players were male, while around 16 percent were female. The number of women is assumed to have grown since then (Yee, 2005c).[7]

Because of the size of the game, this chapter focuses on only one medium-sized population PvE realm in North America (Central Standard Time). Blizzard (Realm FAQ, 2010) does not reveal how many people occupy each realm, instead saying that it has "established an optimal number of players per realm. This number is in the thousands, but manageable enough to foster a sense of community and to prevent overcrowding." Blizzard does classify servers as "low," "medium," and "high" population. In 2010, there were also two major external sites that used different methodologies to guesstimate population: Warcraft Realms and WoW Progress. Warcraft Realms estimates that the population of the realm I will focus on in this chapter was around 21,641 players, with 54 percent playing Alliance and 46 percent playing Horde in 2010. Alternately, WoW Progress estimated that there were 16,184 characters playing, with the ratio of Horde to Alliance being 1 to 0.95.

Cooperation without Mobilization

Unlike the cases of The Pirate Bay and Anonymous, the political impact of WoW is not immediately apparent, as it does not involve public organized political action such as protest and voting. However, even in its most shallow form, game play demands that players engage in debates about norms of fairness, make decisions about the distribution of scarce resources, and answer questions about what constitutes appropriate speech in "public" (e.g., whether it is acceptable to use the word "gay" to mean "bad" or whether it is okay to talk about religion and politics in public spaces). Players' constant negotiation with such questions means that there is politically significant behavior in WoW.

While all players must engage with issues of fairness, resource distribution, and public discourse, the deeper a player's involvement in "end-game" content, the more extensive her experience will be with group negotiations of these norms. End-game content is the content that can be experienced at the highest level in the game (during the course of my research this was level 85) and involves working cooperatively with groups ranging from five to 40 people. End-game content most commonly requires 10 to 25 people.[8] These cooperative group activities usually take hours to complete, with players often having to return to the same site (dungeon) over several days to engage and defeat extremely strong monsters (bosses).

End-game content is available to all players, but researchers—most notably Yee and Ducheneaut—have found that certain types of players are more likely to engage in the highly structured play necessary to complete end-game content. Specifically, young players, and young men in particular under the age of 30, are more likely to engage in the type of focused play involved in end-game content.[9] Yee has also found that young men are more interested than young women or men and women over 30 in having the most powerful characters possible, as well as early access to end-game content (Yee, 2007b).[10]

Thus, Yee and Ducheneaut's large-N studies indicate that the demographic group most likely to be involved in WoW content requiring active negotiation and debate of social norms is the same group occupying places such as IGN and Anonymous. In addition, Yee has found that while younger players are less likely to lead guilds—an in-game institutional tool provided to create stable groups that last over long periods of time (often years)—they are more likely to seek out general leadership roles in the game. Yee notes that these younger players particularly seek leadership roles in "Pick-Up Groups" (PUGs), which are temporary groups formed to accomplish a specific task with a short time commitment (Yee, 2003). Yee also found that this age-based role choice has an inverse relationship to whether a player has a management/ leadership position at work or elsewhere in "real" life. According to Yee, older players with jobs demanding leadership skills enter the game and shun leadership roles, while young people without the same daily external leadership experience are the people most filling leadership roles within the game (Yee, 2007b). This means that the players most frequently in situations where active debate over norms of fairness, resource distribution, and discourse occurs are young men. Yee's research has led to recent leadership studies that focus on the role of WoW in creating leadership skills among young people—particularly young men (Parrish, 2010; Reeves, Malone, & O'Driscoll, 2008; Seely Brown & Thomas, 2006; Terdiman, 2006a).

WoW places young men in large numbers in positions where they are forced to negotiate norms of fairness, resource distribution, and public behavior. The subsequent guidelines for appropriate behavior then have long-term consequences for the people who occupy the in-game space. Thus, the young men who are engaged in these debates, as well as the broader community, exist in a highly politicized in-game universe.

Explaining Political Behavior in WoW

WoW places people in positions where they must negotiate norms of behavior. In contrast to Anonymous and The Pirate Bay, the WoW environment does not foster large-scale mobilization for several reasons. First, the game's architecture divides people into small groups. Second, the space is not anonymous. Players gain in-game reputations and those reputations have meaning for them. Third, much of the player regulation is left up to the players themselves. These characteristics create a structure that fosters small-group cooperation and debates over norms both within and between small groups. Thus, group activity is channeled into smaller groups that, although they require users to engage political questions, create political processes, and make political decisions, are less likely to engage in large-scale political behaviors such as protest.

Spatial Divisions

Unlike The Pirate Bay and Anonymous, WoW's online space does not foster collective political mobilization because it divides people into smaller groups while channeling discussions around norms into negotiating appropriate behavior online. Specifically, while the WoW realm communities are small social universes that are deeply connected and self-regulating, everything about the game architecture pushes individuals into small subgroups within the larger community. The surface game architecture divides players by realms, language, in-game geography, and conversational channels, among other features. Further, the game encourages small-group play—making the most valuable items and the accomplishments with the highest prestige deeply dependent on cooperation between players in groups of 10–40. The structure of the site and game, then, leads to political interaction that is restricted to the interaction within the game itself.

Immersion

The separation between the WoW universe and the offline world constitutes the first level of separation between offline political concerns and online norms. WoW's immersive environment leads to a society separate from the outside world, because the game is not transparent to nonplayers. Players typically dedicate large amounts of time to the game. The time is spent both playing the game as well as "theorycrafting"/planning play time. Therefore, in spite of dedicating large amounts of time to playing, in order to share the personal experience of playing with others, individuals must either make friends with people in the game or bring existing relationships into the game.[11]

Studies show that people do exactly that. In 2005, Nick Yee (2005d) found that 59.2 percent of men and 76.2 percent of women playing WoW found the game through a friend, romantic partner, or family member. He also found that of active players, 25 percent regularly played the game with a romantic partner, 19 percent regularly played the game with a family member, and 70 percent regularly played the game with someone they knew in "real life" (Yee, 2005b). Additionally, in 2007, Yee (2007a) found that most MMO players reported that they had become good friends with someone they had met online.

One of the central reasons that the WoW universe is not transparent to outsiders is that the immersive environment contains experiences, entities, and actions that, while they draw on widely known myths and tropes, do not exist in the offline world. Hence, players have a vocabulary that is distinct to and completely tied up in the foreign world of the game. While all online communities have vocabularies and rhetoric distinct to themselves, WoW ratchets this aspect of online communities up a notch, because the language describes processes, behaviors, and objects that do not exist outside the game.[12] For example, the following are some terms one might use to describe game play:

- Loot = treasure
- AoE = Area of Effect
- Add = An extra monster joining a currently ongoing fight
- Aggro = Gaining the aggression of a monster
- Log = Logging off the game
- Pulling = A player getting the attention of a monster to fight it
- WTS = Want to sell
- LFG = Looking for Group

Thus, it is possible for someone to talk about an experience in the game that is not transparent to nonplayers. For example, below is an excerpt of a guide for a specific fight in the game that my guild spent weeks trying to master:

> This phase is an endurance check—while it may eventually be possible to damage zerg Sindragosa and simply ignore the mechanics,

it is better handled first as a sustained encounter. Be sure everyone is watching their debuffs, both for backlash and for arcane buffet. A second tank is needed during this phase to allow arcane buffet resets—otherwise you will have to use cooldown rotations to mitigate increasingly large Frost Breath hits. (Ciderhelm, 2010)

The time required to play the game and the lack of transparency of the game experience to outsiders, means that players must talk to other players if they would like to share in the game experience.

COMMUNICATION WITHIN THE SPACE

As the section describing WoW outlined, players are not only divided from non-WoW players, but within WoW they are always operating within a subset of the realm community. Players are divided by world region and realms. Players cannot speak to each other across these groups. Furthermore, even though players theoretically share the forums, only a small fraction of players ever use them.

Even within the shared space of the Alliance or Horde faction within a realm, the communication system in WoW pushes the larger community of players into smaller groups and, in doing so, limits the potential for large-group political activity inside or outside the game. The system never allows for a time in the game when individuals can address the entire realm community at once. Instead, players interact in an extremely divided conversation space. Conversation spaces fall into two categories: chat channels restricted to chosen individuals and chat channels tied to a player's geographical location.

There are six major channels restricted to chosen individuals, as follows:

- Whispers—channels for conversations between two people
- Parties—channels for conversations between two to five people
- Raids—channels that allow conversations between two to 40 people
- Guild—channels that allow for contact between everyone in a guild
- Guild Officer—channels for conversations between people designated as guild officers
- Custom Channels—a conversational channel to which players must be invited

These channels are restricted. This means that the people within them know whom they are speaking to at all times and generally have made a conscious choice to enter into the conversational space.

Alternately, there are four major conversation spaces tied to a player's geographical location:[13]

- Say, which reaches anyone in the immediate vicinity of the player
- Yell, which reaches anyone in a large area around the player
- General, which reaches anyone inside the land or major city where the player is located
- Trade, which reaches everyone in a major city within a player's faction

While players can opt out of these spaces, either by turning the channel off or by putting all the players in their immediate area on "ignore," game defaults include players in geographically bound conversations.

Thus, there is never a time in which a player can speak to all people playing on a given realm at once. Even using the realm's official forums does not accomplish this, as only a fraction of players look at those forums. The most highly populated conversational space is the trade channel, whose purpose is to allow players to buy, sell, and trade in-game items. However, the trade channel on most realms also serves as a community channel, although only a fraction of players use it.

Therefore, players are in complete control over whom they speak to and when. Even in the case of default channels, a player's conversational space is always a smaller subsection of the larger realm community.

The Necessity of Groups in a Divided Space

The necessity of being in small groups to fully experience WoW pushes people into cooperative experiences, creating a constant need to address issues of fairness, resource distribution, and appropriate public behavior. Thus, although all the people playing WoW are playing the same game, much as geography and distance divide individuals in the "real" world, the WoW community is also divided in several different ways that have implications for community interaction.

Not only is the player space divided in such a way as to create smaller subsections of the larger community for players, but even though players have the option of playing the game solitarily—and many of them do, particularly the older players—the greatest prestige and best rewards can only be accessed when in a group. The architecture of the game pushes people into forming and participating in groups.

Easy group tasks tend to involve two to five people who work together to kill a monster or accomplish a single task. More complicated group tasks involve five-person "dungeons," which ask players to spend 30 minutes to several hours working collaboratively and using distinct skills to travel through dangerous places full of monsters and extremely dangerous dragons (bosses). Players also end up working in groups if they would like to engage in any of the battlegrounds, where they play other real people in games such as Capture the Flag. Finally, the highest prestige content with the best rewards requires 10 to 25 people (and, in the past 40) working together over hours, weeks, and months to defeat high-level dragons (bosses).

Many of these groups are temporary or "Pick-Up Groups," which allow people to come together for a short period of time to accomplish a specific task. However, even in these instances, players are expected to understand social norms and behave appropriately. The following quotation (which also begins this chapter) from late in the Burning Crusade expansion by a player remembering learning about social norms captures this expectation:

> The first time I ran Gnomer, the cloth helm that shoots lightning dropped, and I rolled need. The mage in the group went nuts. It was the first time I ever ran a dungeon with a group and killed bosses; I didn't know what I did was wrong. I just saw... it was better than... whatever I was wearing at the time. The mage won the roll and proceeded to call me a ninja. I explained that I didn't know what that meant. I think that's when the group actually took pity on me.

As the quotation above also captures, most in-game cooperative endeavors offer treasure as a reward for accomplishing a task. However, the amount of treasure a group receives as a reward for accomplishing an in-game task is never enough so that every member of the group receives a piece of treasure. In raids—collective group activities in which players usually kill a number of monsters—the amount of treasure each monster gives the group on a successful kill is commonly one piece of treasure to five people in five-person groups, two pieces of treasure to 10 people in 10-person groups, four pieces of treasure to 25 people in 25-person groups, and, in the past when there were 40-person groups, between two to four pieces of treasure to 40 people.

The game provides a tool for distributing the scarce resources that is essentially the equivalent of rolling dice, but many players consider this tool unfair. In the minds of many players, a role of the dice can mean that one person receives more of the rewards than others. Thus, in most raids, players circumvent the in-game feature. Blizzard has recognized the inherent problem presented by its rolling feature, so it has also instituted additional features for handling loot—in particular, the role of "loot master."

A group's Loot Master is named by the individual who formed the group. He has complete control over who receives an item. In "Pick-Up Groups" (PUGs)—or groups where people did not know each other previously—the person who forms the group is expected to notify the group as to what the treasure distribution system will be before the group begins fighting monsters. The discussion is necessary, because the group nearly always sidesteps the use of the rolling system for another human-controlled system.[14]

Because treasure distribution tends to be human controlled, concerns and debates about what is fair are common and ongoing. Although groups are brought together for instrumental reasons, such as to be able to see certain types of game content, to gain treasure, or to achieve a goal, the uncertainty about treasure gain creates a demand for predictable and trusted groups with whom individuals might engage in cooperative activities. Blizzard has provided a mechanism for creating a static and "trusted" group with transparent norms—guilds. Guilds also give groups a history of playing time together, which improves their chances for being successful against monsters.

As such, most guilds have long-term, predictable systems for distributing treasure among members. There are many commonly used systems, each rooted in its own set of values, but all aim to distribute treasures fairly enough across members so that they do not leave the guild. Some systems for distributing treasure reward length of membership in the guild; some reward attendance in group activities; some are random; and some are very neo-patrimonial.[15]

Because of the mismatch between the amount of treasure tied to each cooperative task and the number of people required to accomplish those tasks, players are extremely concerned with fair distribution of resources. Hence, although groups are brought together for instrumental reasons— that is, to be able to see certain types of game content, to gain treasure, or to achieve a goal—the uncertainty about treasure gain creates a demand for predictable and trusted groups with whom one can engage in cooperative activities. Blizzard's game architecture offers a solution to this as well in the form of guilds. Most serious players who intend to engage in long-term group activities join guilds. As Scott Andrews (2010a) said in his widely read blog regarding guild leadership strategies:

> In MMOs, distrust is a fact of life. . . . The people in your guild are often the only people in this entire gaming world that you *can* trust.

That's supposed to be the safe place, the place where people aren't out to scam you into giving them too much gold for an item, ninja a trinket or hack your account. If you can't trust the people in your own guild, what's the point of belonging to it? Trust is implicit in the guild experience.

Therefore, the game itself pushes people into groups and cooperative experiences. Once people are in these groups, political issues, such as those around resource distribution, become very important. However, as I will discuss later in the chapter, they become important over the long term because player identity tends to be static over time.

Anonymity and Reputation

In contrast to Anonymous, WoW is not only an immersive experience in which players are divided into subgroups of the larger community, but it is also a space where, through their characters, users have hierarchies and reputations separate from their offline identities. Although there may be the appearance of anonymity for the user, there is none for the user's character. WoW's lack of anonymity creates an in-game environment in which issues of governance such as fair resource distribution are important over time, because violating community norms can lead to long-term repercussions. Additionally, the lack of anonymity creates a situation in which control over the definition of appropriate behavior is important.

The role that the lack of anonymity has in shaping an in-game environment where normative struggles become important is most clear in the way in which individuals relate to and protect their in-game identities. Because a person's in-game identity can have a significant influence on a player's role in the realm community, identities are carefully managed. Thus, even though people in WoW are anonymous in that they use pseudonyms or "avatars" to represent themselves in the online space, people will go to great lengths to protect their primary character's reputations. For example, people are known and evaluated on their choice of character, their customization choices, their gear,[16] their history of playing and in-game achievements, their guild, their server, the "age" of the character, and their PvP scores. This evaluation system creates a hierarchical system that is independent of outside hierarchies. For example, a 15-year-old can be in charge of a 50-year-old in the in-game world.

Although people can create up to 10 characters per realm, most tend to identify one as "main," and the "main" carries their in-game reputation.

Usually players' "mains" are the characters they play the most, that have received the most resources, and that are optimized for the highest level of play. In addition, it is a main character that accrues the social capital of a player's good or bad deeds in the game. Mains also tend to have a privileged position in guilds and other groups. For example, in guilds they usually receive "treasure" before alternative characters (alts) do.

When a player has a bad reputation, her reputation usually travels from player to player on a given realm. For example, if a player misbehaves in a group activity, people in that group usually use a global chat channel and announce her misdeeds to anyone who is present in a major city. People also often go to the realm community forums, posting boards hosted on the WoW website, and announce the person's misdeeds, sometimes including screenshots of the offense. However, if enough people with respected reputations malign a player, their word carries the same weight as a screenshot. The misbehaving player is then ostracized.[17] For example, the following quote is from late in the Wrath of the Lich King expansion:

> I think anyone who joins one of his raids or invites him to theirs deserves what they get. . . . He is notorious for being a bad.

In many cases, after a highly publicized violation of in-game social norms, individuals will transfer the offending character to another realm, changing the character's name in the process. An individual's good or bad behavior in groups can have such a significant effect on game play that Blizzard (2010) includes a "How to be nice!" guide, outlining ways new players can improve their characters' reputations.

Players' behaviors in the game are also transparent in other ways that make people even less anonymous and more accountable for their in-game actions and choices. For example, Blizzard created the "WoW Armory," which contains every character in WoW over level 10. On the Armory, that character's gear, achievements, recent in-game activity, in-game accomplishments, and character customization choices are displayed, as well as other information about the character. The Armory makes it possible for players to examine, evaluate, and rank any character, based on the character's guild, armor choices, specialization choices, and so on.

Another way players' behaviors can be tracked comes from the wide array of external websites not connected to Blizzard created for that purpose. WoW Heroes was one such site. This site provided information similar to that found in the Armory, but it also assigned characters "scores" based on the strength of their gear and suggested what in-game battles are too easy or too difficult for the character based on that score.[18] WoW Heroes also ranked characters in relation to their guild mates and guilds in relation to each other—all based on gear. Another example of a character-tracking website is WoW Census, which gathers census data for WoW and tracks players' guild histories.

The lack of anonymity is not only apparent in the lengths individuals will go to in order to protect a main's reputation but also in the ways in which players will attempt to protect their guilds' reputations. For example, when someone wants to insult another player in the game or on the forums, he will often log into an alternative character, rather than his "main." By using an alternative character, he can protect the reputations of the main and the main's guild, while still saying whatever he likes. The practice is so common that people often chide others to "Post on your main." For example:

> And you totally missed the irony in the previous posts. You told them to man up, yet you're the one posting on an anonymous alt to prevent anybody from being able to put blame on you for this thread. So in your own words, man up and post on your main if you have a legitimate concern... oh wait, that'd probably just reveal the fact that you're probably either a) in the guild and will get gkicked, or b) you're in a much less progressed guild and probably just jealous of their 277's.[19]

As this quotation reveals, players not only refrain from posting on their mains to say something inflammatory but also to avoid comparative assessment of their game play in relation to the person they are criticizing.

Individual reputation in the game is also linked to a player's guild's reputation. An individual player's reputation can negatively or positively impact her guild's reputation, and, conversely, a guild's reputation can negatively or positively impact a player's reputation. The relationship between guild and player reputation is not necessarily linear, with each affecting the other over-time. Thus, people also use alts to protect their mains' guilds. In addition, in order to preserve their reputations, some guilds forbid their members from posting on the forums or in general conversation channels in the game. Therefore, the need to protect the guild reputation means that guilds often highly regulate their members' behavior. Regulation is often acceptable to players because a guild's positive reputation extends to all of its players, as the following quotation suggests:

> One thing I think most people in this thread have thus far agreed on is that trash talking [guild name removed] is kind of like punching

Mr. Rogers. Just goes to show, if you're nice enough and well liked enough, you will never need to defend yourself from people who irrationally trash you. The people you've helped and been cool within the past will willingly do it for you. Kudos to [guild name removed] to achieving that kind of respect on the realm.

On the other hand, a guild's negative reputation also extends to all players, as this quote indicates:

Why anyone groups with [guild name removed] at this point is beyond me. The community has been warned, multiple times now. Stay. Away. From. These. Wankers.

The active maintenance of player reputation is also apparent in the places where players do not work as hard to operate within community norms. For example, players generally agree that they are more likely to behave badly in cross-realm dungeon groups, where they are operating outside their guilds, because of the lack of accountability for their behavior. People are less likely to even say "hello" to each other. The following quotation captures this difference:

On the downside though, the current system has too little ability to police what goes on in these groups. Prior to cross-server dungeon groups, if you acted like a scrub in a group you would probably be kicked by the group leader and depending on the offense, you could possibly be blacklisted on your server.

Thus, although people are not using their "real" names, they are not operating in an anonymous space. Rather, they exist in a space in which they are accountable for poor behavior or even simply for behaving contrary to community norms. The extreme visibility of players means that definition of and adherence to in-game norms is very important.

Regulation

WoW players and the guilds in which they operate end up in a position where they regulate, dispute, and generate community norms because much of the behavior regulation in WoW is conducted by the community itself. While Blizzard has a set of rules for players and has a system by which deviants can be reported to Game Masters for punishment, the regulation of players in WoW is largely left to the game architecture and players. Blizzard outlines some additional rules on their website under the title "In-Game Support Policies." But Blizzard's policies are only sketches of rules. They include descriptions of account penalties; how to interact with Blizzard's in-game "police," the Game Masters; regulation of inappropriate names; harassment of other players; exploitation/manipulation of the server/client (i.e., cheating); and unauthorized account access.

ENFORCEMENT BY BLIZZARD

In theory, WoW players are always being watched, because Blizzard records all chat logs and interactions in the game; however, in practice, for Blizzard to enforce rules it has to be "called in" by other players. Players report other players for spamming chats with advertisements, for using exploiting programs to "cheat" in game, for stealing, for harassment, for hate speech, and a wide range of other concerns. When a player reports an in-game issue, he opens a screen in the game that tries to fix the problem without requiring interaction with a Game Master.

If the issue is more complex, as it often is, the player pushes the "Talk to a GM" button. This button takes the player to a new screen. Once a player has submitted a complaint, a small window appears on the top right of his screen. The window says, "You have an open ticket. We are currently experiencing a high volume of petitions."

The wait for a conversation with a Game Master can be as short as 10 minutes and as long as many days. People report on the forums and in-game that the wait time for a conversation with a Game Master seems to depend on the type of issue. However, Blizzard does not make this process transparent.

In the past, people who were accused of breaking game rules had their characters transported to an island in the game, only accessible by Game Masters, and held in a "prison" (Holisky, 2010) until the issue was resolved. Blizzard has since removed the player "jail," and instead it bans players from the game while resolving severe account violations.

Finally, even if Blizzard's regulation were more extensive and less reliant on player notification, the creators of WoW would have difficulty navigating the dense network of community-generated and community-policed norms.

PLAYER-TO-PLAYER NORM REGULATION

In spite of what seems to be an extensive system of regulation, the fact that players have to call a Game Master in to deal with issues means that much of the regulation of player behavior is done by other players (including players reporting each other to Blizzard). Players regulate each other's behavior in the game in many ways, but the most frequently used method is shaming and/or ostracizing players who violate realm norms or do not adhere to "cookie cutter" ways of customizing their characters or play-style.

Just as it is in "real" life, ostracizing a group member is a very effective way of affirming community norms in WoW, as the following example shows. In early 2010, a player—"Frank"—who organized "Pick-Up Group" raids was accused on the forums of having stolen a valuable piece of treasure. In an additional accusation made soon after, he was accused of having given a valuable piece of treasure to a guild mate rather than to the person who had actually won the item. In response, the raiding class on the server began a systematic effort to ostracize him. For example:

> Frank tried to sneak into one of my PuGs again and ##%@%ed me out when I wouldn't invite. His tears were sweet indeed. No one wants to group with a ninja.

From mid-February onward, Frank's name came up repeatedly on the realm forums and in trade chat channels. When he tried to get raids together or join raids, people would immediately tell everyone that he was a "ninja." A "ninja" is someone who steals something in-game—usually by taking something that other players define as rightfully belonging to someone else. For example:

> I've seen people call this Frank person out in trade when he is spamming for his ICC PUGs.... What am I missing? Why do people still group with this guy and then get upset when he pulls the same crap over and over?

On the realm forums, his name became a joke, synonymous with a player with whom no one wanted to group. For example:

> And to be clear. I'm not as bad as Frank, at least, I hope.

His reputation also extended to his guild, which subsequently had trouble finding partners with whom to collaborate to accomplish in-game goals as the following quotation captures:

For the love of God, do not compare us to Frank's retarded guild.

Although reaching the level of realm-wide ostracism is fairly unusual, individual-level shaming often occurs when a players fails to abide by community norms.

Another informal method of player-to-player behavior regulation is "norming" of play-style. Norming of play focuses on the type of gear players use, the ways in which they optimize that gear, the choices they make to customize their characters, and the strategies they use in different types of encounters. All of these choices and others have been standardized by the guild community in which the players operate. Players who do not follow the guidelines, which are laid out across informational and official WoW websites, are often judged to be inadequate players without any other evidence of their inadequacy, as is illustrated in the following quotation, where a player is judging another player for not adhering to "cookie cutter" customization choices:

> I am all for leveling guilds and learning guilds. Everyone needs to start somewhere. The problem with [guild name removed] is absolutely no one has a clue on how to play their class, class mechanics, or even loot rules. Not many guilds are an actual disservice to the server, but I personally believe that [guild name removed] is exactly that. It is not hard to work the internets and use the googles to understand a class these days. Apparently in [name removed] they choose willful ignorance as part of their core beliefs. I personally would never again run a PUG with one of their members.

Other examples are plentiful. For example, an individual made a thread asking about a dynamic of a particular fight with a monster in the game. As part of the question the individual noted that his guild did not use the "normal" strategy for engaging the monster in a fight. While the player's question was about a detail of the fight, the majority of responses did not even address the question. Instead, most respondents said that it was impossible to conduct the fight in any but the "normal" way. When the author indicated that his guild had, in fact, been repeatedly successful at the fight using an unconventional strategy, posters stated that they did not believe the questioner.

Play style normalization is due in large part to the huge network of non-Blizzard-owned websites that discuss the game in detail, recommending ways of playing, recommending play practices, and offering detailed analysis of in-game dynamics. When the player above stated that people needed to learn to "work the internets and use the googles" to professionalize themselves as players, he was essentially stating that players needed to draw on these third-party sites to educate themselves as to how to play.

My research indicates that the underlying informational network that shows people how to play and what conventional choices ought to be is a network of players. Blizzard's official guides are fairly inadequate to teach players how to play and behave; therefore, the bulk of player resources are created and maintained by players volunteering their time and using cheap or free online tools. A short list of some of the sites that would have been central to a professionalized WoW player's gaming life includes the following:[20]

- Wow.com—formerly (and currently) *WoW Insider*, Wow.com claims to be the largest WoW blog and information site.
- Wowhead.com—a resource for WoW players that includes a huge searchable database of information of all types about the game.
- Thottbot.com—a resource for WoW players that includes a huge searchable database of information of all types about the game.
- ElitistJerks.com—a WoW discussion forum that focuses on high-end raiding and game mechanics. The site was created by a guild with the same name.
- GuildOx.com—a website that tracks guild progress and ranks guilds in relation to each other, player movements, and player gear.
- TankSpot.com—a website created by a guild that houses discussion forums, advice for players, and widely used strategy guides for different in-game encounters. For example, their 10-player strategy for fighting the Lich King has been viewed more than a million times.
- WorldofRaids.com—a WoW guide site that includes a tracker of Blizzard commentary, forums, and guides.
- MaxDPS.com—a site that helps players to optimize their characters for the highest performance levels.
- WowProgress.com—a site that tracks guild accomplishments and ranks guilds in relation to each other, tracks characters, and attempts to track characters that have changed their names.
- Bosskillers.com—a site that focuses on strategy guides for different in-game encounters.
- MMO-Champion.com—an informational site that offers every kind of information about WoW to players.
- Wowwiki.com—a "Wikipedia"-style site about WoW that also includes widely used strategy guides.

- WoW Census—a site that draws on community provided information to track the number of players and player types across realms.

Furthermore, how to find these online resources is not disseminated by online sites, such as links from official websites—but rather through word of mouth—by experienced players who tell other players best play practices and the best websites to use to learn how to play as they do. Even in the cases of forum posts on the official Blizzard forums, the posts are made by players attempting to help the community. Thus, even accessing pertinent information online is a social enterprise and the norms of play are generated and reinforced largely by player-to-player regulation and information sharing.

Guild Norm Regulation

Thus far, I have argued that WoW players are known to each other and extensively regulate each other's behavior. Another common way player behavior is regulated is through guilds. As noted previously, guilds are groups of players who gather together over a long term to accomplish a variety of tasks. Guilds serve many purposes, but one of their main effects is that they regulate player behavior.

While guild creation is provided by the game architecture, guilds themselves are fundamentally political entities with wide variation in purpose, management, and leadership structure. However, in all cases guilds are "owned" by the "Guild Leader" (also commonly referred to as the Guild Master). The game's architecture gives Guild Leaders the power to invite players into their guilds, create guild ranks, promote/demote players, kick players from the guild, allow/disallow access to the guild bank, grant players extensive powers such as the ability to kick others out of the guild or invite new people into the guild, and transfer Guild Leadership to another member. The Guild Leader has ultimate power over the guild, so even when a guild runs in a democratic fashion, guilds are ultimately not democracies.

Guilds often create highly developed rule systems that are housed on guild websites that are external to the game. A comparison of guild rules across guilds on a given realm shows that often they share common rules. For instance, individual guilds often include rules about guild members not behaving "badly" in realm chat channels. For example:

> Fairly simple. Don't be a jackass publicly if it's going to bring large amounts of drama and bullshit on the guild's head. Respect your guildies and allow them the same courtesy that you expect from them.

Do not engage in any activity that would have a negative impact on the name of the guild (Trade chat drama, ninja'ing, trolling)

Some guilds also regulate the type of language that guild members are allowed to use in chat channels. For example:

No excessive cussing, racial slurs, or derogatory comment in ANY chat channel while guild tagged.

Please keep guild and vent PG-13 until midnight server-time.

And guilds that do *not* manage player language also often announce that in their rules. For example:

You should understand that you will be exposed to swearing and topics of an adult nature—but you should also be able to keep it under control without excessive vulgarity and absolutely NO comments that can interpreted as racist or insulting toward sexual gender or preference etc.

This is a guild for mature players. There is no rule against swearing, adult topics, or anything like that.

In addition, guilds often restrict the subjects players are permitted to talk about to minimize conflict among guild members. For example:

Keep chat topics light. There are two things you never discuss openly with your guild mates: politics and religion.

As evidenced here, the ability to mobilize politically is significantly reduced by political speech being forbidden speech in some groups.

While speech is the easiest regulation to spot, most guilds also do not permit their members to break realm norms. When guild members violate realm norms by "stealing," guilds often will "kick" them from the guild. For example:

He was kicked after this was found out. I would like to say that this person does not reflect the people in our guild nor do we support this kind of !#!#.

If a player reports offensive speech or other behavior violations occurring within her guild, most often Blizzard Game Masters will tell the player to take the behavior issue up with the Guild Leader. If the person being reported is the Guild Leader, Game Masters will encourage the complaining player to leave the guild.

In a few well-known instances Blizzard has intervened in the internal matters of guilds, but nearly always in relation to that guild's outward behavior. In one widely publicized event, Blizzard told gay, bisexual, lesbian, and transsexual (GBLT) guilds that they could not restrict recruitment to GBLT members under threat of banning because, in its words,

> topics related to sensitive real-world subjects—such as religious, sexual or political preference, for example—have had a tendency to result in communication between players that often breaks down into harassment. (As quoted in Terdiman, 2006b)

On another occasion, Blizzard forcibly disbanded an extreme erotic role-playing guild that made its nature open in its recruiting. The guild's warning is below:

> NOTE: Be advised that we frequently ERP in guild chat and often engage in even potentially offensive kinks such as (Extreme) Ageplay, Bestiality, Child Birth. . . Watersports, or any other kink those playing may wish to explore. (As quoted in Wachowski, 2007)

It is important to note that Blizzard does not seem to intervene in guilds that allow only male or female players, guilds that only allow people of a certain nationality (e.g., Dutch-only), guilds restricting membership based on age, or guilds that restrict on the basis of language (e.g., French Canadian guilds). There are also many Christian guilds, with places such as the Christian Gamers Alliance hosting lists and contact information for interested gamers.[21] Other religion-based guilds appear to be rarer—with some impossible-to-substantiate rumors that Muslim-only guilds are not allowed. There is no evidence that race-/ethnicity-based guilds exist, which indicates that Blizzard is likely regulating them quickly or there are very few.

As I have discussed, because guilds form little worlds within the larger world, players devote a great deal of effort to regulating behavior inside the guild. However, because of the importance of reputation in WoW, they also expend a great deal of effort in regulating player behavior outside the guild.

REALM-TO-REALM GENERATED RULES

Player-generated rules are the result of extensive negotiation among players over time on each realm, and this is made evident in the normative differences between realms. Such differences can be seen in the places where realms interact.

For example, when Blizzard created cross-realm dungeon groups within Battlegroups, an unforeseen conflict arose within the groups because of differing assumptions about norms that players brought from their realms to the shared space of the battleground.[22] When the last "boss" was conquered in each dungeon, a "frozen orb" would drop. Frozen orbs were mildly valuable items used for in-game recipes. When the final dragon was looted, a loot window would appear that had the same options that appear for any loot. A player could use a "dice" to "need" an item, "greed" an item, or "pass" the item. Each type of roll has its own dice, and each dice rolls 1–100.

In the cases of distinct items—for example, gloves—people would indicate "need" if the item was something they could use, "greed" if they wanted it to sell, or "pass" if they did not want the item. Need has greater weight than greed in the game. Thus, a player who greed-rolls a 100 would lose to a player who need-rolled a five. Therefore, based on the roll, the game would then award the item accordingly.

Frozen orbs presented something of a challenge, because they were useful to everyone and they could be traded among players freely. Therefore, the distinction between "need" and "greed" for frozen orbs was considerably blurred. In this case, the game interface did not provide a clear prescription for action.

Thus, on every realm, different norms appeared for how to deal with frozen orbs. On the realm I observed, everyone in the group used the "greed" option because the item was not technically needed by anyone. However, on some other realms, everyone in the group used the "need" option, because the item was technically of equal value to everyone in the group. On other realms, everyone would pass on the item, and then would do a separate roll between 1 and 100 (in-game this would be referred to as "/roll") to determine who won the item. A "/roll" is a typed command players can use to generate a random number for each player in the group.

For the people from realms that did not "need" frozen orbs, the needers were perceived to have stolen the items (ninjas). Similarly, for the people from realms that did not "greed" frozen orbs but, rather, where everyone passed the item, the greeders were perceived to be ninjas. The debate spilled into the forums with many threads created where players complained about "frozen orb ninjas." Some threads were made across realm forums, whereas others were made in general forums. People from realms that habitually attached "need" to the frozen orbs claimed that everyone technically needed them, because they could be used to make in-game money. People whose servers were not in the practice of "needing" orbs often refused to change their custom, frequently arguing that their choice was the "right" choice and that they were not going to be forced by "ninjas" to change the way they did things.[23] Over time, people in one realm started to watch others' behaviors and modify their own rolls based on what others did. But the debate over what was the "right" way to roll did not subside on the forums. Thus, after a few months of debate, Blizzard modified the interface so there was no longer an option to do anything else but "need" the frozen orbs.

In an older example, before the player-versus-player aspect of the game involved cross-realm interaction, players could earn titles and rewards based on their success playing other people in their realm's battlegrounds (e.g., games where members from the Alliance and the Horde compete in games similar to Capture the Flag). The most difficult to obtain titles and rewards could only be earned each week by a tiny fraction of players—with the most prestigious title, Grand Marshal / High Warlord only being awarded to a single player in each faction. On some realms all of the players who were pursuing the Grand Marshal / High Warlord title would organize them-selves, decide who would earn the title each week, and monitor each other's progress. Anyone who threatened the chosen player's acquisition of the title was deterred in his or her own progress by the organized players who had guaranteed the chosen player's success. In return, players who were "good" community members—that is, who supported the group's decisions—were rewarded when it was their turn to acquire the title. Players who adhered to this system argued that not only was it more fair, but it prevented players from having to dedicate hours and hours of their life to win a title—or from violating game rules by having many individuals play one character in order to continue play for 24 hours a day.

However, on other servers, the title was rewarded through open com-petition between players. The tensions between the two systems would be revealed when Blizzard would open up new realms and allow people from established realms to transfer for free into the new realms. Players would arrive with a set of expectations about appropriate or fair play that was, in many cases, in direct opposition to the expectations of players from other realms. In the weeks that followed, players would try to convince players from other realms that their realm's system was the best one. This was often a process accompanied with threats of ostracism for players who did not agree to change behavior.

It is important to note that there are also many instances of shared norms across realms. For example, during the game-wide holiday "Children's Week," in which players from all realms can choose to participate in various holiday events in player-versus-player battlegrounds, cross-realm players from both Horde and Alliance factions worked together, bypassing the game architecture, to help each other fulfill holiday objectives. The majority of Horde players would stand by (instead of attempting to attack or kill Alliance players) while Alliance players achieved holiday goals and vice versa. Meanwhile, players in both factions who tried to undermine the cooperation were ostracized, censored, and shunned by the majority of the players who were cooperating.

The difference between realm norms is evidence of the "domestic" processes of norm debate and development on realms. The development of realm norms is due to the division of in-game space, the need for small groups, the lack of anonymity, and the necessity of players to regulate each other's behavior. However, even in cases where realms share some norms, there is always some mismatch between beliefs about appropriate behavior.

Normative Conflict

As in the cases of The Pirate Bay and Anonymous, users do not arrive in WoW as blank slates, but rather their preexisting beliefs about fairness, resource distribution, and appropriate public behavior shape player choices in the game. The manner in which divergent offline normative contexts are filtered through the game architecture can be seen in the short life of most guilds and in the durability of the small groups of players that find each other in the game and play together over very long periods of time.

Research on WoW guilds has found that most guilds have very short lives (Ducheneaut et al., 2007). Ducheneaut et al. argue that guilds do not endure for a variety of reasons, such as leadership, burn-out playing the game, "drama," and in-group politics. However the work of Ducheneaut and colleagues does not indicate why these factors might destroy guilds; instead, the authors' focus is on optimal group size for accomplishing collaborative tasks successfully (which they conclude is about 35).

As Ducheneaut et al. (2007) and others have noted, guild culture is not only about the distribution of treasure; it is also a social environment that regulates player behavior. Because so many guilds limit discussion about politically divisive topics such as politics and religion, value fault lines tend to concern other types of belief systems. All cooperative activity in the game involves players acting on their individual moral values, especially concerning how scarce resources should be distributed, what is appropriate language, what is offensive, and how people should treat one another. Thus, even in a space in which political discourse seems to be limited and players appear to be held together for instrumental reasons, the different ways in which guilds attempt to control and reward player behavior can come into conflict with individual player beliefs. Therefore, in the crowded marketplace of guilds, while players may look for guilds that can achieve their desired in-game goals, guild instability is caused because players also look for guilds that fit their own individual beliefs about appropriate behavior and sometimes it takes a while to find such guilds.

My research indicates that guilds themselves have value subgroups within them that ultimately create larger group instability and guild collapse. In addition, my research shows that the smaller value groups do not break up when the guilds break up; rather, the smaller value groups continue to play together—often moving through many guilds. This means that new guilds may tend to be less stable, because when player values do not overlap with guild values, eventually the rewards of guild membership no longer keep the individual in the guild. Either the individual leaves with her friends for another guilds or she creates conflicts in the guild that overwhelm normal interaction and cause the guild to fracture. In contrast to new guilds, stable guilds tend to have a core of players whose personal beliefs match guild beliefs, with new members either agreeing to those beliefs or leaving after a short period of time.

WoW value subgroups within larger guilds can be observed through longitudinal study. For example, I tracked a group of people originally in one guild from 2005 to 2010. The original guild—Guild Zero—broke up in 2006, after nine months of guild activity. When it broke up, it dissolved along value lines. About 25 percent of the guild, including about two-thirds of the guild leadership, formed a new guild—Guild A—that had most of the same rules and values as the original guild. Another 25 percent, including one of the guild officers, formed a second guild—Guild B—with a different set of rules. In this guild, the treasure distribution system was changed, the prohibition on certain types of language was loosened, and the leadership model changed. A third group within the original guild—again about 25 percent—including several of the guild's longtime, influential members, also formed its own guild—Guild C—with an entirely different set of rules. This group also changed the treasure distribution system. In addition, the group completely removed any prohibitions on language and changed the leadership model. The final quarter of the original guild members scattered into other guilds.

Since the 2006 guild split, these three cohesive value groups have moved together through the game. For example, Guilds A and C have maintained the guilds they formed after Guild Zero broke up and these guilds remained intact from 2007 to 2010 with their numbers remaining relatively static. Alternately, Guild B has moved through many guilds, sometimes forming and disbanding guilds under its control and sometimes joining and then leaving guilds under other players' control. However, the same core group of people has stayed involved together. These three groups have also collected new players around them, and while some of the new group members stick to each group, others do not. But the original value groups have remained somewhat the same.

Thus, while Yee points to issues such as leadership and the game architecture as a limiting factor on the life of guilds, my research reveals that there is an external factor influencing the life cycle of guilds: the individual values that players bring to the game. Guild culture and the ways in which guilds break up and form, as well as the enduring nature of smaller groups in the game, indicate that players' in-game experience is significantly shaped by their own beliefs about appropriate behavior. Furthermore, my research suggests that using guilds as the lens of understanding groups in WoW hides the endurance of friendship networks that are often based on shared values.

Offline normative beliefs are filtered through this in-game structure and the demands of game play rather than being projected outwards. As mentioned in the first chapter, in such a context, small differences in beliefs about appropriate behavior can become significant distinguishing features between groups, in contrast to the broader strokes of belief apparent in Anonymous or The Pirate Bay. The norms of behavior and beliefs about resource distribution seem to crosscut national groups in the English-speaking American/Oceania realm groups. Therefore, there seems to be no pattern of grouping—for example, Canadians are not all forming Canada-exclusive guilds because of beliefs about resource distribution. Even language-specific guilds appear to be fairly rare.

The only obvious value divisions can be seen in age restrictions on player membership in guilds—as well as a few highly publicized cases of high-end raiding guilds stating they did not want female members. This also means that in addition to the bonding activity that Yee discovered in his studies (i.e., closer ties with people previously known), players are engaging in cross-national cooperative activities and value negotiation, which could be considered bridging activities (i.e., building ties with people not previously known).

Conclusion

Because WoW's durable groups are based on common values, one would expect to see types of political action similar to those I found with Anonymous and The Pirate Bay. However, my research also seems to indicate that online, larger anonymous groups are more likely to engage in large-scale online and offline political behavior.

It is widely documented that when the smaller WoW groups do cross over into "real life," it is in the form of friendships and small-group meet-ups. However, unlike the cases of Anonymous and The Pirate Bay, the larger group stays internal to the game, and people clearly see a line between the in-game world and the "outside world." Guilds continue to make rules forbidding the discussion of politics, and offline organization remains fairly nonexistent. Instead, the political behavior arising from this space is the internal debates about value systems, in which individuals' external belief systems come into conflict with the beliefs of others. The political behavior in this case is the constant negotiation between players over questions such as fairness in resource distribution and appropriate speech.

5

IGN.com

Conversation without Mobilization

10 years I have been on this forum. . . and what do I get in return? A wonderful, awesome community that has become a great place for me to let out my anger, my hostility and to be among a great group of people. . . I just want to say in this thread that I love you guys so much and thanks for being part of my life.

—IGN.com user celebrating 10 years of participation

The highly anonymous and relatively unregulated online communities of Anonymous and The Pirate Bay have produced widespread political mobilization, including online hacktivism, offline activism, online and offline protest, and support of political parties. In World of Warcraft (WoW), a social space in which people are not anonymous and are moderately regulated, people engage in debates about norms of fairness, speech, and resource distribution. These debates have tangible consequences for the participants, and differences of opinion splinter players into small groups and cause players to form long-lasting "real life" relationships. But, in spite of the close personal relationships, WoW players have not produced any meaningful political mobilization. IGN Entertainment's online discussion board system (formerly Imagine Gaming Network) is characterized by political conversations and debates but no political mobilization.

Of the four cases in *Expect Us*, IGN's board system is the most similar in technological form to Anonymous's board systems. However, in contrast with Anonymous groups' homes, the board systems attached to IGN.com are not anonymous and are highly regulated. People on IGN.com's posting boards engage in conversations about every subject possible. Thus, they also end up vigorously debating everything—politics, religion, ethics, food, bathroom habits, race issues, social policy, video game quality, and which actresses are hotter, among other topics. In spite of the constant debate and the fact that people in the space splinter into small groups and form long-lasting relationships, the space has not produced any widespread political mobilization, making its political outcomes more analogous to those of WoW—a video game—than to those of the other community that emerged from posting forums considered here—Anonymous.

Indeed, much as it does in WoW, the lack of anonymity on the IGN. com posting boards means people form smaller groups within the larger group. These smaller groups tend to weaken large-group cohesion, which is further weakened by an extremely accessible board format. Such a format allows for private conversation between users and minimizes a need for a strict lexicon or knowledge of community history to indicate belonging. These factors, tied to a high level of regulation of speech and behavior on IGN.com, undermine collective group mobilization. However, even though there is no political mobilization, there is extensive debate about politics and some indication that these conversations influence user beliefs.

What Are IGN.com and the Vesti?

IGN Entertainment was created in 1996 as Imagine Gaming Network. It has since changed its name to "IGN Entertainment." It is owned by Rupert Murdock's News Corporation, and its headquarters are in San Francisco. According to IGN Entertainment, the combined IGN online products/ websites are the most visited group of online locations by 18- to 34-year-old American men (IGN.com, 2010). In the United States, IGN.com is in the top 200 most visited websites and in the top 300 visited websites internationally according to Alexa.com in 2011. Its users are 69 percent male, and IGN claims its users spend up to 40 percent more time with their content than the online average (IGN.com, 2010).

The IGN.com array of online brands includes the extremely popular subsidiaries Askmen.com, Gamespy Industries, and GameStats. As part of their many services, IGN houses widely respected video game reviews, movie reviews, video game walk-throughs, comic book reviews, and trailers for upcoming releases, among other content. In this chapter, I focus on a subsection of IGN.com, the IGN.com-housed posting board system.

The IGN posting boards were initially developed in 1999. In an interview, the lead programmer and administrator of the boards at the time, Brian Claridge, said that the board system accounted for about 30 percent of IGN's overall traffic.[1] The board system includes a range of boards, the majority specific to certain games or TV shows (e.g., Prince of Persia or Lost), some loosely grouped around a topic (e.g., Australia board; PC Games; Movies; Sex, Health, & Dating), and a few "community" boards, each with its own community. The most trafficked IGN board is "the Vesti"—originally named "the Vestibule." Perhaps counterintuitively, although the board's name means "entryway," most users report they find their way to the Vesti via other boards on IGN.com. In 2011, the number of registered users, as measured by Big Boards, was around 1,255,254.

IGN's board format is essentially the same as most message board systems.[2] The forum is subdivided into posting boards. One could consider a message board system as a house with each room in the house an individual board. Each board contains many threads, and each thread is made up of individual posts. In the house metaphor, those threads would be the conversations occurring within the "rooms" of the message board. Threads are most frequently organized chronologically, arranged on the page by the time/date of the last post within the thread.

Each thread could be considered a "conversation" with users responding to each other's posts. These conversations are considered "asynchronous" because they do not have to occur at the same time, such as conversations in a chat room do. The "conversation" is archived and, usually, remains visible even if there is a large gap in time between posts. Thus, a user may begin a thread by making a post and not receive a reply for days. When a thread receives a reply, that thread is "bumped" to the top of the list of threads on a given board.

On the Vesti, with the exception of the hours from 1:00 to 7:00 a.m. PST, so many people are posting responses to threads that a thread receiving no replies can disappear off the front page of the board in a matter of seconds. Thus, even though the format is set up for "asynchronous" communication, at peak hours the Vesti operates more like a threaded chat room, with many conversations essentially occurring in real time. As a user said in response to a thread asking if people remembered the first time they saw the Vesti:

I joined IGN right around the time GTAIV was coming out to post on the GTA boards. . . . I remember someone over there talking about it so I ventured to the magical land. I made a thread here and it was off the page in about a minute. I was shocked.

Posters on the Vesti can include any IGN user. They tend to be mostly male and younger than 25, but because so many posters have "grown up" posting on the boards, users between 13 and 60 post together at various times of the day, with the majority being between the ages of 15 and 26.

My research focused on the Vesti but takes into account other IGN boards as well. This is because the boards as a whole could be considered a social system, with the Vesti serving as the heart. Many users very occasionally post on the Vesti or "lurk" there without posting anything. The large number of lurkers became apparent in 2005 when several pranksters posted a link on the Vesti that, when clicked, changed the user's icon to a picture of a steak and caused the user to repost the link in a new thread with the title "STEAK!!"[3] The script quickly spread to boards across IGN.com as lurkers clicked the link.

Additionally, not only does the Vesti have the highest traffic of all the boards in the IGN board system, but users across boards have an awareness of Vesti events. For example, in one case the news broke on the Vesti that a well-known and popular moderator (who happened to be the mother of another well-known user) had taken an unemployed and also popular user into her home and had engaged in an ongoing affair with him with the consent of her husband. The news was widely commented on across posting boards even by people who were not Vesti users.

Conversation without Mobilization

As was true for the cases of Anonymous, WoW, and Pirate Bay, the IGN posting boards are also an unlikely location for any type of political behavior. While IGN sites span entertainment genres, many people using the IGN posting boards report finding them because they are searching for IGN's video game boards. Thus, users frequently arrive at the board system for entertainment purposes and stay to socialize. Additionally, while I was studying IGN, there was no "politics" board among the general topics boards. While there was a "current events" board, it had very little traffic or discussion; only a handful of users actively participated on the board.

Also as was true for the other three cases, there are no links or connections to political sites or resources from the board systems other than links offered by posters. Snapshots of discussion topics show that the majority of topics discussed on the Vesti are not political. For example, the first 50 threads on February 7, 2011, around 4:25 p.m., are listed below. The italicized threads are those that were still on the first page two hours later:

1. Board code is not working because[4]
2. ——— *Official Monday Night RAW Thread (February 7, 2011)* ———
3. Which movie should I watch 1st: Slumdog Millionare, Inglorious Basterds, or Inception?
4. you know that their is a problem with.athiest......
5. Not eating meat will lower your testosterone and turn you into a pansy
6. *With all the available meat-substitutes, how's it even possible for meat-eaters to continue killing?*
7. *How do you pronounce "McDonalds"?*
8. You think you can change the way things are done in CHICAGO?!?!?
9. Don't you guys feel sorry for Alaska, Delaware, Montana, Vermont, Wyoming & North/South Dakota?[5]
10. Why do non-Americans bash us so often YET they continue to post on this AMERICAN website?
11. Icon doesn't show when PMing
12. Do you think you will ever directly kill another human in your life?
13. ** Mr McMahon Returns tonight as Monday Night Raw!!**
14. 82 percent of Egyptians Believe adulterers should be stoned
15. Shounen Big Three Manga—Naruto, One Piece, Bleach—Which is your favorite?
16. *i hate liberals*[6]
17. Holy ****. Never **** with Anon
18. Vince returns to RAW tonight
19. DAMN IT... my girlfriend just dumped me on my birthday today.
20. ITT: You post with yourt eyes closed an d, kidrubf gyer hanbds
21. Vesti Soul Silver adventure
22. lol at people who go to community college to be a cop
23. What's the best Digital Audio Workstation software?
24. Funny story inside, WOW people are idiots
25. Best "superpower" ever
26. Why is the Dyson vacuum guy obsessed with balls and suction?
27. I'd get KZ3, except Rico is in it
28. Vesti, what do you usually talk about with a girl you met & aren't sure if you share a common interest
29. My Girlfriend's Ass Flatulates like a mother****er

30. ITT: use this video game name generator and post the name of your video game, would you play it?
31. *110 MILLION people tuned in to watch Super Bow XLV; becomes most watched program in US history*
32. ITT: You post with your eyes closed. . . WITH YOUR NOSE
33. Hockey > Football
34. SCENARIO: Kim Kardashian does a shake weight commercial
35. lol at people who go to community college for 7 years.
36. ATTN: MeatIsMurderSoStop
37. quote = dr.Indiana]Indy's Board Code Quote-a-thon [/quote][7]
38. By Primus, the Transformers: Prime Toys look ****ing gorgeous
39. Did anyone feel a little sick after watching the Taco Bell commercial with the 4 steak taco?
40. What do YOU post from most? (browser)
41. 4Chan sucks
42. ITT: Nostalgia NEEDED DESPERATELY
43. So, the guy I know dropped another song (Gorilla Warfare Tactics)
44. Favorite part of the male body? (Besides penis)
45. Are there any other cliques on the Vesti besides "Hotties 18+/Cat People"?
46. Seriously, what the hell did professor Ivy do to Brock?
47. Question. . . if i play psn games on 2 diff systems do trophies sync on both?
48. *Dragon Age 2 is looking pretty good*
49. I love anti-jokes
50. Who else avidly enjoys KILLING animals to eat their flesh?

During the late afternoon, there is a far larger and more diverse crowd of posters on the Vesti. The mix includes people posting from work, young people in the United States posting after school, and, because of the time compatibility, people posting from all over the world. Alternately, late at night, the number of posters decreases. For example, on February 3, 2011, at around midnight PST, the first 50 threads were the following:

1. Board code not working because. . .
2. ALL of my Steam games are ****ed up, need some help ITT[8]
3. One of the funniest troll face cartoons I've seen in a while [physics related]
4. Battle of the IGN younglings

5. Just heard a lound bang, power went out and. . .
6. Why do some Religious people believe being an Atheist makes you immoral
7. Which southern state do you associate with the most inbred, uneducated, lazy rednecks?
8. What are you bros getting your lady for Valentine's Day?
9. Whatever happened to JongaBonito?
10. How many Lil B songs are in your iTunes?
11. Damn playing K23 with the Move is awesome.
12. BREAKING NEWS: Mark Up now available for IGN Insiders!
13. Those 10 (16) ranked. (FAIL ITT)
14. The Greatest user in the History of IGN hasn't posted since Aug of 09
15. Lebron James has 23 points in the 1st quarter
16. All the best sitcom dads went BOWLING. . . weird
17. If the Wolverines beat the Buckeyes in basketball tonight I WUL the entire thread
18. Post your Marvel Vs. Capcom 3 team
19. Obama's and US Government's stance on Egypt has been shameful.
20. Changing aim sensitivity in Killzone 3
21. any sims players? looking to get my first sims 3 expansion
22. Official No Markup Length Predictons Thread
23. ~*~ The Official Vesti NBA 2k11 Online Association Thread ~*~
24. Tonight Michigan beats Ohio State and the Magic beat the Heat
25. My first attempt at a troll-face comic
26. Killzone 3 has some insane graphics
27. What is the maximum amount of $ you're willing to drop for the PSP2
28. you people do the "but that's _____" thing all wrong
29. So the markup being down has pretty much ruined MUs for a month
30. If you have steam and play CSS or TF2
31. CNN said i'll be dead by 21.
32. I've never heard a little b song.
33. ~~** Official Vesti Mafia NHL '11 Team Thread **~~
34. have u ever smelled ur pee after u ate asparagus before
35. Religion has no place in a thinking man's society. . .
36. ATTACK OF THE SHOW JUST MENTIONED THE IGN BOARD CRASHES
37. ITT: The VESTI builds a Minecraft EMPIRE!
38. What are you doing tonight, Vesti?
39. Its like Egypt up in here
40. Vampire Diaries or American Idol?

41. After reading this preview, I'm almost drooling with anticipation for Deus Ex: Human Revolution
42. Can you make your iTunes library available to all users on a PC?
43. First 10 ranked.
44. So, what are your feelings on the KZ3 beta so far?
45. Do threads automatically lock at 3 pages now?
46. ITT: My favorite Lil B line
47. THE Ohio State University will win the NCAA Title this year
48. ITT We sing WWE superstar Alberto Del Rio's theme
49. THANK YOU ACID GOD
50. WHY CAN'T IGN IP BAN WTF MAN!!!!!!!!!!

These two lists show the range of topics discussed on the Vesti. Within the list of titles, there are obvious political conversations—or in the case of the first list, a debate about meat eating that spilled over into multiple threads.

Threads discussing politics are not uncommon. For example, in May 2007, there was a poll on abortion, in which users debated when abortion might be appropriate. At the time, 51 percent voted that the mother should decide whether/when to have an abortion, while 44 percent voted that it was "never" appropriate. Three percent were undecided. The thread directly next to the abortion debate was filled with photos of nearly naked women. Other threads on the board at the same time were: "WE LIVE IN AMERICA WE DO NOT NEED SIGNS IN SPANISH"; "PC Vista > PS3, 360, Wii"; "I'm about to be a father"; "rate what I've been doing before I go to bed lately"; "why do liberals love partial birth abortion but not the death penalty"; and "Kobe was elbowed in the face today by Gasol" among many other threads. At any given time there are roughly two explicitly political threads for every 25 threads with the possibility that politicized topics are being discussed in threads that seem to be unrelated to politics. As the above example of the 50 threads on the board on February 2011 indicates, a discussion confined to a single thread, such as the one about eating meat, can explode across the board with multiple threads being created around the topic.

Although no traceable political activism has occurred because of interactions on IGN, extensive political discussion can be construed as a political outcome. Additionally, there is some indication from users that posting on IGN has caused them to consider perspectives that differ from those they hold or to change their mind about those beliefs. However, in contrast to the political outcomes from participation in Anonymous and The Pirate Bay, the political interaction on IGN has yielded no obvious political mobilization, making its political outcomes more analogous to those of WoW, a game. This unexpected similarity raises the question of why IGN's political outcomes more closely resemble those of a video game than another posting board system.

Explaining Political Behavior on the IGN.com Posting Boards

As in the other three cases, on the IGN posting boards, the levels of anonymity, regulation, and type of spatial divisions influence the type of political behavior apparent in the space. On IGN.com, the lack of anonymity, the high level of regulation, and the division of the space foster personal relationships rather than large-group identity and thwart high levels of political mobilization.

Anonymity

The IGN board system is a community in which people are known as individuals. This lack of anonymity is created by attributes of the technological space, such as user names, registration dates, icons, post counts, and profiles, among other factors. As in the WoW community, the ability to know each other means that people form individual personal relationships rather than a single group identity and, as a result, divide into smaller subgroups within the broader community.

The initial reason the IGN posting boards are not anonymous is because users must register an account to be able to post on the boards. In doing so, individuals choose a user name that is then associated with all of their posts. While users could register a new email address with IGN, and, therefore, a new user name every time they post, most users tend to use one user name for all of their posts. Therefore, user names become "real" names in the online space to such an extent that IGN rules forbid impersonating a user. The rule states: "You may not impersonate another board member or create an account specifically for the purpose of provoking other users."[9]

User names and styles are not the only features that distinguish individuals from each other. User names also come with registration dates, titles, and post counts, which further "customize" a user name and increase identifiability. Thus, when a user makes a post, it includes the information distinct to the user. Users can also add icons—or images—to their user names.[10] Users are very proprietary about their icons because they become their "face" on the board system. In threads discussing the use of another user's icon, most people frown on the practice and say that no one else uses their particular icons—indicating that people attempt to avoid copying each other.

For example, in a thread in early 2010 asking how many other people have the same icon as another user, a poster stated, "None. It would be weird if someone else had an icon of me." Furthermore, posters will attack users who use recognized icons of well-known posters.

Additionally, users can include a "signature" with every post they make. These tend to be less static, but can also become part of the recognizable "face" of a user. Users have profiles, which they can customize to some extent. Finally, it is also possible for users to have a blog. However, this feature is not widely used and was not present when I began my research.

The fact that people have distinct identities in the space means that IGN users are familiar with each other. Therefore, individual users can accrue reputations. As with any social group, reputations can be positive or negative. For example, a user can gain a reputation for being particularly knowledgeable about politics, history, or science. Other people can have reputations as a gay person, as a female poster, or as an "attention whore."[11]

One of the reasons it is easy for users to gain reputations, particularly on the Vesti, is that every post made on any IGN board is publicly viewable.[12] Additionally, all user posts are available via the user profiles—making it possible to view all posts by a given user at once across boards and threads.

User reputation is often based on distinct posting styles that are commented on, admired, reviled, and/or emulated. One prominent example is that of a user who gained an extremely high post count by posting bland one-line responses to a huge number of threads that contained just enough information to not count as spamming, but not enough information to be meaningful. For example, in response to a thread in which "John" complained about something this user might have posted, "I am very sorry to hear that, John." The responses were so formulaic that at one point another user did a fake expose of him that claimed he was actually a robot. This user became notorious on the boards entirely because of his distinct posting style.

The ability to be known means that people can publicly approve of others, and there is a board mechanism for publicizing support of a user. Users can "watch" other users by adding them to their "watched user list" (WUL)—referred to as "WULing" on the boards. WULS are a commodity on the boards because they are an indication of social acceptance. People trade them like currency, offering them for help or in even exchange. However, most people treat them as a meaningful indication of liking another user. WULs are listed in user profiles under the heading "Watched by count" and so can be seen by other users.

The importance of these features in identifying users is illustrated in a debate on the boards about the board format. After more than 10 years, the IGN engineers are voicing a need to "fix" the boards by changing the format. In line with this need, they have begun polling the users to ask them what kind of format they would like the boards to have. In response, many users have posted expressing concern that IGN maintain the identifying elements of users, rather than retain a particular board format. For example, the following quotes capture the sentiment:

> Overall I've had experience with all the mentioned forum types and would have to go with phpbb. However, I mainly just want to know if I'm gonna lose all my important info (reg date, post counts, wuls).

> But what about post history/WULs/reg dates? That's the stuff we REALLY care about. PLEASE listen to us this time; there's a breaking point, and who knows what could happen if that point was crossed.:(

> I'd say the way that makes it so that we can still keep old post counts/reg dates/icons/sigs/old threads/post history/same look. I honestly don't want to have to re-register, deal with people who changed names, and so on, so if you can do that, that'd be the best option. Theres been a lot of memories made on this site. I'd like at least to still be able to do this.

Thus, much like WoW, the lack of anonymity allows personal connections to form on the board because people are identifiable and gain reputations over time. The individuality of posters is the first aspect that leads to the creation of subcommunities within the broader community and the generation of one-on-one relationships. And, as the continuing debate about a board restructure indicates, people are emotionally connected to the space and each other.

Regulation

Weaker large-group identity is not the only factor that limits political mobilization arising from the IGN.com posting boards. IGN's aggressive policing model of regulation and its formal rule systems also minimize on-board mobilization. Specifically, the extensive rule system has prevented IGN users from engaging in empowering group activities because nearly all of the necessary abilities for mass mobilization are either discouraged or forbidden. For example, users are discouraged, and sometimes banned, for posting links to other social sites; users are forbidden from engaging in illegal or quasi-legal actions or for linking to any online location where such illegal behaviors or conversations may occur; and users are forbidden from having conversations about anything that could have questionable legality. These rules effectively minimize the ability to organize online. The official list of IGN rules includes the following:[13]

1. No flaming and bashing other users, groups, or the board system—including posts meant to illicit a negative response.
2. No pornography or sexually explicit content. This includes sexually explicit stories. And there is a detailed guide of what is forbidden in terms of imagery ("no ass cracks," "no bushes," "no camel toe," "no nipples," "The Lesbian Rule,"[14] etc.).
3. No pedophilia: "This includes but is not limited to all images, 'friends' pictures or pictures taken from social networking sites, school sites, any joke-style images, written stories, jokes or remarks."
   No explicit content: "Explicit images/videos, which include but not limited to death scenes, death pictures, torture, mutilation and human feces, are not allowed. Explicit written descriptions of these acts is also not allowed on the boards."
4. No posting "real life" information
5. No Racism/Hate[15]
6. No Trolling: "If you are knowingly or purposely posting to incite anger/negativity on the board or from the community, you will be banned for trolling. These boards are meant for meaningful discussions and debates, not a place for you to start trouble."
7. No Profanity
8. No Criminal Activity: "No discussions of illegal activity will be tolerated on the boards. Any instruction on how to carry out illegal activity or admission of illegal activity will be dealt with harshly."
9. No Spam
10. No Circumventing a Ban—essentially, if a user is banned for breaking a rule s/he should not create another account to post with while banned.
11. No Copyrighted Material
12. No System Wars—essentially, no long arguments about what kind of video gaming system is better.
13. No Advertising and Solicitation: "Posting for the pure purpose of driving traffic to your own website is not allowed." This rule seems to

also encompass telling people to use another forum or conversation space to discuss actions that are against the rules on the IGN boards.

14. No Piracy, ROMs, and Warez: "Linking to or giving information about any site that distributes illegal software, ROMs, media, or emulators, seeking help to circumvent any copyright laws, admitting to possessing and/or distributing illegal copyrighted material, or encouraging software or media piracy is grounds for an immediate ban. It is also unacceptable to post first-hand impressions, reviews or screenshots of known pirated material. This goes for all copyrighted material, including but not limited to games, movies, music and television broadcasts."

15. No impersonating other users/accessing another user's account

16. No Altering Board Code

17. No Off-Topic Posts: "Try to post suitable subjects on each of the appropriate boards"

18. No Spoilers—a spoiler is giving away a surprise ending such as Darth Vader being Luke Skywalker's father

19. No Posting Huge Images / Fake Signature Pics—essentially, a rule to avoid the images one user posts crashing the computer of another user.

20. Questionable Content Rule: "Since we can't have a rule to cover everything, this is the rule to, well, cover everything. These are public boards, so act like you would if you were in a public place. IGN reserves the right to choose the guidelines of objectionable content based on its knowledge of users and company policy."

The result of this list of rules is that the community cannot use the community space to organize or engage in any collective online action. Thus, the only community collective action that arises are "riots" in which users attempt to disrupt normal board use by flooding it with threads that have a specific title and theme.[16] Usually riots are started by a single user or a small group of users who are then joined by a critical mass of other users creating a waterfall effect.

Therefore, the only substantive collective action on the IGN posting boards is IGN users mobilizing briefly against IGN itself. The effectiveness and frequency of riots have significantly decreased over time as moderators have become faster at stopping them, and board code has been changed to prevent automated riots such as the STEAK!! script riot.

Rule breaking is aggressively monitored and punished. When a user violates a rule, occasionally he is warned to not do it again, but most often he is banned. Banned users are forbidden from posting on the boards, and when they attempt to log in they receive a message telling them that they are banned. Additionally, their profiles are marked as "unavailable." Bans vary in length depending on the severity of the offense. Bans can be permanent (perma-bans) or they can be for as little as a few hours. If a user is banned repeatedly for the same offense, the ban length will increase each time.

While being banned may seem like a trivial penalty for a non-community member, it is a fairly severe penalty for people who spend hours on the boards every day. It means that for the duration of the ban, the offender may not interact socially with the community without using third-party sites or methods. Because there is a norm in the space against revealing "real life" information, in particular people's legal names, users are bound to the board system as their only way to communicate with friends. Therefore, users often choose to reveal their "real life" information to people with whom they are close. Names are usually not revealed until users have known each other for extended periods of time—often years. When a user is banned, he may have no way to contact other users and, therefore, is essentially socially isolated.[17]

To have a ban removed, a user has to submit a ban notice. In the notice, the banned user must state what she did to receive the ban, apologize, and promise not to reoffend. Once the user submits the "unban" notice, a moderator will read it and unban the user if her response is deemed sufficient. While bans themselves are time-bound and users know how long they will be banned for, moderators are not required to read the unban request in a timely fashion. Moderators report on the boards that they read unban notices when they "have time" (or "feel like it"). Thus, it is possible for a user to be banned longer than her sentence.

Bans usually only apply to a user name. However, if a user attempts to "circumvent" the ban by creating or using another user name, the poster can be "IP banned," a ban that applies to anyone posting from that IP address. Users adept at circumvention are known to use proxies to access the boards during ban times. However, the use of a proxy slows down posting time, and those found using proxies are subject to harsh penalties. It is not uncommon for a circumventing user to be "recaught" by the moderators, because she often will reveal her "real" identity to her subcommunity on IGN. Then, once her friends begin interacting with her as if they know her (and WUL her), moderators are able to identify the user and reban her.

The boards are policed and rules are enforced by a group of volunteer moderators. IGN's moderation system is far more aggressive than those of either WoW or Anonymous. The ability to aggressively police speech in the space is due in part to the continual archiving of conversations in the space—which allows moderators to search archives for violations. These moderators are the main mechanism of social control on the boards. They are volunteers, selected from the posting population, although the criteria for selection are unclear and are surrounded by rumor. Officially, IGN states (2011) that "a Moderator is a volunteer chosen by the Community Manager from among the user base who gives of his/her valuable time to help keep the boards a fun place for everyone."

Due to the presence of moderators and the archiving system, social control on the IGN boards is similar to social control methods in broader society in that there is always a chance that any action could be observed. Additionally, the ability of moderators to search board history and user posts means that any rule violation could be caught weeks after it occurs. The extensive nature of the board rules in addition to the inclusion of "judgment" clauses allow moderators to exercise considerable discretion in banning or editing.

Threads that moderators decide should not exist are usually locked. When a thread is locked, people can see the thread, but they cannot post in it anymore. Occasionally rule violating threads are "disappeared" from the forums, and users can no longer see the thread. When this happens, users attempting to access a disappeared thread will see a message that tells the user that she does not have permission to access the thread.

However, unlike other systems, unless the thread is full of rule-violating language/images, moderators usually leave threads intact with the rule-violating content edited out, or the thread locked to prevent additional posts. This approach of identifying how they have altered the posts allows moderators to leave a mark of their authority on the board.

In addition to moderator regulation, users also regulate each other's behavior. As in offline communities, user norms are often policed by other users. For example, as mentioned previously, users who "put on" a known community member's icon are shamed by the community. Also, users who post outside community norms, particularly on the smaller boards, are ostracized and shamed. If they continue to post, some moderators consider their intrusion "trolling" and will ban them for continuing to transgress community norms.

Additionally, users can report each other's bad behavior to moderators. The board system includes a list of all moderators who are online, and users can send a moderator a private message. Users can also report bad behavior on the "Contact a Moderator" thread. However, public complaints about other user behavior can also open the reporter up for ostracization for being a "snitch" or a "junior mod" as there is a board norm against reporting other users publicly for bad behavior.

Thus, the high level of moderation on the boards also serves to thwart mass mobilization by the community for or against any political cause, because many of the techniques that community members use to organize in other online forums are not available on IGN. This feature combined with the community's focus on interpersonal relationships means there is little mass mobilization other than occasional board riots aimed against the board itself. Presumably, because IGN users know about the actions of groups such as Anonymous, those interested in engaging in political action use other online locations to do so.

Spatial Divisions

In addition, the possibility of a larger group identity is undermined by the board structure itself, which fosters small groups instead of one large group. The boards have two distinctive features that undermine larger group identity: private messaging and archiving.

First, while the IGN boards are entirely public—in other words, any conversation on any board can be seen by anyone who visits the site (including people not registered on the site)—the private messaging feature allows users to engage in private conversations.[18] IGN users can send private messages (PM) to other users, which offers users a venue for people to get to know each other and for having more extensive conversations outside the view of the public.

Second, nearly all threads on IGN are archived and can be accessed for years after their posting. Functionally, this means that every conversation that occurs on IGN is accessible for a long period of time. Thus, a user who would like to become knowledgeable about the community can simply access the post history of prominent users or read the archive of a given board.

Therefore, the nature of interaction on the board is much different from that among Anonymous users. Unlike Anonymous, on IGN there is little need to assert in-group status by using distinct lexicon or showing knowledge of history in every post. "In group" membership is apparent from other markers. Users show a wider variety of posting styles than they do on Anonymous, and those with older registration dates are assumed to know board history. Belonging is not determined by performance but rather by identity markers external to the user's text. Like Anonymous users, those using IGN participate in community jokes. For example, an enduring joke is to reply "Because you touch yourself at night" to any "why" question posed on the board. And, like Anonymous users, long-time users are often assumed to know about the board's history. However, in IGN, these factors are less important to asserting membership in the community than they are in Anonymous.

The peculiar outcome of the lack of anonymity is that on IGN.com knowledge of board history and community events is more ephemeral than it is in Anonymous, even though IGN.com keeps archives of threads and Anonymous boards do not. The ephemeral nature of IGN.com members' knowledge of IGN.com history is because identifiable users are assumed to be the holders of community history and, thus, the same effort is not put into recording knowledge. Evidence of this is the contrast between Encyclopedia Dramatica—the storing house of a sometimes accurate Anonymous history—and the Vesti Wiki—which is extremely limited and is missing mention of many key Vesti historical events, jokes, and people. Additionally, in any thread on IGN.com that asks about "best users" or most important events, older users may cite events from years past, but newer users nearly always cite more recent users/events.

In addition, the lack of anonymity, the ability to accrue reputation, and the board format lead people to form smaller groups and relationships within the larger group. Larger group identity is less cohesive. The lack of large-group cohesion is most obvious on the smaller boards where communities develop and exist over long periods of time. For example, on one of the general topic community boards in IGN, the population has developed such extensive friendships that people have dated, flown across large distances to see each other, and annually have a "Secret Santa" drawing.[19] The deep interpersonal connections between people also occur on the Vesti, and there are many instances of people who met on the boards meeting in "real life," forming long-term friendships, dating, and other meaningful relationships. People also have "left" the boards in small groups and moved their communities to other online locations where they are not subject to the regulation of IGN or to people outside their subgroups participating in their conversations. And, while the Vesti's "reputation" is that of a heartless mass just making fun of each other, over time, I have seen people turning to the boards in the wake of breakups or deaths in the family, for help dealing with addictions or disorders, for consolation about anxieties or worries about physical features, and out of openly admitted loneliness.

Normative Conflict

As is true of the other online spaces discussed previously, users come into the IGN space with previously held beliefs about the world. Because they are in a space that carries the expectation of discussion, their beliefs shape the

Table 5.1   **Responses to Informal Poll on IGN: Have You Changed Your Mind about an Issue Based on a Discussion on the Vesti/IGN?**

Poll Answer	Number of Votes	Percentage of Total
Yes	12	19.0
No	10	16.0
Some of the discussions here have made me think harder about my own stance on issues	34	54.8
Nothing people say here affects my opinions	5	8.0
I don't know	1	1.6

constant political discussions occurring in the space. While political conversations are the minority of threads on the Vesti, except during times of high political excitement, such as election night, there is always at least one thread about a political topic on the front page. The structure of the IGN boards themselves filters the users' behaviors and shapes the community in such a way that individuals remain fragmented politically.

When I was an IGN community member before I began my formal research, I asked the Vesti if the daily debates I was observing had any effect on people's thinking. I asked: "Have you ever changed your mind about an issue based on a discussion you've had on the Vesti/IGN?" I gave respondents five response options: "yes," "no," "some of the discussions here have made me think harder about my own stance on issues," "nothing people say here affects my opinions," and "I don't know." Sixty-two people responded to the question, and their responses are illustrated in table 5.1. As the table shows, 24 percent of the respondents said they had not changed their minds about an issue based on a discussion. In contrast, 74 percent reported either changing their minds or having thought harder about their own beliefs based on a discussion. Interestingly, a look at the textual responses in the thread revealed that many people who chose the "think harder" option reported that this meant that their minds had been changed though they did not select the "yes" option.

Political conversations in the space can often bear the stereotypical characteristics of online political conversations, including hyperbolic shouting and parallel argumentation. However, they also display other attributes such as the following:

- Posters requesting recognized "experts" in matters such as Middle East politics to weigh in on a debate
- Two Americans in different states asserting that the "US is like X" and having a conversation about the differences in their perception

- American users questioning whether Canadians actually like their healthcare system and Canadian users answering that they would not trade it for the US system
- Longtime users coming out as homosexual to the community and users grappling with that revelation
- Religious users being challenged on their religious beliefs and engaged in conversation
- Non-US users criticizing and questioning US policy in various parts of the world and engaging in conversations about appropriate policy
- Debates about the meaning of marriage
- Longtime users revealing that they are African American or Mexican (two groups who are heavily criticized/stereotyped in the space)
- Conversations about what is sexually normal
- Discussions about the appropriate role of women
- Threads where longtime users reveal physical disabilities, such as deafness, and then answer questions about what life is like for them
- Notification and conversation about big political events around the world, such as the 2009 protests in Iran, with Iranian users and expats weighing in with their experience
- Support offered to people having a difficult time because of ostracization at school or rules set out by parents

These conversations mean, if nothing else, that users are exposed to alternate views of reality regularly. Further, the presence of recognized experts on subjects also means that they are given evidence of different realities and ways of viewing the world. While these may not change their beliefs, the indication is that they do make them think about their beliefs. The exposure to such a wide range of beliefs and experiences is not available to people who are not online. Even in cases where an individual is not surrounded by a community that shares his views, there are extremely limited opportunities for exposure to as many different perspectives any time of day in one space. Users expect that any time they post a belief—political, social, aesthetic—that belief could be challenged, rejected, or affirmed. Thus, while there is no recognizable political mobilization on IGN, there is important cross-national interaction on the boards, which exposes users to alternate arguments, ways of seeing deeply held beliefs, and debate from other national contexts.

A good example of this occurred during the healthcare debates in 2010. While the media in the United States were demonizing or praising the healthcare systems in other countries, users who repeated these claims on the IGN boards were challenged by people who actually lived in those countries. When users stated that the US system was better than any other, Canadians and Australians said that they would not trade their systems for that of the United States. When users stated that socialized medicine systems were better than the US system, users from England would post their frustrations with the British system. Thus, the cross-national nature of the space meant that the young people in it are exposed to perspectives and beliefs that they might not otherwise experience.

Additionally, even within the United States, users often are exposed to other ways of viewing their own realities. Gay users facing offline bullying are told that things are better in other places. Users expressing frustration with immigrants are told that their online friends are immigrants themselves. Users making racist jokes are confronted by online friends. While it is difficult to claim unequivocally that the conversations in the space influence the developing political beliefs of IGN's young users, there is some indication that they challenge individuals' perspectives.

Conclusion

Group mobilization does not arise from the IGN boards because the technological space does not afford users anonymity, allows them to accrue reputation, includes a board structure that fosters small-group interaction, and includes an aggressive moderation system that prevents large-scale mobilization. However, even in the absence of political mobilization like that arising from sites such as Anonymous and The Pirate Bay, IGN users spend time in extensive debates about politics. There is some indication that these conversations challenge individual belief systems.

The comparison of IGN to WoW, Anonymous, and The Pirate Bay indicates that having the ability to know and be known by others in online spaces thwarts wide-scale political mobilization—channeling interpersonal connections into one-on-one and small-group relationships rather than an overriding large-group identity that can serve as a foundation for mobilization. In the cases of both IGN and WoW, although users interact around political questions and debates, there is little indication that these conversations, however heated, translate directly into actual political mobilization. Additionally, in both cases, aggressive moderation and regulation interrupt large-group mobilization within the space, making it difficult to organize or build a history of collective action.

In contrast, in Anonymous and The Pirate Bay, the high levels of anonymity allow users to conceive of themselves as part of a larger group—a
status that, in the case of Anonymous, must continually be reiterated and
proven through performance. Furthermore, the lack of regulation in the
space allows users to mobilize in and around the space in ways that build a
history of group mobilization.

6

Expect Them

> A common thread that binds many internet users and impels them toward
> Anonymous is the concept that information, by its nature, is free; and that
> communication should be unfettered.
> —Statement on WhyWeProtest.net[1]

The highly populated, seemingly chaotic online social sites in *Expect Us*
represent the many densely packed online social spaces that overlap with
our offline lives. As their stories show, these spaces have critical relevance to
offline political realities.

In every social space online, there are heated discussions about political topics. In communities where participants have mobilized on behalf of
political ideals, such as Anonymous and The Pirate Bay, the groups have
fundamental conflicts with offline norms that are strong enough to compel
them to mobilize politically. The normative conflicts that propel such mobilizations are deeply intertwined with the nature of the Internet itself as well
as participation in online spaces that fosters certain types of interactions and
frustrates others. Central to stories about this type of transformative conflict seem to be communities that foster a set of beliefs grounded in deeply
liberal ideologies about freedom of expression and techno-utopian ideals
about collaborative culture—combined with the creativity that is fostered
in environments where there is a lack of individual ownership over content.
These types of communities emerge in online spaces with high anonymity,
low levels of formal regulation, and limited spatial divisions.

The research and findings in *Expect Us* suggest two important implications: first, nonpolitical social websites are central to understanding civic
engagement in the information age; and second, although we do not yet
know what the future holds for the type of political activism I have discussed

in this book, there is some indication that we are seeing the emergence of a freedom-of-information-based social movement.

Civic Engagement in the Information Age

As *Expect Us* has shown, nonpolitical social websites are important for understanding how we conceive of ourselves in relation to political processes. Throughout *Expect Us* I explicitly and implicitly discuss the political conversations and important political processes that are occurring in these online spaces. The subsequent political mobilization of Anonymous members and file-sharers is evidence of the importance of these political conversations happening in unlikely places online, but so are the findings of extensive negotiations over norms in World of Warcraft and the indication that IGN users have changed their minds based on conversations on the IGN posting boards.

Indeed, while the sites in *Expect Us* differ from each other in many ways, over the course of my research I observed impassioned political conversations in all of them. This was the case even in World of Warcraft, where the overriding reason individuals were in the space was to play a game. Even there, politically significant interactions permeated micro-interactions, such as the informal regulations players laid out for each other in one-on-one conversations in terms of acceptable speech, and macro-structures, such as the realm that has become a widely known as a "safe haven" for GLBTQ players and women because of the presence of large and powerful GLBTQ-focused guilds on the realm that discourage hateful speech and encourage inclusion.

Expect Us also indicates that nonprofit organizations such as the MacArthur Foundation (Bennett, 2008), which seek ways to facilitate youth civic engagement using the Internet, should be looking to the creators of Anonymous community spaces and The Pirate Bay for lessons. And when thinking about fostering civic engagement it is important to remember that the central factors in political mobilization—anonymity, regulation, small-group interaction—are the products of conscious site design. My research indicates that the intentions of site creators and owners have powerful effects on the shape of online spaces. As I have shown, the construction of online spaces matters for the type of community that emerges in the space.

This is something that other scholars have noted in relation to the private ownership of many of the websites that activists use daily (MacKinnon, 2012; Morozov, 2010b), but work still needs to be done examining the implications of creator belief on site design. The construction of business-owned sites is, by necessity, driven by bottom-line concerns. Worries about making a profit drive company decisions about these spaces. For example, IGN specifically lists its population as part of its marketing to advertisers (IGN.com, 2010). Blizzard is so proprietary about information about its customers that it only releases data on its number of subscribers.

Thus, in the conversation about the Internet's public role, it is unwise to forget that profit drives considerations of many online spaces and, therefore, heavily affects the shape of online space. For example, commercially owned sites tend to push the boundaries of privacy because information about users is valuable for advertising and for product creation. The outcome in these cases is that speech is curtailed, controlled, observed, and pruned so as not to limit the marketability of products.

Alternatively, non-commercially owned sites, at least until they attempt to make money, tend to be more protective of individual privacy and more permissive of different types of speech. However, even though spaces such as those occupied by Anonymous are not corporate-owned, their owners still have their own agendas and desires for their online communities. While these agendas may be more normatively satisfying to researchers such as myself, they are agendas nonetheless, and site owners code them into the designs of their sites. For example, the "birthplace" of Anonymous, 4chan. org, was created by Christopher Poole when he was 15 years old. Poole is vocal in his belief in anonymity online. In a talk, Poole stated (2011):

> We believe in content over creator. . . . When you look at most other communities things that are really important are when you registered, what your user id is, you know how many thanks you've gotten, what kind of points you've accumulated, things that aren't really that important. If any of you have been a member of an online community, you know there starts to be these known persons within communities and their contributions are weighted in a way that isn't quite right, because people start to bandwagon around certain individuals. . . . In a place like 4chan you don't have that. People are all judged the same way, which is, by what their contribution is.

Similarly, The Pirate Bay's administrators are activists. For example, when asked where The Pirate Bay's servers are located, Peter Sunde has stated that no one person knows anymore (Jardin, 2009)[2]:

> The servers were in Sweden but they aren't now. I'm not aware of the location of any servers. In fact no one from what used to be TPB is

aware of where they are. After the raid servers were given to people and they were told to set up a VPN to them, and we said "don't give us the real IP, just give us a tunneled IP." So someone knows where one of the web servers is, another person knows where one of the database servers are and they don't know each other.

Each site's format has its owners' beliefs coded into it on multiple levels including, in the case of The Pirate Bay, the underlying infrastructure of the site, which is built to prevent external entities from being able to take the site down.

Because most online social sites are privately owned, the values of the site owners are then encoded into the site designs, which, as the four cases in this book show, can have major implications for the types of communities in each space. Two broad value groups illustrate an important divide in online communities that complicates discussion of these places as public spheres. In the first group are corporations, which encode profit-driven logic into online spaces. Google and Facebook are interested in providing a service that is largely connection based—the connection of information, people, and products to people. Creating these connections involves the erosion of personal privacy and reifies traditional gatekeepers and owners of information, such as corporations. For example, in an interview, Mark Zuckerberg, Facebook's CEO and president, stated (Kirkpatrick, 2010, p. 199):

> You have one identity. The days of you having a different image for your work friends or co-workers and for other people you know are probably coming to an end pretty quickly. Having two identities for yourself is an example of a lack of integrity.

Zuckerberg has also stated in other interviews that the "norm of privacy" is dead and that Facebook attempts to reflect this changing value in its site design. Critics of Facebook point out that Facebook itself is constantly eroding privacy in an effort to make more money, and Facebook users may grumble, but they generally accept the changes. Thus, in this case, it is difficult to know which comes first: the chicken of Facebook's profit-driven logic or the egg of individual beliefs about what kind of privacy one can expect online.

The second group illustrating the divide in online communities includes sites where site creators, such as Christopher Poole and Piratbyrån members, consciously encode their values into their online spaces. Entities such as Anonymous and the multitude of The Pirate Bay-sponsored projects, argue for freedom of information, lack of censorship, contributory culture, sharing, privacy, and user-generated content, stating that they are not only essentially about human rights, but also that people want societies based on such values. For example, in a recent speech, Christopher Poole argued that the anonymous nature of 4chan.org allows a contributory culture to flourish in a way that nonanonymous sites do not (Poole, 2011):

> Zuckerberg is totally wrong on anonymity being total cowardice. Anonymity is authenticity. It allows you to share in a completely unvarnished, raw way.

A study of a range of online spaces makes clear that the drive for profit and the drive for sites that encode certain societal values both have important implications for the design of online spaces. The research in *Expect Us* indicates that the profit-driven logic may thwart political mobilization. For example, for a time the Anonymous website WhyWeProtest.net stated:

> This potentially powerful expansion of goodwill and information-sharing challenges current social and political structures and thus presents a likely target for powerful entities whose interests rely on the status quo. It may be only a matter of time before the information shared via social media is by default compromised and censored.

There is some indication that this statement is correct. Facebook and Twitter have been lauded as contributing heavily to the "Arab Spring" in the Middle East, allowing activists and protesters to organize quickly and effectively against repressive regimes. However, some commentators have noted that much of the organization happening on Facebook, in particular, was happening in spite of the Facebook design, which appears to make political organization difficult (Chen, 2011). In contrast, Twitter's owners had a value system that led the company to support the protests, for example, by rearranging maintenance times (Pleming, 2009). Unlike its stance with the Arab Spring protesters, Twitter has not been as kind to Anonymous activists, whose accounts have been banned, particularly during high-profile collective action, such as their protests in support of WikiLeaks. Because the transformative effects of these online spaces on political mobilization are just beginning to appear, we will not know for some time whether the Why We Protest activists are correct, but my research indicates they may be.

I do not intend to demonize or laud either type of ownership but rather to point out the realities of an Internet built by corporations. These realities are particularly important to note because corporate-owned sites, such as IGN.com, often have a higher level of discourse—conversation that is considered normatively good—but the maintenance of this discourse level by site owners thwarts spontaneous challenges to the status quo. In contrast, individual- or activist-owned sites are often filled with speech, imagery, and behavior that many would consider offensive, but these sites also seem to be creating the type of political engagement and mobilization on behalf of rights that we would consider normatively "good." The complicated realities of the groups that emerge from such sites are evident in Anonymous, where Anonymous's activism focused against the Westboro Baptist Church's hateful message can coexist with the use of homophobic language.

Complicating this picture is the normative assumption that the public sphere in a healthy democracy would be full of high discourse, something similar to that found in the famous online community The Well,[3] where users must use their real names, are highly educated, and interact in a polite manner.[4] However, a look to 4chan.org—and even to cases outside this book such as Reddit—indicates that in places where there is a wider range of conversation, including content that can be deeply disturbing, there will be more opportunities for political action. The cases in *Expect Us* suggest that there is value not only in the places online that fit our expectations of civil society but also in the places online that make us cringe. Before simply eliminating spaces from the Internet because of their content, we need to ask whether, with such censorship, anything of value would be lost.

The Future of Online Political Mobilization

If the findings of this book are significant for those wanting to understand civic engagement online, what do they indicate for the future of online political mobilization?[5] While the "stories" of Anonymous and The Pirate Bay are still in their infancy, it is not clear whether their political mobilization will sustain itself over time. For example, the success of Anonymous groups' 2010 protests on behalf of WikiLeaks serves, ironically, to highlight the groups' weakness as political actors. Following the DDoS attacks, some Anonymous sources stated that it was time to change tactics, as the attacks were becoming less effective. Thus, it was proposed that Anonymous members begin going through the diplomatic cables on WikiLeaks looking for examples of political misconduct. A website[6] was set up to facilitate this operation and its birth was announced with a YouTube video. The video stated (anonopleakspin, 2010)[7]:

> We have already made it very clear we will fight for freedom of speech and a free press, but we have, at best, given them a black eye. The game has changed. When the game changes, so too must our strategies. We are now moving forward to phase two of our war on disinformation terror. Introducing Operation Leakspin. Become part of the hive and join us. This is a fight we can only win with information. Begin searching through Wikileaks for the best, least exposed leaks you can get your hands on. Post summaries of them, along with the complete source... make one to two minute YouTube videos reading the leaks. Use misleading tags. Post snippets of the leaks everywhere on the Internet.

The move to Operation Leakspin was largely unsuccessful, with very few summaries of cables posted on the website. This is not to say that Anonymous is not still committed to freedom of information or that its support of WikiLeaks had lessened. Rather, this example suggests that Anonymous's ability to sustain political mobilization depends on both the participation of the new Anonymous members and on the entertainment value of the protest. DDoS attacks are fun, but careful research may not be.

In addition to the Anonymous example, the steadily dropping Swedish Pirate Party membership numbers may also indicate weaker "staying power" for Internet-generated political campaigns (Fiveash, 2010). As I discussed in chapter 3, Pirate Party membership numbers surged in the wake of the Pirate Bay trial. In Sweden, where the party had great initial success, the Swedish Pirate Party received 7 percent of the vote—gaining a place in the European Parliament. However, following this election, support for the party appeared to be dropping (Foresman, 2010).

In spite of these examples illustrating the potentially weak staying power of this type of online activism, with each collective mobilization, some individuals "stick" to issues, remaining and becoming committed activists. Why We Protest is a good example. It began as part of the Anonymous protests against Scientology. As time passed, the Why We Protest activists opened a forum to provide support to Iranian protesters and to the Pirate Bay administrators. They also engaged in other online and offline activism. In 2011, they launched a new, more broad-based website focused on pursuing freedom of information online.[8]

Another example of this kind of "stickiness" is the "failed" Crowd Leaks website. This website has become a citizen journalist website attempting to foster "crowd journalism." Over time, Crowd Leaks has turned its attention to making sure the information on WikiLeaks is available in multiple languages.[9] Contributors write articles, translate materials, edit articles, and provide technical support for the site. The project is still young, but there is a slow, steady stream of articles on the site.

Therefore, while some evidence suggests that sustainability is an issue for political mobilization online, the long-term impact of the political mobilization by online communities is still unfolding. The political performances I observed may be episodic, but the activists who "stick" after the surges may form a core of activists who then drive the next eruption of political mobilization.

In addition, there is some indication that the multitude of Anonymous groups, the Pirate Parties, and other activists are coalescing into a transnational social movement focused on freedom of information. Online rhetoric about the potential of the Internet to change society, the need to reform intellectual property laws, and the evils of censorship of any kind is becoming similar across sites.

Anonymous's press releases increasingly frame its online activities in terms of the United States' civil rights movement and other civil disobedience. For example, on January 27, 2011, in response to the arrest of five young men involved in the pro-WikiLeaks DDoS attacks, an Anonymous press release stated:

> It is important to realize what a DDoS attack exactly is and what it means in the contemporary political context. As traditional means of protest (peaceful demonstrations, sit-ins, the blocking of a crossroads or the picketing of a factory fence) have slowly turned into nothing but an empty, ritualised gesture of discontent over the course of the last century, people have been anxiously searching for new ways to pressure politicians and give voice to public demands in a manner that might actually be able to change things for the better. Anonymous has, for now, found this new way of voicing civil protest in the form of the DDoS, or Distributed Denial of Service, attack. Just as is the case with traditional forms of protest, we block access to our opponents infrastructure to get our message across. Whether or not this infrastructure is located in the real world or in cyberspace, seems completely irrelevant to us. . . . Hacking as such is defined by the law as "unauthorised access to a computer or

network," whereas a DDoS attack is simply a case of thousands of people making legitimate connections to a publicly accessible web-server at the same time, using up the entire bandwidth or process-ing power of the given server at once and thereby causing a huge "traffic jam." It is clear then, that arresting somebody for taking part in a DDoS attack is exactly like arresting somebody for attending a peaceful demonstration in their hometown.

While the characterization of a DDoS attack as the equivalent of a sit-in is contested (Morozov, 2010a; Sauter, 2013), a German court has upheld the right of activists who wanted to use a DDoS attack against Lufthansa as part of a human rights protest (Frankfurt Appellate Court No. 1 Ss 319/05).[10] The group was protesting Lufthansa's collaboration with the German gov-ernment in deporting asylum-seekers.

Further, the ability of groups such as Anonymous to channel the power of like-minded but not tech-savvy allies is increasing. As groups become more organized and focused in their protests, activists "sticking" to issues may be able to recruit others to use online tools. Doing so would allow Anonymous activists to draw on supportive individuals whose protest stay-ing power does not last past a burst of DDoS attacks.

For example, while Anonymous has a long history of online mobili-zation, its breathtaking impact in December 2010 on the normal business operations of multinational corporations such as MasterCard was the result of Anonymous members overcoming one of the principal barriers to mass online hacktivist protest—supporters' lack of technological know-how. Since 2008, every time Anonymous (or 4chan.org) has been in the news— or news of Anonymous action online has spread across online sites—new people arrive in Anonymous community spaces. Many among the nonactiv-ist Anonymous groups regard these new people as "the cancer that is killing" Anonymous, but for activist Anonymous members, these new users repre-sent untapped potential.

In the past, activists in Anonymous have hosted detailed guides to help new Anonymous members learn to engage in actions such as DDoS attacks. For novices, the technical details are difficult to understand, and these new actors have often put themselves at risk of being identified. However, with the WikiLeaks protests, activist Anonymous groups simplified and stream-lined the education process to bring new Anonymous users to important information sources and coordination locations. Additionally, Anonymous participants more widely used a tool that they had used in other attacks— the "Low Orbit Ion Cannon" or LOIC. The LOIC is a way for people who do not know anything about technology but who want to help out to engage in DDoS attacks. To use it, people download an application onto their computer with a field in it to enter the target. The application also includes a giant push-button. Once the user has "pushed the button," the application then manages the user's actions—either directly engaging with the site in question or routing through an IRC server, which allows someone else to unleash the traffic all at once on a target. While the use of LOIC has since proved to be problematic because of security issues with the tool, it shows the potential of designing tools to bridge the gap between technically savvy online activists and novices (Sauter, 2013, discusses LOIC in great detail).

The highly publicized arrests in the wake of the WikiLeaks protests show that groups such as Anonymous may frame their actions in terms of online protest, but governments frame them in terms of criminality. The effects of this action-reaction from governments on Anonymous-fostered online mobilization are still unclear.

Although a tension between activist opinion and state interpretation of law clearly exists, the public's opinion about such matters may also be changing. Over the past five years discussion of and support for the idea of "freedom of information" has increased over time among the online communities I observed. My findings from observing this diverse group of highly populated online communities are supported by polls regarding WikiLeaks, as well as by the amount of money donated in support of the project. In many widely reported surveys, pollsters have found that the majority of US citizens did not support WikiLeaks. For example, a CNN poll (2010) found that 77 percent of the people polled in the United States disapproved of WikiLeaks for placing leaked diplomatic cables online. However, when public opinion polls were broken down by age group, a different pattern emerged.

In a telephone survey taken in December 2010, 59 percent of those interviewed said that individuals who publish secret US documents should be prosecuted, with only 31 percent responding that the publication of such secret documents should be protected by the First Amendment. However, 52 percent of the individual respondents aged 18–29, agreed that publication should be protected by the First Amendment (Marist College Institute for Public Opinion, 2010). These numbers raise the question of whether the CNN poll results would be different if CNN had only polled people under the age of 30 or analyzed results by age.

American youth are not the only people who support WikiLeaks and Julian Assange. In Australia, 59 percent of the population supported WikiLeaks' choice to make the diplomatic cables public, while 25 percent opposed that choice. The percentage of supporters increased among younger voters (Lester, 2011). In Britain, older individuals were far more likely to support Assange's deportation to Sweden as well as his prosecution for releasing secret diplomatic documents than were those between the ages of 25 and 34 (Martinez, 2010).

These polls asked different questions, and so should be taken as illustrative rather than definitive proof of public opinion. For example, polls that asked about WikiLeaks' mission and then separately asked about the release of the secret diplomatic cables tended to find higher levels of support for WikiLeaks itself than for its choice to release the diplomatic cables. Additionally, the phrasing of questions seemed to make a difference. For example, a FOX poll (2010) found high levels of disapproval for WikiLeaks but phrased its questions about WikiLeaks in terms of "treason."

Support for a more aggressive conception of "freedom of information" can also be seen in the financial donations WikiLeaks received in 2010. A German foundation, which processes most donations given to WikiLeaks, reported that in 2010 WikiLeaks received about $1.9 million in donations and that more than $700,000 of that was donated at the height of WikiLeaks' difficultly finding a stable home, in November and December 2010 (Zetter, 2011). The foundation also reported that around 35 percent of the donations came from the United States, 14 percent from Germany, 12 percent from Britain, and about 6 percent from Australia and Canada. Other countries also donated in smaller amounts (Zetter, 2011). The foundation reported that the average donation was €25, but that it also occasionally received large donations, such as a donation from a single person of over €50,000.[11]

Iceland has also stepped into this fray. Before the US actions against WikiLeaks, Iceland was designing a new set of domestic laws configured to create a media haven for journalists, publishers, and threatened media. In June 2010, the Icelandic Parliament unanimously passed the Icelandic Modern Media Initiative (IMMI). The IMMI is a proposal to turn Iceland into the leading media haven with the strongest protections for journalists and publishers in the world. The Icelandic Parliament's vote began a process of changing Icelandic law through borrowing the most stringent national legal codes governing these aspects of information policy from around the world. The IMMI specifically proposes changing Icelandic law to match various aspects of US, European Union, Belgian, British, Estonian, Georgian, Norwegian, Scottish, and Swedish laws.[12] The revisions attempt to incorporate "best practices" of strong legal protections for speech from countries around the world while eliminating the weaknesses of each national legal context. The IMMI also modifies the Iceland Freedom of Information Act and creates an international prize for freedom of expression. The hope of the IMMI is that if materials are housed, routed, and published from Iceland, Icelandic law will provide protection, and thereby, increase worldwide media freedom.

Julian Assange was consulted during the drafting of the IMMI and in the "FAQs" attached to the proposal the IMMI cites the example of WikiLeaks, which distributes its infrastructure across national contexts to take advantage of strong legal protections for journalists, sources, and publishers. For example, until December 2010, WikiLeaks was routed through Belgium and published from Sweden, a process that theoretically protected WikiLeaks under the Swedish constitution's provisions for source anonymity and the Belgian laws regarding communications confidentiality.

Iceland has long been considered one of the countries with the most freedom of the press protections in the world (Freedom House, 2010). The IMMI represents an effort to take a more aggressive step to protect freedom of information. The timing of the IMMI, the involvement of Julian Assange and mention of WikiLeaks, and the concerns of the United States and other governments about WikiLeaks' actions mean that the IMMI also represents a normative statement about freedom of information. However, a considerable barrier is the resistance of power holders across national contexts to WikiLeaks' model of whistleblowing.

While small-state theory posits that small states can influence international affairs as norm entrepreneurs (Ingebritsen, 2006), Iceland's vulnerability to outside pressure is sometimes mentioned in news stories in relation to the IMMI. Often journalists ask IMMI authors about the possibility of pressure from powerful governments such as the United States and China. The question is in relation to responses to the IMMI such as Marc Thiessen's. A former George W. Bush administration staff member, Thiessen wrote a blog post (2011) condemning the IMMI, stating, "The IMMI calls into question Iceland's seriousness as a NATO ally, and Iceland needs to realize there will be consequences for its actions." In response to journalists' questions, Icelandic policymakers have acknowledged the pressure from outside governments but state that they do not consider it a reason to stop the revision of Iceland's laws. Instead, supporters recognize that whether other countries' courts decide to honor these legal frameworks or not is discretionary; concern over diplomatic ties offers some restraint (e.g., Chu, 2011).

Evidence suggests that the US government is willing to use political pressure against supporters of WikiLeaks. For example, in January 2011, the US Department of Justice subpoenaed[13] the content of the Twitter accounts of individuals associated with WikiLeaks, including Julian Assange, the spokesperson and founder; Chelsea Manning (previously Bradley Manning), the most well-known "leaker" associated with WikiLeaks; Birgitta Jónsdóttir, a former WikiLeaks volunteer and current member of the Icelandic Parliament; and Jacob Appelbaum and Rop Gonggrijp, activists associated with WikiLeaks (Singel, 2011).[14] Iceland's foreign ministry demanded a meeting with the US ambassador to Iceland in response to the subpoena, and the Icelandic interior minister described the action as "very odd and grave" (Iceland Review Online, 2011).

It is also unclear whether the US government, as its policies dealing with this new online challenge to its authority evolve, will act with as much coercive power as it has in the area of intellectual property. Because actors such as WikiLeaks are releasing classified documents, and, therefore, are engaging the US government in areas defined as security issues, the US government is likely to react strongly.

In the area of intellectual property the United States has used threats of trade sanctions to encourage a wide range of countries to contradict and/or change their intellectual property law. For example, although the claims are contested, there are allegations (and some evidence) that Sweden (Ahrens, 2006; Ernesto, 2010c), Russia (Anderson, 2006), Spain (Elola, 2010; Wilson, 2010; Geist, 2010), Australia (TVNZ, 2011), and Costa Rica (Long, 2010), among others (Linkletter Knapp, 2000), have all succumbed to US government pressure regarding intellectual property laws. Because the international center of the recording and film industries is in the United States—with major domestic branches of this industry in most Western countries—the push has, over time, become more and more a push for harmonizing other countries' domestic law with the United States' intellectual property laws through the use of international treaties and trade agreements.

The United States' action in the realm of intellectual property suggests that, were there to be a safe harbor for WikiLeaks or WikiLeaks-like sites, the United States might take action against it. US pressure against corporations in an attempt to remove all WikiLeaks infrastructure could be widened to include governments in ways similar to its attempts to harmonize intellectual property standards across contexts.

In spite of such pressure, a broad-scale "freedom of information" movement would represent a mobilization around ideas that are organic to the Internet and information technology and would involve online actors, such as Anonymous and Telecomix; "offline" organizations, such as the Electronic Frontier Foundation working on behalf of freedom of information; and states, such as Iceland. Whatever the future of this newly forming freedom-of-information movement, its emergence from the online world offers an indication of the power that the Internet and online communities have in shaping participants' political beliefs and actions. Young people online are willing to mobilize on behalf of abstract rights claims, and that willingness has spread quickly across the social spaces online.

Conclusion

Every day, people, mostly young, arrive in countless online spaces from all over the world. They come to socialize, play games, and find music. While together online, they make new friends, hear about life in other countries, are confronted with ideas and opinions different from those of their parents, fall in love, and become closer friends with people they already knew, as well as with young people who were once strangers and whom they will never meet face to face. Whatever their reasons for coming to these online spaces, once there, young people end up engaging in intensely political conversations and even political activism, such as protest.

As people share their lives in myriad and constantly multiplying online spaces, it should be no surprise that upon seeing each other's stories and hearing other's joys, injustices, and sorrows, they would find ideas and experiences they share. And when they learn about these ideas and experiences, it is also unsurprising that they would find they share beliefs that run counter to those of existing power structures. Those of us lucky enough to be watching have begun to witness what happens when the mismatch between those beliefs, norms, laws, and governance propels individuals online to work together to challenge powerful actors. We have begun to expect them.

Appendix: Research Methodology

The purpose of this appendix is to make my methodological choices transparent. In this appendix, I outline the following processes used in my research of political mobilization and online communities: the choice of ethnographic methods, the use of the comparative method, the case selection, the data-gathering methods, the operationalization of the central concepts, and central ethical issues addressed.

Before beginning, it is important to note that *Expect Us* uses a small number of closely examined cases to build theory about political mobilization online and the relationship between the online world and state-society relations. The research is inductive, rather than deductive, and not meant to test hypotheses but, rather, to generate concepts and an understanding of a set of understudied phenomena. This goal is in line with a qualitative research agenda meant to use targeted case studies to refine concepts and generate theory (Munck, 2004, p. 119). Thus, the purpose is not to create generalizable causal frameworks; future research will test the arguments articulated here on a larger number of cases.

Ethnography

The first major methodological choice I made was to use an ethnographic approach to the study of the four online communities because an understanding of community culture was essential to understanding why each community behaved as it did. I would characterize this as deep holistic watching—a method that includes hours of observation and/or participant observation; creating physical maps of the online space (e.g., formal rules, internal geography, spatial divisions, and conversation flow); attempting to gain a deep understanding of community norms (e.g., informal rules, culture, and expectations); becoming well versed in community history, stories, and inside jokes; and creating a mental map of connections of the foundational community space to other online spaces.

My choice of ethnography was informed by the long lineage of ethnographic methods in Internet studies. Pathbreaking research into online communities such as Rheingold's (1993) study of The Well, Baym's (1999) examination of a soap-opera fan community, and even nonscholarly but academically influential work such as Dibbell's (1993) look at rape in cyberspace, established ethnography as a central research method for understanding the dynamics of online communities. The consistent inclusion of ethnography as a method in methodological volumes such as Hine (2005), Boellstorff et al. (2012), and Baym and Markham (2008) further establishes the centrality of the method in Internet research. Thus, it is no surprise that technology researchers (e.g., Dányi, 2006) and new media researchers (e.g., Garcia et al., 2009) have long drawn on ethnographic research to record important online spaces (e.g., Schaap, 2002); build theory about communication, interaction, and information flow (e.g., Nahon & Hemsley, 2011); and generate the tools for large-*N* analysis.

In contrast, ethnography is a far less used method in political science than other methods are and, indeed, is a methodology that is less appreciated by the discipline than are other methodological choices (see, Aronoff, 2009, p. xi), likely due to the hegemony of statistical language and conceptualizations within the discipline (Schatz, 2009, p. 2). In a volume meant to argue the case for ethnography, Schatz asserts that ethnographic approaches have long informed political science and works to elucidate the concept of "political ethnography." Schatz argues that ethnography has many components. First, he asserts that participant observation is the most common definition of ethnography—by which he means some kind of immersion in the context under study. Second, he asserts that ethnography is a "sensibility." This "sensibility" means that the approach sets out to "glean the meanings that the people under study attribute to their social and political reality" (Schatz, 2009, p. 5). Under such an understanding, ethnography is not only participant observation, but it is also the "close familiarity with and analysis of any collection of human artifacts (texts, cultural products, and so on)... revealing the meanings people attribute to the world they inhabit" (Schatz, 2009, p. 6). As part of the same book, Jourde asserts that ethnography allows political scientists to uncover "unidentified political objects"—or "political relations and sites" that have not yet been examined (Jourde, 2009, p. 201). Jourde quotes Martin's (2002) claim that political science often examines a "limited repertoire of political objects" rather than expanding to include new places and questions (Jourde, 2009, pp. 202–3).

Expect Us operates within both of these traditions—the long-standing respect for ethnography as a way to understand online community and the struggle in political science for ethnographic methods to gain recognition. Much of the research in *Expect Us* would not have been possible using other types of research methods. Online communities are difficult to study, not only because of the ways in which they confound traditional conceptual frameworks, but also because many of them also confound attempts to datamine content (e.g., using large data scrapers or crawlers that collect massive amounts of text to be catalogued). For example, Issuecrawler.net, a nonprofit service that creates hyperlink network maps for scholars, has difficulty gathering links from posting boards, chat rooms, blogs, social networking pages, online video games, and many of the other types of forums that contain and foster online communities. When researching World of Warcraft, for example, I attempted to use hyperlink network mapping to understand the boundaries of the WoW community outside the game itself. In doing so, I discovered that it was impossible to map the community without doing it "by hand." The network map of the community—including instructions of where to find key informational nodes for novice players—is communicated by word of mouth. Furthermore, archiving attempts such as the Internet Archive often do not capture much of the interaction in these spaces. Another example of the ineffectiveness of data-mining tools for gathering reliable information about online sites is the famously ephemeral /b/ board on 4chan.org, described in chapter 2. Thus, as Internet scholars have long known, without ethnographic research or close observation, the interaction in these sites will be lost, and the networks of sites that intersect and contain these online communities will not be analyzed.

Comparative Method

The second major methodological choice I made was to use the comparative method. The comparative method involves the comparison between and within cases in order to gain analytical and causal leverage in explaining a given phenomenon (see Lijphart, 1971 or Collier, 1993 for more). It usually involves examining a small number of cases in order to use the comparison itself to highlight key similarities and differences. The method is most closely associated with comparative politics (Lijphart, 1971), a political science subfield, and so has traditionally focused on cross-country comparison or cross-temporal comparisons within a single context (e.g., Ragin, 2004, pp. 133–34).

The research in *Expect Us* is not only comparative but explicitly case-based. My use of case-based research follows Gerring (2004), who argues that case study is "an intensive study of a single unit for the purpose of understanding a larger class of (similar) units." Gerring further argues that a case is a "spatially bounded phenomenon—e.g. a nation-state, revolution, political party, election, or person— observed at a single point in time or over some delimited period of time" (Gerring, 2004, p. 342).

Defining Communities as Cases

In *Expect Us* I treat each online community as a case and define the case along two separate parameters—the cultural boundaries of the community and temporally. Throughout the chapters of the book I examine the way that the communities articulate themselves, the core norms and practices shared by each community, and, to the extent that it is possible, the amorphous boundaries of these anonymous and semi-anonymous communities. I also examined each community within a specific time frame (primarily 2007–10), something that is important to note as all of these communities still exist and have evolved over time.

Also important is that I treat the communities themselves as the cases rather than the websites where the communities were born. While part of my argument is that the structure of the birthplaces of each of these online communities shaped the communities themselves in profound ways, in every case the communities soon drew upon a wide array of online spaces. The decisions over where the boundaries lay in each case posed a set of challenges as discussed by Hine (2005).

In the case of *Expect Us,* this methodological choice is heavily informed by new institutionalist theory, in particular, historical institutionalism and theory focused on organizational culture. To conceive of the birthplaces of each online community, I was informed by historical institutionalist explanations. According to Hall and Taylor (1996), historical institutionalism defines institutions as the "formal or informal procedures, routines, norms, and conventions embedded in the organizational structure of the polity or political economy." Social spaces online could be considered a collection of formal procedures and informal norms that are encoded into the technological design of the space. For example, anonymity itself is formally encoded into site design. First-time posters on IGN.com are required to choose user names and provide email addresses. The link between the user name and email address makes it cumbersome to create a new account every time a user wants to log into the website and post something. In contrast, there is no need to create user accounts in most Anonymous sites, and all users post under the name "anonymous." In each case, these formal procedures have created informal norms and ways of existing in each community. In Anonymous sites, anonymity has become a social value, and in many cases non-anonymity is punished. In contrast, in places such as IGN.com, posting under a "fake" user name is considered duplicitous.

In addition, I also drew on a historical institutionalist approach to define my cases because when conceiving of home websites, historical institutionalists also offer valuable insight into the interaction between individuals and rule systems. Historical institutionalists consider actors to be operating within a social context (Migdal, 2001, p. 246), but calculating (often rationally) within those frameworks (Migdal, 2001, p. 255). The historical institutionalist focus on the agency of the individual within the institutional context also provides an explanation for online social spaces, where the diversity of users' "real worlds" means that individuals' external contexts and value systems make it difficult to generalize about individual motivations. This is particularly important because the social spaces I study are not constant presences in the lives of users as people must log in to be a part of them, and so it is difficult to conceive of them as all-encompassing regulatory presences.

Additionally, a historical institutionalist approach was useful for defining my cases because it considers the relationship between the individual and the institution as a process in which the past has an impact on future choices. The central articulation of this idea is the concept of "path dependence"—or the outcomes of critical moments that establish distinct trajectories (Collier & Collier, 1991). These distinct trajectories are laid out in critical moments of institutional change, or "critical junctures." Path dependence does not follow a deterministic logic, but rather it is probabilistic—certain outcomes are more likely than others.

Finally, a historical institutional approach helped in case definition because the approach tends to view the rules and the individual as engaged in mutually transformative relationships (Migdal, 2001, p. 254). Social variables are not necessarily independent but are mutually constitutive. Thus, "preferences, interests, and identities" are not just causes; they are also products of the institutional framework. In every case in this study, users arrive in the spaces with distinct preferences, interests, and identities. These then shape how users interact with other people. In IGN. com, for example, users' preferences, interests, and identities dramatically shape the types of conversations people have in the space, and in World of Warcraft, they determine how people divide into groups.

When attempting to define the parameters of each "case"—or community—I also drew upon an organizational culture approach. An organizational culture argument would define the object of study as the online community. Kier (1999, p. 28) defines organizational culture as the "set of basic assumptions, values, norms, beliefs, and formal knowledge (within an organization) that shape collective understandings." Institutions in this sense would be very broadly defined as symbolic systems, mental scripts, morals, formal rules, norms, procedures, and even culture. According to Kier (1999, p. 28), organizational culture defines problems and "determines the range of possible solutions and strategies appropriate for solving it." To understand what the culture is, Kier argues, scholars should look for consistency among members of an organization. Kier asserts that "satisficing" actors use the institutionalized behaviors to pursue goals. In such a paradigm, actors and structures interact, with, as Kier argues (1999, p. 33), actors being both "the products and the producers of their cultural environment."

Using this conceptualization, I defined the online communities as having a culture separate from, but also found in, their "home" websites. This culture would be created in large part by the structure of the initial online website, which would continue to shape individual choices even in other online spaces. For example, Anonymous communities may make use of tools such as the IRC, in which users can have distinct user names; however, community members continue to value anonymity and attempt to exist online within the anonymity value guidelines from 4chan.org.

An organizational culture approach helped me to define my cases and examine the tensions between the communities and their birthplaces, but it did not help me understand the splintering of the online communities into clear value subgroups. For example, in chapter 2, I track the initial fracturing of Anonymous into three factions, and currently the number of Anonymous activist groups and approaches has multiplied even further. While many of the basic values exist across the factions—for example, most recognize the value of anonymity online—there is a wide divergence across groups in other value areas, most notably adherence to legal versus illegal protest strategies. Similarly, in the case of WoW, individuals also splinter into small groups based on values that are exogenous to the space—such as appropriate public speech. The divergence in approaches indicates that while users are bound by community values to some extent, they are not only looking to the organization (or institution) to identify appropriate strategies for dealing with a given problem, but they are looking outside it as well.

Finally, using an organizational culture approach also helped me understand the interaction between the communities as cases and offline contexts. In an examination of French and British military doctrine, Kier (1999, p. 21) argues that the constraints of the domestic political arena (based on civilian political culture) and the military's organizational culture shapes the choice between offensive or defensive military doctrine. As part of this argument, Kier (1999, p. 32) asserts that organizational culture does not explain a change of doctrine on its own, but rather, there has to be an associated change in the organization's external domestic political environment that the organization then reacts to. Thus, the external context of an organization matters in outcomes.

Case Selection

The third major methodological choice I made was regarding case selection. The initial research project that served as the foundation of *Expect Us* was driven by the hypothesis that everyday interactions in online social spaces led to individual-level political change, such as introspection and belief evaluation. Studying these changes, I believed, could enrich theoretical understandings of youth civic engagement. This hypothesis was shaped by Habermas's conception of political discourse—specifically, that the online conversations and debates about political issues had significance in the outside world.[1] It was also based on initial observations of IGN.com and drew on studies focused on legal consciousness (e.g., McCann, 1994; Ewick & Silbey, 1998; or Nielsen, 2004).

The four online spaces included in this research are the following:

- Anonymous, a community that was born from 4chan.org but now crosses many posting board systems and websites that share some common characteristics such as extreme anonymity.
- The Pirate Bay, a community whose symbolic heart has become the file-sharing website Thepiratebay.se (previously thepiratebay.org).
- World of Warcraft, a massively multiplayer online role-playing game (MMORPG).

- IGN.com's posting board system, a system whose community is relatively contained to IGN.

I used seven criteria to select the four cross-national online sites that form the basis of this research. First, the sites needed to be apolitical. In other words, their central purpose could not be political discussion or action, and they could not be connected to online political forums, blogs, news providers, or groups associated with building civil society. I was interested in social sites that had no political purpose because as a community member in two of them, I had observed politically significant behavior in the sites.

In addition, I not only specifically looked for spaces where no political mobilization had occurred but I chose spaces where the majority of the participants were in the space for nonpolitical reasons. It is important to underline this point because of what subsequently happened with Anonymous and The Pirate Bay. While both Anonymous and the community that coalesced around The Pirate Bay ultimately mobilized politically, in 2007 when I began observational research, neither community looked like political actors. Just as World of Warcraft players arrived in WoW to play a game, Pirate Bay users arrived on The Pirate Bay to download files and Anonymous members arrived on the /b/ board on 4chan.org to socialize and be entertained.

My second criterion for site selection was to choose spaces that were highly populated. Although counts are difficult to conduct, at the time I began my research The Pirate Bay had around 25 million peers sharing files at any given time.[2] Anonymous is a more difficult entity to measure. In August 2008, 4chan.org saw 3.2 million visitors. In August 2008, the most trafficked Anonymous space, 4chan.org, was accessed by 3.2 million unique visitors (Poole, 2013). In August 2012, the founder of 4chan.org reported that 4chan had just had its one billionth post. As part of the news post on 4chan with this information, he also stated that as of the beginning of August 2012 4chan had been accessed by 134 million unique visitors and had 4.5 billion page views. He further stated that since 2008, 4chan has had more than 500 million people visit the site (Poole, 2012). World of Warcraft has more than 11.5 million users worldwide (Blizzard Entertainment, 2008), and I estimated around 21,641 people played on the realm I observed.[3] External estimates of IGN.com's population have placed its membership at around 1,250,000 users.[4] I chose communities with large populations as a proxy for impact because the collected populations of the home websites of each community are millions of people.

The choice of high-population social spaces was not only a methodological choice but also a practical one. Initially I included a general topic posting board in my research design with a fairly small community and before I began formally gathering data in the community, it disappeared from the Internet. Thus, selecting cases on the basis of their large size and popularity make it possible to track activity over time. In the constantly shifting terrain of the online world, highly populated cases are often the most solid ground for researchers to stand on. While the ephemerality of online content makes this concern particularly pertinent to Internet research, it is in line with Ragin's (2004, p. 125) claim that most case study research involves a process of "sifting" whereby researchers drop and add cases as concepts are revised.

Third and fourth, I excluded sites where users are identified by their legal names, and I looked for spaces where users do not have the option of completely removing, filtering, or tailoring the type of interaction they experience. I chose sites where users did not use their legal names because I was interested in the role of anonymity in shaping interaction online. When I began my research I conceived of anonymity in very naive terms, grouping all websites together where users did not supply their legal names to interact with the community. It was only as I began gathering data that the differences between anonymity in each community began to emerge as an important factor. Additionally, I focused on sites that did not give users control over the type of information they saw or the individuals they interacted with because this lack of control characterizes many social sites online. Thus, I explicitly excluded prominent social networking sites such as MySpace, Facebook, and Twitter where users can block or hide information and where users choose their interaction partners. I was interested in spaces where people were thrown together, usually from different parts of the world, and where filtering out content had to be a continuous decision.

The fifth criterion was that even though site populations could be cross-national, English had to be the language participants used to interact. The English-speaking criterion was based on preliminary research in IGN.com's posting boards where I had shaped the initial parameters of the study.

Sixth, in order to have diversity in my cases, I chose to observe a variety of interfaces. This criterion allowed me to determine whether the interface had an impact on the type of interaction in the space. The way that people interact with each other in each of the four cases is dramatically different, with the most similar interface being that between 4chan.org and the IGN.com posting boards. However, even between these two cases, there are significant differences in the way that one posts and interacts with other users. My focus on different types of posting interfaces was informed (perhaps strangely) by neo-institutionalist theory, in particular historical institutionalism, as I discussed above. New institutionalist literature is characterized by a concern with the ways in which structure—formal and informal regulation—shapes individual action.

Finally, the above criteria meant that I was also selecting sites with an estimated average age for users of 30 years old. I triangulated this average age based on a range of sources. First, the Pew Internet & American Life Project (PIALP) has found that different groups of people use the Internet in different ways (Purcell, 2010). Specifically, although approximately the same percentage of teenagers and adults use the Internet to send and receive email and to read the news, adults tend to use the Internet primarily as a research tool (Gross, 2004; Roberts, Foehr, & Rideout, 2005). In contrast, people under the age of 28 use the Internet to talk to each other in social spaces online. The PIALP reports that 93 percent of American youth have used the Internet at some point (Purcell, 2010). Second, Nick Yee's work has found that the average age of MMORPG players is 30 years old (Yee, 2005c). Third, IGN.com reports that its demographic is 18- to 34-year-old men (IGN.com, 2010). Therefore, once I had chosen to study social sites, I had also chosen to study young people.

Epistemologically, the case selection could be considered to be a focus on "crucial cases" as defined by Brady and Collier (2004, p. 283) drawing on Eckstein (1975). Scholars such as Abe Gong (2011) have criticized Internet researchers for small-n studies that are focused on prominent cases, noting that such cases do not always represent larger groups. Criticism of small-n studies on the basis of representativeness and choosing cases on the basis of importance is not uncommon; however, as Ragin (2004, p. 129) argues, this criticism is based on a fundamental misunderstanding of case-based research. Among other arguments, Ragin points out that social scientists often choose to study things that are culturally or historically important *because* they are culturally or historically important and necessitate illumination. The intent here has been examining each case holistically to understand an understudied phenomenon (Collier, Mahoney, & Seawright, 2004, p. 87).

Data Gathering

The fourth major methodological choice I made was in relation to data gathering. Most of the research in *Expect Us* was conducted between 2007 and 2010. In all cases I used participant observer and observational research methods. I engaged in textual analysis of materials in community spaces. I also used news reports of behaviors, archived community documents and artifacts, and published interviews of prominent community members. In addition, I pieced together narratives from a range of Internet sites. Much of this could be characterized as "process tracing"—which, George and Bennett (2005, p. 206) claim, "attempts to identify the intervening causal process—the causal chain and causal mechanism—between an independent variable (or variables) and the outcome of the dependent variable."

Because I was unable to watch all things happening at all times and I needed to know key historical events for communities, a central component of the research was also piecing together chronologies and understandings of what had happened, when and how. This work was helped by the data-rich environment of the Internet, where I could find artifacts of most online content in some form. For example, if something major occurred in World of Warcraft while I was not logged in, people would often speak about it on forums or in blog posts. However, piecing together chronologies and events was also hindered by the data-rich environment of the Internet, where artifacts of events could be fragmented, incomplete, and in some cases misleading. Often, the only way to verify information was through the stories community members told, the ways in which events were referred to, and my judgment calls about whether someone was telling the truth.

In cases of contradictions between narrative accounts, I either used accounts that were reported in more than one source or found an average point between reports, particularly when numbers were reported. In cases where I make assertions about community culture, I also triangulated across online resources or drew upon my knowledge of the community.

Field notes were kept using Zotero, most commonly screen-captures of public content. Any cited online content I also captured because of its ephemeral nature, except in cases when it contained information that could be traced back to users who were not explicitly operating as public figures. I also kept extensive handwritten and typed field notes, including tables filled with coding of behaviors.

The traditional ethnographic "year" model whereby a researcher spends a year living somewhere does not necessarily work in the online context, particularly when attempting to compare cases. Thus, I approximated this type of immersive experience as best I could. I began in each space by spending time observing interactions. After observing each, I began an intensive immersive experience in each case. While I was immersed in one community, I kept tabs on the others but did not necessarily spend focused research time in them. If something "big" happened while I was immersed in another case, I would move to the case in question—and this is what happened with Anonymous groups' mobilization against the Church of Scientology in 2008. When I was not immersed in a case, I still visited community spaces every few days (at the least), kept up with major community events, and tried to maintain an insider's understanding of the community.

My research methodology also varied slightly across cases based on the opportunities and restrictions provided by each case. In the case of Anonymous, I engaged in observational research. As the scope of chapter 2 illustrates in the case of Anonymous, the bulk of my research time was between late 2007 and early 2009. I began my research on the website 4chan.org in 2007 and was focused on the no-topic (/b/) board. However, I expanded my "net" to include other online spaces such as 7chan. org, 711chan.org, 888chan.org, enturbulation.org, and partyvan.info, among others, particularly once Anonymous began mobilizing against the Church of Scientology.

In the case of The Pirate Bay, I also engaged in observational research, but I did not interact with the community. The bulk of my research time in The Pirate Bay was focused between late 2008 and early 2010. While research within Anonymous involved extensive observation of interactions between individuals, research into The Pirate Bay included far more extensive piecing together of community history—including the history of file-sharers; file-sharing sites; and international, US, Swedish, and European Union law related to intellectual property. This search was complicated by the fact that these issues are not reported on systematically outside of topic-specific online publications such as *Torrent Freak*, particularly when I was engaging in observational research. In this case, much of the background research into issues such as the ways in which US copyright law interacts with other national laws through the filter of US government pressure never made it into the final accounting of The Pirate Bay in this book. In the case of The Pirate Bay, like Anonymous, the community spaces I explored included a range of places that were not part of the original space, including other file-sharing websites such as OiNK. Unlike Anonymous, many of these other places were not interactive spaces, but rather were text and video archives such as documentaries, news reports, government documents, interviews, and legal texts.

I focused on World of Warcraft most intensely between late 2009 and late 2010. This meant that the bulk of my research occurred during the Wrath of the Lich King Expansion. Unlike Anonymous and The Pirate Bay, I had previous experience with World of Warcraft as a nonresearcher and so had an understanding of the game prior to the research time period. In WoW, I engaged in participant observation research. As part of this, within the game I was heavily involved in two raiding guilds, including observing guild chat, listening into voice software interactions, raiding with one of the guilds regularly, and informally speaking to guild leadership and members. I also observed the general conversation channels within the game. As in the other cases, the boundaries of the community spread beyond the immediate community space. For that reason, I also read forums, blogs, how-to guides, wikis, guild websites, and WoW-focused news websites. I also did some comparison to other realms and online conversations happening among European WoW players.

IGN.com's posting boards were where I conducted the preliminary research to create the research design for the entire study in 2007. It was the location where I first observed intensive political conversation happening in an unexpected place. I returned to IGN.com's posting board repeatedly throughout my research, and it served as something of a touchstone for the rest of the project. I was a participant observer in the system in late 2007, for some time in 2008, and again during 2010. My research in IGN.com's posting boards focused on the general topic board—the Vestibule—although I also studied other community spaces within the broader board system. Unlike my other cases where the community had come to sprawl out across a range of online spaces, the IGN.com posting board community was more spatially bound. This meant that although I also used tools that were external to the IGN board system to interact, such as MSN Messenger, some off-site board systems, informal conversations with longtime and influential community members, and community-created archives such as the Vesti Wiki to build my understanding of the community, unlike my other cases, the majority of my IGN research was focused on the boards themselves.

Central Concepts

The fifth major aspect of my research methodology was less a choice than an iterative process that developed over time as I dealt with the central concepts that emerged from my study. As part of my argument, I work to articulate and build the central concepts of anonymity, regulation, and spatial divisions within online spaces.

I used an inductive process to generate categories and measurement criteria for each that was specific enough to define each concept within a given space but was flexible enough to avoid the dangers of "concept stretching" (Sartori, 1970). To do this, I drew heavily on social science literature discussing concept formation. For example, Becker (1998, p. 133) argues that concepts are relational. In a discussion of social class Becker states:

> Terms like "middle class" or "working class" only have meaning in relation to one another or to the "upper class," and the meaning is the character of the relationship. . . . That seems obvious enough. But it's one of those obvious things that people acknowledge and then ignore. How do they ignore it? By imagining that a class, by having a characteristic culture or way of life, would be what it is no matter what system of relations it was embedded in.

Becker argues that for a concept to "work" it must be put into the context of "the full set of terms they imply" (1998, p. 138). To develop concepts in such a relational manner, Becker argues, scholars should "forget the name entirely and concentrate on the kind of collective activity that is taking place" (1998, p. 144).

Keeping Becker's argument in mind, to generate and measure the central concepts, I engaged in a process of coding for each space that was iterative and similar to the process of coding open-ended responses to surveys or interviews, with categories emerging from the space and sometimes remaining and sometimes being revised or reabsorbed into other categories. When a new category emerged, I would go back to all of the other spaces and check the new category against each space. This inductive method of analyzing qualitative data is sometimes called the "constant comparison" method (e.g., Merriam, 2001). As will be apparent below, some of the categories or questions asked about the space do not have dichotomous answers (yes/no). Instead, many have more graduated answers that also required additional analysis and consideration. At the end of the research process, I also analyzed two other online spaces to test my coding in order to check for bias. This process involved note-taking and often large and constantly expanding tables as I attempted to simplify, filter, and group the information I was processing from a range of sources.

Anonymity

Regarding the first central concept I put forth, the level of anonymity in a social site is key to determining the type of political activity that develops. Measuring the level of anonymity a user has in a space also can be framed as how difficult it is for a person to gain an individual identity and reputation in the community. I coded the level of anonymity in each community based on characteristics of each the online space. The central categories that emerged were the following:

- Can users interact in the community without going through a registration process? When users have to register to participate, they have a lower level of anonymity on the site than they do when registration is not required.
- Do users have a name in the space, such as a user name? Users who are named have lower levels of anonymity than those who are not.
- Are users required to use their legal names? The stronger the link between the online persona and the offline identity, the lower the level of anonymity a user has on the site.
- Do users have fixed avatars and/or other pictorial representations of self that can come to be identified with them? The greater number of identifiers, the less anonymous the user is.
- Does the site have searchable/readable archives of conversations/interactions available? If everything a user says can be recalled weeks later, users have lower levels of anonymity than they would if such information were not available.
- Is there a way to formalize connections between users in the space, such as joining groups or guilds? When a user's individual identity is tied to other users, the user's level of anonymity is lower than when such linkages do not occur.
- Is a user immediately identifiable by a visual or word cue as being a part of a group? Such cues decrease the level of anonymity users have on the site.
- How large is the population of the community? Highly populated communities make it more difficult for a user to be known in the space.
- Does the site keep track of who is there, such as IP tracking? In sites where users' IP addresses are tracked, users have lower anonymity than they have in sites where IP addresses are not tracked.[5]

It is possible there are other parameters of anonymity—and in early iterations there were far more categories. However, those listed above emerged as the central measurement criteria.

Regulation

Related to anonymity, regulation in a site is central to the development and shape of online communities and the political action that emerges in them. Regulation includes both "formal" regulation—that enacted by website owners and administrators—and informal policing, which is conducted by community members. Much like anonymity, the type of regulation in a space can be determined by responses to a range of questions. Following are the central questions I used to determine the level of regulation:

- Are there many official rules designed to regulate behavior in the space? Roughly, more than five rules, extensive Terms of Service/Use, End User Licensing Agreements, or other kinds of regulations indicate high levels of regulation on a site.
- Are there open-ended rules that allow moderators to sanction users who have not violated a specific rule? For example, IGN has a "catch-all" rule to cover any behavior not specifically covered by its official rules, giving moderators the right to decide rules on the spot. The presence of open-ended rules, particularly when coupled with many official rules, indicates a highly regulated site.
- Is there a regulatory presence in the space? If so, is it constant or do regulators have to be "called in" via users submitting notices? A highly regulated site will have a constant "police" presence and easy ways for users to report rule violations.[6]
- Are there searchable archives of user behavior that moderators can look through to sanction behavior after it occurred?[7] When a user's bad behavior can be found and punished weeks later, the site can be said to be highly regulated.
- Is speech regulated? For example, are offensive words or phrases forbidden, such as derogatory terms for groups or obscenities? The degree to which speech is regulated indicates the level of regulation in the site.
- Are types of conversations regulated—for example, erotic role-playing or stories? When conversation topics are monitored and managed, sites can be said to be highly regulated.
- Are types of images, such as pornography, regulated? As noted with speech regulation, the degree to which images are regulated indicates the level of regulation in the space.
- Does the community police itself, regulating norm violations through informal sanctions such as shunning? All communities self-regulate. However, high levels of community regulation coupled with high levels of site regulation create highly regulated sites.
- Are there unwritten rules that differ from the formal rules? These rules are difficult to operationalize as they can only be discerned through long-term observation. However, they can be loosely defined as behavioral expectations— deviations from which open the offender to sanction or ostracism by the community. Highly regulated sites often have many of these kinds of rules.

As with anonymity, there are other possible parameters, but those above were my central set of criteria.

Spatial Divisions

Unlike anonymity and regulation, the components of spatial divisions are less tidy to operationalize. Below, I list four major questions I used to map the spatial divisions in each online community. However, the response to these questions varies widely for each online space and the answers to each were far longer, more descriptive, and more complicated than simply clean categories for measurement:

- How is the conversational space divided?
- Is a single community space where all users can interact simultaneously available and used?
- How difficult is the communication interface to use?
- Are there searchable archives of community history or do participants have to be present to experience community events?

The four online communities in this study represent widely divergent types of online communication spaces.

Research Ethics

Finally, the sixth major methodological choice I made had to do with research ethics. Appropriate online research methodology is debated within the research community and it is not a debate people are necessarily aware of outside the community.[8] Thus, to form my own ethical stance in doing this research, I engaged with three of the central debates about research ethics.

The first debate is about what online text actually is—a cultural artifact or a conversation. Scholars who treat online text as a cultural artifact argue that online text is much like a book in library, because it is (*a*) published and (*b*) always accessible.[9] In this conception of online spaces, as long as the scholar can access the material without special permission, she can treat the text as an object, the produced work of an individual, placed by that individual into a public space. In this conception, the study of these "cultural artifacts" online is not a study of active human interaction.

Alternately, some argue that reading the text is the equivalent of an ongoing conversation that they are observing.[10] They argue that researchers have a greater ethical obligation because the text is attached to individuals interacting and is not a stand-alone object.

My research fell between these two perspectives. On the one hand, I spent much of my time trying to understanding a macro-level phenomenon—the relationship between a certain segment of society and the state—through watching the multiplicity of every day interactions occurring in social spaces online. Thus, in these cases, the text I was interested in was most often not an artifact, but a living conversation. On the other hand, I also analyzed many different types of media, including flyers, videos, news reports, interviews, and other imagery. In such cases, I was examining cultural artifacts.

The second debate is about what is public and what is private online and what that distinction means in terms of our ethical obligation to our subjects. This debate is intimately wrapped up in the issue of informed consent because it considers the question of whether people in online communities fully appreciate the implications of their actions when posting. This question is particularly pressing because my own experiences in these communities showed me that although the participants are anonymous and disconnected from "real" identities, the thoughts they express often represent their real ideas.[11]

Scholars universally agree that a single ethical rubric is not sufficient for all online research because of the diversity of place types online.[12] I agree with the assessment of the literature; however, I expanded some of the rubrics of others concerning what kinds of protections are necessary for online researchers.[13] Perhaps unsurprisingly, this understanding of privacy is very much informed by my understanding of anonymity and included the following:

- Degree of connection to offline identities
- The size of the population of the community
- The stability of the population (i.e., are the users constantly turning over?)
- Participant beliefs about who can see interactions
- Participant beliefs about privacy
- Participant agreements about privacy
- Level of archiving of participant-generated text
- Subject of focus of the community
- How one gains access to the community
- Whether the conversations are viewable without membership
- Researcher intentions/level of analysis

For example, research that is the highest risk to community participants would have the following characteristics:

- Researcher can connect individuals to "real life" information.
- The population of the community is small (fewer than 50 people)
- The population is extremely stable over time.
- Individual believes conversations are between himself and a few people whom he has selected specifically.
- Individual expects information about herself to only be accessible to people she chooses.
- The site has no privacy agreement and users have not been warned in any way that what they post may be viewed by third parties.
- Individual expects conversation to be ephemeral—in other words, not archived.
- Community is "sensitive" in nature—dealing with highly emotional topics or a vulnerable community.
- To gain access to the community one must be invited or given membership.
- Outsiders cannot view conversations without membership.
- Researcher is interested in profiling individual experiences or psychologies.

Ethically, in the case of a community like the one described above, researchers would need to treat their research as extremely risky to individuals. In contrast, research that is the lowest risk to community members would occur in communities characterized by the following:

- Individual is completely anonymous or uses an alias not connected to "real life" information.
- The population of the community is large (more than 200 people).
- The population is unstable—that is, constantly changing.
- Individual believes anyone can observe conversations and gather information.
- Individual believes the conversation is public and expects any personal information revealed to be available to anyone who happens upon the site.
- The site has a privacy agreement and users are warned that what they post may be viewed by third parties. In the most secure example, users would have the power to modify their own privacy settings.
- Individual believes the conversation will be accessible after it has occurred—that is, it is archived.
- Community is no-topic in nature or deals with topics that are not sensitive—such as video games.
- Anyone can make an account/participate in the community.
- Anyone can view conversations, even without an account.
- Researcher is interested in profiling aggregate behaviors not telling individual stories.

By my measurement, the spaces involved in my research were in the low-risk category. Even so, these considerations are a balancing act for all researchers. The burden is on researchers to make sure that no ill effects are visited on our subjects, including among an individual's fellow community members who may recognize him from a quote or other information provided about a speaker or participant. Researchers can mask a member's identity in a number of ways, including changing the person's gender, locale, and so on—methods familiar to all qualitative researchers seeking maximum protection of subjects and groups under study. For this reason, I slightly altered the language without changing the meaning for any illustrative quotes I used throughout *Expect Us* that could be traced to an individual.

A third debate in the literature is the question of the expectations of the subjects.[14] This issue is also intimately involved in the question of informed consent. The expectations of the subjects, which are often connected to forum privacy agreements, are important because sometimes even in online venues with an extensive agreement structure outlining the public nature of conversations in the community, researchers should still consider whether subjects expect their conversations to be public.

Again, in the online world, the way to deal with this issue is somewhat subjective and based on the communities under study. The Association of Internet

Researcher's 2002 guidelines to ethical online research argue that community member expectations are shaped by a wide array of factors including the venue, the ability to indicate if a conversation is private, and the content of the conversation. In my research, I shaped my design in relation to participant expectation.

Further, AOIR argues that the venue in which interactions occur shape participant expectations of privacy. Sites with explicit statements notifying users that the domain is public and statements as to whether conversations are archived make it reasonable for researchers to assume that users are aware of the limits to their privacy in the space.

Additionally, the AOIR ethics committee argues that in sites where users can indicate that their exchanges have become private—such as private messaging or moving conversations to "private" boards or rooms—also make participant expectations of privacy clear to researchers. Users' understanding that some exchanges are public, as well as signaling that they are moving to private conversations, allows the researcher to adopt the participant's public/private consideration (see also Reid, 1996).

The AOIR ethics committee also asserts that researchers should consider the content of conversations. For example, if the content of user conversations were to become public, would the users be harmed? Conversations about intimate topics such as psychological issues, sexual experiences, or "deviant" identities should be treated as highly sensitive.

Conclusion

In conclusion, the research in this volume blends long-used methods from Internet research and political science and engages in research methods shaped by the central research question as well as the practicalities of the online spaces.

Notes

Chapter 1

1. Alexandra Samuel (2004, p. 2) defines "hacktivism" as the "nonviolent use of illegal or legally ambiguous digital tools in pursuit of political ends. These tools include web site defacements, redirects, denial-of-service attacks, information theft, web site parodies, virtual sit-ins, virtual sabotage, and software development."

2. A distributed denial-of-service attack is a coordinated attack intended to make a computer resource (such as a website) unavailable. This is accomplished by flooding the target with so many external requests that the servers cannot answer requests from legitimate users.

3. This is not a technological deterministic argument; rather it would be analogous to Howard's argument of "soft" technological determinism, which recognizes that technologies "provide capacities for and impose constraints on users" (Howard, 2010, pp. 16–17). Or, in line with Winner (1980) and others (e.g., Neff & Stark, 2004), using an approach that focuses on the political implications of technological design in facilitating or discouraging certain types of interactions; creating opportunity structures for certain types of political mobilization; and producing specific desired outcomes, such as learning goals (e.g., Jones & Rafaeli, 2000; Freelon, 2011; Kafal, 1995; and Dickey, 2009). It is also analogous to the concept of "path dependence" in historical institutionalist theory, as I discuss in the appendix.

4. A troll is a user who tries to goad others into responding in a certain way. Usually this means the troll posts inflammatory, off-topic, or ludicrous material in the hope of generating an emotional response. In most social spaces online, if someone responds emotionally to a troll, it means that the troll has won.

5. For example, Brosky & Giles touch on the issue of anonymity, 2007, pp. 94 and 106. See also Mulveen & Hepworth, 2006, pp. 284 and 293; Greenberg's

coverage of the anonymous drug trade, 2013; Chen's coverage of pedophile communities, 2013; and the United Nation's Interregional Crime and Justice Research Institute's work on jihadist networks, 2013.

6. Alternately, as Gray (2009, p. 15) argues, young rural youth may not draw on new media to "escape their surroundings" but rather to "enhance their sense of inclusion to broader, imagined queer communities beyond their hometowns."

7. Internet Relay Chat is a form of synchronous online text communication designed for group communication in channels. It also supports one-to-one communication and file-sharing.

8. An example of such a group would be the Rough Trade Gaming Community, which operates under the guild tag <Taint> in World of Warcraft and describes itself as "a group of Lesbian, Gay, Bi-Sexual, and Transgender (LGBT) online gamers that have a presence in multiple MMO's. . . . We offer a safe and fun gaming environment for thousands of LGBT players and supporters." As of November 2013 their website could be found here: http://taint.rtgc.org/.

9. Originally called "Caturday," lolcats are images with amusing and grammatically incorrect phrases superimposed over photos of cats.

10. Rickrolling is when a user provides a link that is supposedly related to a discussion topic but instead is a link to Rick Astley's 1987 song "Never Gonna Give You Up." The song could be buried as a surprise—for example, in the middle of what seems to be a "serious" YouTube video. The "Rickrolling" meme was credited with Rick Astley being asked to perform in the 2008 Macy's Day Thanksgiving Parade.

11. A word cloud is a visual representation of text that gives more frequently used words visual weight, showing them as larger or in specific colors.

12. Because of the changing nature of the list, this data was gathered through analyzing discussion threads in which people mentioned/complained about certain words being on the list.

13. Another way of framing this is in terms of "legal pluralism" (Merry, 1988).

14. The Cybernorms Research Group at Lund University has done extensive work examining social norms and file-sharing. As of November 2013, its website could be found here: http://cybernormer.se/.

15. This term was first used by a Los Angeles Fox affiliate KTTV on July 26, 2007, during a news report describing Anonymous' MySpace hackings. As of August 15, 2011, Know Your Meme provided background to the reference including the original news clip here: http://knowyourmeme.com/memes/internet-hate-machine.

16. This phrasing is an online joke that originated on 4chan.org. Most now refer to the phrasing as the "Pretty Cool Guy Meme." The original phrasing is, "i think halo is a pretty cool guy. eh kills aleins and doesn't afraid of anything."

17. Anonymous gained access to HBGary Federal's documents about Anonymous, as well as a multitude of internal documents, and published them online in February 2011 (Cheng, 2011). While the actors who engaged in the DDoS attacks on WikiLeaks have never been revealed, in the online communities I studied members generally believe that the US government was involved.

18. Even searching for "Because no one of us is as cruel as all of us" without reference to Anonymous will list Anonymous sites and references primarily.

19. Please note that while I use the categories of "old" and "new" for analytical clarity, as I discuss in chapter 2, the lines between Anonymous groups are blurry, and it is likely that many members participate in more than one Anonymous community.

20. Wikis are websites in which users create and edit linked pages. The most famous wiki is the collaborative online encyclopedia Wikipedia.org. An imageboard is a type of posting board centered around the posting of images. A very famous imageboard is 4chan.org. Social networking sites are websites whose purpose is to connect people who share interests or activities. In their most basic form, social networks tend to include individual profiles, as well as links between the individual's profile and other profiles. Two famous examples are Facebook and Twitter.

21. A mirror is a complete copy of a website placed online for download. Often individuals copy a site to prevent it from being "disappeared" from the Internet. In these cases, the mirrored site is usually downloaded by many individuals, who then remirror it. The redundancy serves as security for the site content.

22. Pirate Party International kept a record of all mirrors with some information about each on a publicly available website—and this record of mirrors was also mirrored, in case the original site went down.

23. When I was studying World of Warcraft it was divided into four regional blocks: North America / Oceania, Asia, China, and Europe. The Chinese block is separate from Asia because the Chinese government requires Blizzard to change the game in line with Chinese government regulations. For example, the Chinese government prohibits Blizzard from displaying any skulls in the game. Within each regional block, the community is divided by "realms." When I was conducting my research there were around 241 North America / Oceania realms and 263 European realms. Each realm has over 10,000 people playing on it.

24. For example, WhyWeProtest, an Anonymous group, states in its "Vision" statement, "As new technology enables activists to bridge the boundaries of distance and language, momentum is gathering and possibilities for social change are opening up." As of August 15, 2011, it could be found here: http://www.whyweprotest.net/vision/.

25. This was in a thread posted in early December 2010. The text about Amazon burning books is a reference to a WikiLeaks' Twitter post that said, "If

Amazon are so uncomfortable with the first amendment, they should get out of the business of selling books."

26. All threads were posted in early December 2010.

27. As I discuss in greater detail in chapter 4, to play World of Warcraft, an individual must create a character. Part of the creation process is giving the character a distinct name. Only one character per realm may have any given name.

28. All of this data was from the World of Warcraft Armory. Accessed on July 17, 2011.

29. All threads were posted on IGN's "Vesti" in early December 2010.

Chapter 2

1. I gathered the numbers in this chapter from various websites where participants reported about their local protests in the days following the protests.

2. Anime is the Japanese term for "animation." Generally, in English it is used to refer to the subset of animation that originates in Japan. Manga is Japanese term for cartoons or print form animation.

3. The use of offensive language in Anonymous communities is a complicated topic and not one that should be treated in simplistic terms. Experts in Anonymous such as Norton (2011a) and Auerbach (2012) have stated that the use of such offensive language does not necessarily mean that the speakers are racist, homophobic, or sexist. Norton (2011a) argues that the intention of offensive language, such as the widespread use of the words "fag" and "nigger," is to keep non-community members out, rather than indicating actual hatred. Similarly, Auerbach (2012) argues that the offensive language is meant to "drive away anyone who is not sympathetic to the general libertarian mindset." These arguments are in line with my findings—that the use of offensive language and imagery serves to create community boundaries. However, it is important to note that even in the cases where these words are not used as instruments of hatred, studies have found that they have that impact. For instance, Gray (2012) examines the process by which African American Xbox Live players are treated as deviant and subject to racist speech while playing. Gray argues that this leads to the normalization of racist speech and discriminatory events and that African American players come to view this treatment as a normal part of playing. Gray also finds that those using words such as "nigger" often justified it by saying that they used the word no matter the skin color of the target, that the word no longer had the same meaning that it previously did, and that they use the same word around African American friends. Gray's findings are consistent with my 2011a findings in a study of female World of Warcraft players. In that study, I found that women develop different types of coping strategies in the face of being treated as "the other" in the game.

Thus, even when the speaker using derogatory terms does so without negative intent, such language can isolate and ostracize. In spite of the openness of online communities such as Anonymous, the foundational idea that nothing is sacred can lead to language and image use that marginalizes. Reagle (2012) finds, paradoxically, that in communities associated with the free culture movement some participants (particularly women) can be informally alienated, in spite of foundational values such as freedom and openness. His argument is in line with Herring's findings (1996) that men and women articulated different ethics for online discourse and that the male ethic was the dominant one online. I do not tackle these issues here, although simply reading some of the quotations in this book may raise serious questions about misogynistic, homophobic, and racist language. The unintended normalization of hate speech and the impact of such language (and imagery) on different groups is an important aspect of the culture of many online communities and warrants its own volume.

4. Doxing someone means that an individual's personal information is found and posted online. This can include legal names, address, phone number, and other information. Doxing is frequently followed by the type of "real life" harassment in this example. The idea of "doxing" has particular power in online spaces where anonymity is valued.

5. Leet = elite; V& = "vanned" as in "partyvanned," which means arrested by the FBI.

6. Chofagwannabes = people who want to be Cho, the man who killed 31 people at Virginia Tech in 2007.

7. Another famous example of an early large-scale Anonymous-organized activity was the Habbo Hotel incident, which was discussed in Knappenberger's 2012 documentary, *We Are Legion*.

8. This is the same news story I mentioned in chapter 1. Please note that the bomb threat campaign referred to in this show is a story that has long since been discredited.

9. There is also a celebratory webpage of the success showing downed Scientology websites that as of August 2013 could still be accessed here: http://epicscientologywar.ytmnd.com/.

10. There were many systems with /i/ boards or related content, such as 789chan.org, 808chan.org, insurgen.info, rockstararmy.com (rockstarchan). In this chapter I only mention systems that no longer exist online—with the exception of WhyWeProtest.net and 4chan.org.

11. By 2008, organizing raids was no longer allowed on 4chan.org.

12. Because of the repeated claim that some Anonymous spaces host child pornography, I would like to make sure this information is clearly understood. The board was a /loli/ board. "Loli" is short for "lolicon"—a type of Japanese manga or anime that depicts underage individuals in sexual situations. While

the term "loli" is sometimes also used to describe pornography depicting real children, it technically refers to this subtype of sexually explicit Japanese manga or anime (hentai). Anonymous systems that allow loli will usually explicitly state that child pornography involving real children is forbidden. For the purposes of this chapter, rather than entering into this debate about whether lolicon should be differentiated from child pornography, what I want to note is that this "new" organizing space was not necessarily a media- or novice-friendly space.

13. Mirrors of this site still exist online.

14. The video stated: "Rule #0: Rules #1 and #2 of the internet still apply. Your memes are not, at this juncture, something that the real world can appreciate. Although meme speak between fellow Anonymous is acceptable, focus on the target and keep it to a minimum." Rule 0 is, "don't fuck with cats, or we'll find you." Rules 1 and 2 are, "do not talk about /b/" and "do NOT talk about /b/." There is some debate over whether rules 1 and 2 apply outside of raids, but for many Anonymous the "real life" protests would have been considered part of a raid.

15. Enturbulation.org no longer exists, but this site eventually became Why We Protest. This site has gone through much iteration since 2008 but could be found at https://whyweprotest.net/ as of August 2013.

16. This rule stated: "Absolutely no discussion of anything illegal. Enturbulation. org is here to foster discussion and encourage learning about scientology, and to organize peaceful and legal protests. Do not tarnish this idea and intention, as well as invite legal action against this site, with any sort of discussion about illegal acts."

17. This rule stated: "Keep racist and offensive language to a minimum. Regardless of the other internet forums you may have came from, Enturbulation.org is meant for the general public, it's important to keep it welcoming and friendly."

18. In these rules, "CP" refers to Child Pornography. "When I was" refers to a type of thread that begins with that phrase. "When I was" was considered a "forced meme"—or a meme that did not emerge naturally from the community but was a studied attempt to produce a meme. In these rules the reference stands in for any posts that violate the community posting norms, particularly when combined with "no faggotry."

19. See, for example, Beyer, 2014; Coleman's 2011 and 2012c analyses; Norton's coverage of Anonymous for *Wired*, 2011a, 2011b, 2012a, 2012b; Chen's coverage of Anonymous for Gawker.com, e.g., 2012; Olson's 2012 book about LulzSec and Anonymous; and Knappenberger's 2012 documentary, *We Are Legion*.

20. While members of the community maintain extensive archiving and encyclopedic resources for the board systems such as the 4chan Archive and Encyclopedia Dramatica, these do not necessarily capture the entirety of the

interaction on the board or the complete history. Some, such as Encyclopedia Dramatica, can be inaccurate. Also, these sites are external to the board systems themselves—meaning users have to find them.

21. For example, Whitney Phillips (2012a) discusses one such rule change in a blog post.

22. ZOMG = Oh My God with a "Z" in the front of it. It is pronounced, "Zoh My God."

23. A "shock image" is an image that is intended to garner an immediate visceral reaction from viewers. Famous shock images depict the human body in sexually related but shocking ways, dead bodies, or photographs of extreme cases of sexually transmitted infections. Some shock images have been so widely circulated online that their names have become inside jokes.

24. Coleman (2012a) and Olson (2012) have noted that as Anonymous became a more practiced political actor, different wings of Anonymous appeared and that the IRC, in particular, facilitated these personal and small-group relationships. These small vanguards groups appear to primarily use the IRC as a way to communicate, but do so within the framework of the Anonymous culture that rose from 4chan.org.

Chapter 3

1. A 2008 Pirate Bay blog post stated: "TPB is not just a website. TPB is not just a file sharing network. TPB is not just a movement. TPB is also art. TPB is a performance. It's a long running art project. Very long. TPB was initiated by Piratbyrån—The Bureau for Piracy. Read the activity report for year 2007 to understand more about their work. TPB and PB are the best of friends. That's why we're making more art together—but now we need your help!"

2. Piratbyrån is no longer in existence. On its former website is a sign that states in Swedish, "Closed for Reflection." In an interview for *Torrent Freak*, Peter Sunde reported the decision was due to the death of Ibi Kopimi Botani, a founding member (Ernesto, 2010b). Many of the members have continued to work on other projects related to intellectual property and copyright.

3. This claim was first made by Sveriges Television. Other evidence often cited is letters from the MPAA and other organizations to Swedish officials. There is additional evidence of US preoccupation with this issue and communication with the Swedish government in a leaked cable from the US embassy in Stockholm. See Stockholm 09-141, written March 2, 2009, and released August 30, 2011, on WikiLeaks. Diplomatic cables Stockholm 09-276 and Stockholm 09-546 also discuss The Pirate Bay.

4. Amelia Andersdotter received her seat following the ratification of the Treaty of Lisbon changing the number of representatives sent to the Parliament from some European Union members.

5. Argentina, Australia, Austria, Belgium, Bolivia, Bosnia and Herzegovina, Brazil, Bulgaria, Canada, Chile, China, Colombia, Costa Rica, Cyprus, Czech Republic, Denmark, Ecuador, El Salvador, Estonia, Finland, France, Germany, Greece, Guatemala, Ireland, Israel, Italy, Kazakhstan, Latvia, Lithuania, Luxembourg, Mexico, Morocco, Nepal, Netherlands, New Zealand, Norway, Panama, Peru, Philippines, Poland, Portugal, Republic of Korea, Romania, Russia, Serbia, Slovakia, Slovenia, South Africa, Spain, Sweden, Switzerland, Taiwan, Tunisia, Turkey, Ukraine, United Kingdom, United States, Uruguay, and Venezuela either have or are starting Pirate Parties.

6. As of September 2012, a list of German Pirate Party seats could be found here: http://wiki.piratenpartei.de/Mandate.

7. Use figures are on the front page of The Pirate Bay, constantly update, and are time stamped.

8. Registered users have no profile page—but they can gain "trusted" (pink/purple skull), VIP (green skull), Helper (blue skull), or moderator/super-moderator/admin status (moderator icon), indicated by small colored skulls next to their name. According to the site, trusted means, "We have checked some uploads from him/her and they are ok." VIP means, "Long time hangarounduploader with good uploads." Helper means, "Can edit torrents, move them and check torrents as ok. Also able to report torrents to mods." All the moderator ranks have various levels of power, but they are, "The assholes that fight spam/fakes/Trojans." To gain a rank, users must be recommended by Helpers to a moderator.

9. There are some external sites that try to help regulate torrents—such as Torrent Spam, where users can paste the name of a torrent to see if it is fake or dangerous or flag torrents that are fake/dangerous.

10. A "Trojan" or a "Trojan Horse" is malicious software that looks like software that is already present on a computer or software that will fulfill a useful function. However, Trojans allow access to a computer by nefarious outsiders and can cause other kinds of damage.

11. Please note I differentiate The Pirate Bay from other sites in two ways. First, while site administrators/owners such as Napster's owner asserted he was not breaking the law and fought a legal battle in line with his claim of innocence, he did not aggressively seek out opportunities to hassle and clash with the recording industry as The Pirate Bay has over time. Second, Isohunt's Gary Fung could be seen as similar to The Pirate Bay in that he seemingly moved to Canada with the intention of escaping the United States' more restrictive legal findings on file-sharing. However, Fung also did not aggressively seek conflict with the recording industry in spite of his willingness to fight it in Canadian courts. For example, he agreed to block US traffic to his site.

12. For example, see the case in the Netherlands of antipiracy group BREIN versus Svartholm/Neij/Sunde. The controversy was outlined on Sunde's blog at the time.

13. The Jesper Bay is no longer online.

14. This number was cited on the Open Internet Homepage. The page no longer exists.

15. The Pirate Bay merchandise site is linked off of the main Pirate Bay website.

16. This service is no longer online and the URL appears to have been bought by another entity.

17. The Baywords homepage is still linked off of the main Pirate Bay website. However, as of August 20, 2011, the website no longer displayed.

18. As of August 2012, the BayImg homepage was located at http://bayimg.com/.

19. As of August 2012, the Paste Bay homepage was located at http://pastebay.com/.

20. As of August 2012, the IPREDator homepage was located at https://www.ipredator.se/.

21. A sea fort is a platform on pontoons and stilts in the middle of the ocean. Please note that although Prince Roy of Sealand has claimed it to be sovereign, the United States and Germany have both publicly stated that it is not a recognized sovereign state.

22. What became of the money is unclear. *Torrent Freak* reported that the men had used the money to buy trees that were planted in Cambodia, but I was unable to verify this claim.

23. I have tried to verify this number. It is repeated across interviews and reprinted in many news sources, but no one has any link to the original number (Ekman, 2006).

Chapter 4

1. For the purposes of this study, the following well-known WoW events are not considered the same type of political phenomena as the Anonymous and The Pirate Bay mobilizations due to their small size and preoccupation with in-game issues. First, in 2005 people who were playing the warrior class converged on a realm to protest changes to warrior abilities and caused the realm to crash. Second, there was a protest by a handful of Zul'jin players at the World of Warcraft booth at Gencon 2006. Third, there were also rumors in 2008 that warlocks were protesting in-game by using a special warlock spell to bring dangerous creatures into a city—but this was never confirmed to be widespread or formalized. Fourth, there have also been other small-scale "protests" conducted by small numbers of players such as shamans who protested shaman changes by making a trail of player bodies between two cities. Fifth, in 2009, some of the mainstream news media reported that PETA was planning an in-game protest to bring attention to the killing of baby seals in the real world. PETA later said that no actual protest was planned; rather it was just a creative way to bring attention to the issue. Finally, in 2010, when

Blizzard Entertainment announced that it was going to begin attaching legal names to posts on the public game forums (Real ID names) there was widespread anger at the change, which ultimately led to Blizzard deciding not to change its policy. However, this anger only manifested itself as text-based complaints on forums and blogs. Finally, there are some rumors online that Chinese players have used the game to protest the government's slowness in approving the release of a World of Warcraft expansion; however, the Chinese realms are outside of this study and I was unable to confirm these accounts.

2. See, for example, the 2010 *Journal of Virtual Worlds Research* special issue "Virtual Economies, Virtual Goods and Service Delivery in Virtual Worlds" edited by Salomon and Soudoplatoff outlines many of the debates.

3. There has been research examining the range of options available upon character creation and the relationship between "evil" characters, beauty aesthetics, and race such as Cornelliussen and Walker Rettberg (2011). There have also been comical looks at the same issue. See, for example *Dark Legacy Comic's* "World of Whitecraft," which as of November 2013 could be found here: http://darklegacycomics.com/190.html.

4. Alliance races are Human, Gnome, Dwarf, Draenai, and Night Elf. Horde races are Troll, Undead, Orc, Blood Elf, and Tauren. Since conducting my research, three new races have been added—Worgen, Goblins, and Pandaren.

5. When I conducted my research and wrote this chapter, Blizzard still used Battlegroups to structure play. Since then, Blizzard has removed all Battlegroups.

6. Please note that the game was not always divided this way. As the game has become bigger and more tools for interaction, such as the random dungeon finder, have appeared, Blizzard has created more complex systems of organization. As these systems increase, the interaction between realms has increased but player accountability to distinct communities has decreased.

7. Studies find that women now are around 30 percent of all gamers online, although numbers of WoW specifically have not been studied.

8. Please note, until the launch of Mists of Pandaren in 2012, 40-man raids were a thing of the past except in PvP.

9. In their most recent work, Yee and Ducheneaut use the number of characters a person has as a proxy for in-game focus. In past work, Yee found that there is a positive relationship between age and type of content players prefer, with younger players focusing on the more high-reward/high-prestige end-game content and older players preferring to play alone (Yee, 2009). There is also an interesting gender dimension to in-game motivations, with women overwhelmingly stating that their primary motivation is relationships (Yee, 2005a).

10. Interestingly, after age 30, even though the number of player interested in character power and access to end-game content is far smaller than for younger players—women are more interested in these two aspects of the game than men.

11. It is also worth noting that playing MMORPGs still carries some level of social stigma, which is likely to further divide players from discussing the game with offline communities.

12. My sister calls talking about WoW "speaking in nerdish." Blizzard (2010) has provided a glossary, although it is not complete.

13. There are also two other channels—a defense channel and a guild recruitment channel—that are not used by many players.

14. See Mark Chen's *Leet Noobs* (2011) on the changes in raiding in WoW overtime for an excellent in-depth look at raiding.

15. I mean neo-patrimonial to describe a relationship in which group-gained resources are distributed by a single leader (or small group of elite) in reward for loyalty in a way that supplants all other administration, bureaucracies, or structures. The relationship removes the distinction between group-earned public resources and the private resources of the leadership. In such cases, the rule systems in the guild are often arbitrary, constantly changing, or nonexistent. Because of the game architecture, nearly all guilds have some neo-patrimonial characteristics, even when they have extensive rule systems. Eisenstadt (1973) was the first to adapt Weber's idea of "patrimonialism" in this way.

16. Gear is a catch-all term that encompasses the armor a player wears, the weapons the player carries, and other items such as rings. Gear comes in varying quality depending on the difficulty of the task required to receive the gear.

17. Please note that this is not straightforward. Because there are thousands of individuals on every realm, and people can opt in and out of public channels, it is very rare that an individual can be completely ostracized. However, it is possible for an individual to be blocked from lucrative group activities with the more active and highly accomplished groups/guilds/players. As Blizzard has changed the structure of the game in ways that have weakened realm communities, this type of community regulation has diminished.

18. As of 2011, Blizzard had incorporated gear scores into the game interface.

19. This quote is from late in the Wrath of the Lich King expansion. "277s" refers to the gear score of items that come out of beating the current hardest content in the game. Thus, he is basically saying that the original poster is jealous of the guild's accomplishment, and is posting on an alt to hide that he has not accomplished as much.

20. During the Cataclysm expansion, many of these sites fell into disuse with other sites becoming prominent. There does seem to be an overall decrease of this

type of website overtime as related to WoW, which may be an indication of the declining popularity of the game or an indication of Blizzard incorporating many of the services into the game that were formerly provided by third parties.

21. For example, see the Christian Gamers Alliance Forums. The forums were available as of August 2013 at http://www.cgalliance.org/forums/.

22. While Battlegroups no longer exist, the same type of conflict can arise between people from different realms.

23. The problem was also compounded by players who would identify the other players' realms in the group—and knowing that they were all from realms that used a greed-based system, would wait for everyone else to roll greed and then would need—thereby ensuring that they received the item.

Chapter 5

1. Claridge, known as ZeroSleep on the boards, gave this interview to Big Boards between 2003 and 2005. Unfortunately, the website did not mark the interview with a clear date.

2. The format differs in appearance and user interface from an imageboard system, but has a very similar basic purpose.

3. The riot initially was based around a specific user's icon and changed to focus on steak. However, due to the script using the "STEAK!!" motif, it has become known as the "STEAK!! Riots."

4. This thread was "stickied" to the top of the list of threads, meaning an administrator or moderator "stuck" it there so it would be at the top of the list of threads no matter when the last post in the thread occurred.

5. This thread was about their small number of representatives in the House that turned into a conversation about rural versus urban life.

6. This thread would be a good example of a thread that appears to be about politics from the title, but was not about politics.

7. The broken mark-up is included in the thread title as a joking reference.

8. ITT is an abbreviation for "In This Thread."

9. The rule states: "Impersonating Other Users/Accessing Another User's Account. You may not impersonate another board member or create an account specifically for the purpose of provoking other users. Also, accessing or using someone else's account or attempting to access another poster's account is strictly prohibited. If you engage in this type of behavior, you will be barred from the boards permanently" (IGN.com Rules, 2011).

10. When I first began studying IGN.com only the people who paid a subscription fee could have an icon. The rule has since changed. People with subscriptions are called "insiders" on the board.

11. For example, in 2011 the externally hosted Vesti Wiki had a section entitled "Controversial Users." However, the list was woefully incomplete.

12. When I started my research, only subscribers could see all posts on all boards. However, the Vesti has always been publicly viewable by anyone.

13. A series of norms/rules about selling stuff on the classified boards is not included in this list although it is included in the list of board rules.

14. This rule states: "Yes, lesbians are very titillating (ha ha) but this is still a PG-13 board. Some lesbian pics that have been posted go too far. Just because you can't see anything doesn't mean that it's not too sexual. Sex toys in pics are a no no. Lots of groping is not allowed as are pics that simulate oral sex or nipple sucking."

15. Interestingly, this rule includes use of the word "gay" in a derogatory manner, although this part of the rule has not historically been universally enforced.

16. The Vesti Wiki's list of famous riots is fairly complete. As of August 2013 the list could be accessed here: http://vestiwiki.yabd.org/wiki/index. php?title=Category:Riots.

17. There was a time when some banned users would simply move to a board system that was owned by IGN but that did not have any community—the board system had been bought out by IGN and had died. However, after this option became too popular, IGN shut down the board system entirely.

18. Please note that when I began my research this was slightly different. First, while all boards could be viewed by nonsubscribers, only subscribers could read the threads. The Vesti was readable by nonsubscribers as were all video game topic boards. Second, only subscribers could send private messages. While nonsubscribers could receive them, they could not read them without a subscription.

19. This group of people also left the IGN board system as a group for another online location and in doing so "killed" the board they posted on regularly. After they left, no one posted on that board anymore. They carefully did not mention where they relocated in public so undesirable community members could not "follow" them.

Chapter 6

1. WhyWeProtest.net is the home of an online activist group born from the Anonymous versus Church of Scientology campaigns. This quote is no longer available on their website, but was accessed August 12, 2011.

2. He has stated this in other interviews as well (for example, Fiveash, 2010a).

3. The Well can be found at http://www.well.com/.

4. See, for example, Freelon et al., 2011.

5. Portions of this section are also found in Beyer, 2014.

6. The site has now become a citizen journalist website: http://crowdleaks.org/.

7. This video had been viewed 51,383 times as of March 1, 2011.

8. As of August 2011, Why We Protest could be found here: http:// WhyWeProtest.net.

9. As of August 2011, the Crowd Leaks website could be found here: http://crowdleaks.org/.

10. The full decision can be read (in German) at http://www.libertad.de/service/downloads/pdf/olg220506.pdf as of September 15, 2012.

11. These numbers come from a *Der Speigel* interview with Hendrik Fulda (2011), who is on the board of the foundation that is one of WikiLeak's main funding channels.

12. The entire proposal is housed on the IMMI website https://immi.is/ as of August 2012.

13. As of August 2011, the full subpoena could be found here: http://www.salon.com/news/opinion/glenn_greenwald/2011/01/07/twitter/subpoena.pdf.

14. It is important to mention that the initial request for information placed a gag order on Twitter that would have kept Twitter from notifying the users. Twitter successfully challenged this order in court (Singel, 2011).

Appendix

1. Habermas' (1989) argument about discursive communities roughly fits the patterns of interaction on posting boards. Habermas looks to the inherent "politicalness" of discursive communities, because they are the sites where meanings are articulated and negotiated, thereby creating a collective body. This connection has been explored by many scholars, e.g., Papacharissi, 2010, p. 39; Dahlberg, 2001; or Froomkin, 2003.

2. The Pirate Bay's use figures are on the front page of The Pirate Bay, constantly update, and are time stamped.

3. This data was gathered May 2010 using Warcraft Realms.

4. This number was generated using Big Boards, which no longer exists, but had a daily updated list of message board forum usage.

5. I include this in my operationalization of "anonymity" because in the simplest sense, an IP address gives an individual an identity. Therefore, in places that track IP addresses, individuals are known to site management. However, I should also note that this feature of online spaces has some implications for regulation. When a user's IP address is tracked, the IP address can then be used to punish (e.g., IP banning).

6. I do not discuss punishment as part of regulation or anonymity in this chapter because of the diversity of punishment forms across cases. However, I do discuss it in the Chapters 2–5 in relation to regulation.

7. Although I include this question in the operationalization of "anonymity," it measures different factors in relation to regulation. In relation to anonymity, the archives allow other users to access an individual's contributions to the community weeks after submission. The accessibility facilitates the process by which an individual is known—as any present behavior can be

immediately contextualized with past behaviors and statements. In relation to regulation, archives allow regulatory actors to look for rule violations after they have occurred in order to punish the user for past behavior. An example of such regulation involves a moderator on IGN.com who would search the boards for the word "fuck." If she found that a user had posted the word, she would ban him, even if he had posted it weeks prior to her search. In contrast, an example of archive searches related to anonymity would be IGN.com user who searches another user's posts to see if she is the type of person who uses naughty language. The knowledge gained about the user's language choices would then become part of an understanding of the individual's character, which has an indeterminate effect on regulation.

8. Ess (2002) asks the question of whether there is convergence in online research ethical standards and finds there is some convergence but a lot of heated debate.

9. This definition of the online world has been extensively debated on the Association of Internet Researchers listserv; and is also discussed in the following publications (among others), Bassett and O'Riordan (2002), Ess (2002), and the Association of Internet Researchers Ethics Working Committee Report (2002).

10. The distinction between the two approaches is often seen as a difference in social science and humanities approaches to Internet research. See, for example: Association of Internet Researchers Ethics Working Committee Report (2002); Waskul (1996); and Elgesem (2002).

11. For a widely cited discussion of how researcher legitimacy comes from being a community member, see Hine (2005). Also, Orgad (2005), Sanders (2005), and Rutter and Smith (2005).

12. This is widely argued. See, for example: Allen (1996), Ess, C. and the AoIR Working Committee Report (2002), Kraut et al. (2004).

13. My rubric includes, and was inspired by, Kraut et al. (2004).

14. Again, there is a large body of literature on this issue. See, for example: Pace & Livingston (2005) and Thomas (1996).

Bibliography

Ahrens, F. 2006. U.S. Joins Industry in Piracy War. *Washington Post*. June 15, http://www.washingtonpost.com/wp-dyn/content/article/2006/06/14/AR2006061402071_pf.html (accessed August 17, 2011).

Allen, C. 1996. What's Wrong with the "Golden Rule"? Conundrums of Conducting Ethical Research in Cyberspace. *Information Society 12*(2), 175–87.

Allen, K. 2009. Pirate Party Fires Broadside at German Political Establishment. *The Local*. September 28, http://www.thelocal.de/politics/20090928-22209.html (accessed January 15, 2010).

Allen, S. 2013. Boob Sliders, or How Role-Playing Games Helped Me Transition. *The Border House*. January 15, http://borderhouseblog.com/?p=10009 (accessed November 10, 2013).

anakata. 2004. Response to Dreamworks. *Legal Responses: The Pirate Bay*. August 23, http://static.thepiratebay.org/dreamworks_response.txt (accessed August 25, 2011).

Anderson, N. 2006. US Government Helped Sink The Pirate Bay; Goes After Other Sites. *Ars Technica*. June 16, http://arstechnica.com/old/content/2006/06/7072.ars (accessed August 18, 2011).

Andrews, S. 2010a. It's a Secret. *Wow Insider: Officers Quarters*. August 2, http://www.wow.com/2010/08/02/officers-quarters-its-a-secret/ (accessed July 15, 2011).

Andrews, S. 2010b. *Strategies and Guidance from a Battle-Scarred MMO Veteran*. No Starch Press.

anonopleakspin. 2010. Operation: LeakSpin—A Message from Anonymous. *YouTube.com*. December 12, http://youtu.be/fLcUVNee_UI (accessed August 25, 2011).

AnonymousHateMachine. 2007. Re: Anonymous on FOX11. *YouTube.com*. July 29, http://youtu.be/uZ1qi9gz7UU (accessed July 17, 2011).

Aronoff, M. 2009. Foreword. In Schatz, E. (Ed.), *Political Ethnography: What Immersion Contributes to the Study of Power*. Chicago: University of Chicago Press, ix–xii.

Auerbach, D. 2012. Anonymity as Culture: Treatise. *Triple Canopy*. February 9, http://canopycanopycanopy.com/15/anonymity_as_culture__treatise (accessed August 12, 2013).

Bakioglu, B. 2009. Spectacular Interventions of Second Life: Goon Culture, Griefing, and Disruption in Virtual Spaces. *Journal of Virtual Worlds Research* 1(3), http://journals.tdl.org/jvwr/index.php/jvwr/article/view/348/421.

Bakioglu, B. 2011. Governance in Virtual Worlds: Grief Play, Hacktivism, & Leakops in Second Life. February 1, http://ssrn.com/abstract=2179886.

Bassett, E. & O'Riordan, K. 2002. Ethics of Internet Research: Contesting the Human Subjects Research Model. *Ethics and Information Technology* 4(3), 233–47.

Baym, N. 1999. *Tune In, Log On: Soaps, Fandom, and Online Community*. New York: Sage.

Baym, N. 2002. Interpersonal Life Online. In Lievrouw, L. & Livingstone, S. (Eds.), *Handbook of New Media: Student Edition*. London: Sage, 35–54.

Baym, N. 2007. The New Shape of Online Community: The Example of Swedish Independent Music Fandom. *First Monday* 12(8), http://firstmonday.org/htbin/cgiwrap/bin/ojs/index.php/fm/article/view/1978/185.

Becker, H. 1998. *Tricks of the Trade: How to Think About Your Research While You're Doing It*. Chicago: University of Chicago Press.

Bell, M. 2010. Online Role-Play: Anonymity, Engagement, and Risk. *Educational Media International* 38(4), 251–60.

Belmonte, E. 2011. Manoli, la primera concejal pirata. *El Mundo*. May 23, http://www.elmundo.es/elmundo/2011/05/23/barcelona/1306103816.html (accessed July 10, 2013).

Bennett, W. L. (Ed.) 2008. *Civic Life Online: Learning How Digital Media Can Engage Youth*. Cambridge: MIT Press.

Bergstrom, K. 2011. Don't Feed the Troll: Shutting Down Debate about Community Expectations on Reddit.com. *First Monday* 16(8), http://firstmonday.org/ojs/index.php/fm/article/view/3498/3029.

Bernstein, M., Monroy-Hernández, A., Harry, D., André, P., Panovich, K., & Vargas, G. 2011. 4chan and /b/: An Analysis of Anonymity and Ephemerality in a Large Online Community. *Association for the Advancement of Artificial Intelligence*, http://www.icwsm.org/2011/papers.php.

Beschizza, R. 2010. More Than 1000 WikiLeaks Mirror sites Spring Up in a Week. *Boing Boing*. December 8, http://www.boingboing.net/2010/12/08/more-than-1000-wikil.html (accessed July 17, 2011).

Beyer, J. 2011a. Women's Engagement with Male-Dominated Online Communities. In Gajjala, R. & Ju Oh, Y. (Eds.), *Cyberfeminism 2.0*. New York: Peter Lang, 153–170.

Beyer, J. 2011b. Youth and the Generation of Political Consciousness Online. Doctoral dissertation, University of Washington, Seattle.

Beyer, J. 2014. The Emergence of a Freedom of Information Movement? Anonymous, WikiLeaks, the Pirate Party, and Iceland. *Journal of Computer Mediated Communication* 19(2), 141–154.

Beyer, J. & Hussin, I. 2012. Making Authority Online: Muslim Fatwa Sites after the Arab Spring. American Political Science Association Annual Conference, New Orleans.

Big Boards. Interview: Brian Claridge, IGN-VNBoards Programmer and Administrator. http://www.big-boards.com/int.php?n=327 (accessed August 25, 2011).

Blizzard Entertainment. European Battlegroups. http://eu.worldofwarcraft.com/pvp/battlegrounds/battlegroups/ (accessed May 15, 2010).

Blizzard Entertainment. Glossary. http://www.worldofwarcraft.com/info/basics/glossary.html (accessed May 15, 2010).

Blizzard Entertainment. North American and Oceanic Battlegroups. http://www.worldofwarcraft.com/pvp/battlegrounds/battlegroups/ (accessed May 15, 2010).

Blizzard Entertainment. 2008. Press Release: World of Warcraft Subscriber Base Reaches 11.5 Million Worldwide. November 21, http://us.blizzard.com/en-us/company/press/pressreleases.html?081121 (accessed August 15, 2011).

Blizzard Entertainment. Realms FAQ. http://www.worldofwarcraft.com/info/faq/realms.html (accessed May 15, 2010).

Blizzard Entertainment. Tips on Being Nice! http://www.worldofwarcraft.com/info/basics/benice.html (accessed May 15, 2010).

Blizzard Entertainment. World of Warcraft, In Game Policies. http://us.blizzard.com/support/article.xml?locale=en_US&articleId=20309 (accessed August 15, 2011).

Boellstorff, T., Nardi, B., Pearce, C., & Taylor, T. L. 2012. *Ethnography and Virtual Worlds: A Handbook of Method.* Princeton, NJ: Princeton University Press.

Brady, H. & Collier, D. (Eds.) 2004. *Rethinking Social Inquiry: Diverse Tools, Shared Standards.* Oxford: Rowman & Littlefield.

Carey, R. F. & Burkell, J. A. 2007. Revisiting the Four Horsemen of the Infopocalypse: Representations of Anonymity and the Internet in Canadian Newspapers. *First Monday 12*(8), http://firstmonday.org/issues/issue12_8/carey/index.html.

Chen, A. 2011. Why Facebook Should Do More to Help Egypt's Protesters. *Gawker.com.* February 5, http://gawker.com/5752904/why-facebook-should-do-more-to-help-egypts-protesters (accessed August 15, 2011).

Chen, A. 2012. 4chan's Moment Is Over Even Though It's More Popular Than Ever. *Gawker.com.* July 12, http://gawker.com/5925535/4chans-moment-is-over-even-though-its-more-popular-than-ever (accessed September 15, 2012).

Chen, A. 2013. Dark Net Busted Wide Open after Child Porn Arrest. *Gawker.com.* August 5, http://gawker.com/dark-net-busted-wide-open-after-child-porn-arrest-1030239391 (accessed August 12, 2013).

Chen, M. 2011. *Leet Noobs: The Life and Death of an Expert Player Group in World of Warcraft.* Bern: Peter Lang.

Cheng, J. 2011. Anonymous to Security Firm Working with FBI: 'You've Angered the Hive.' *Ars Technica.* February 7, http://arstechnica.com/tech-policy/2011/02/

anonymous-to-security-firm-working-with-fbi-youve-angered-the-hive/ (accessed August 2012).

Chesney, T., Coyne, I., Logan, B., & Madden, N. 2009. Griefing in Virtual Worlds: Causes, Casualties, and Coping Strategies. *Information Systems Journals 19*(6), 525–48.

Chu, H. 2011. Iceland seeks to become sanctuary for free speech. *Los Angeles Times.* April 2, http://articles.latimes.com/2011/apr/02/world/la-fg-iceland-free-speech-20110403 (accessed August 12, 2011).

Church of Scientology. 2008a. Call to Action. *YouTube.com.* January 27, http://youtube.com/watch?v=YrkchXCzY70 (accessed August 15, 2011).

Church of Scientology. 2008b. Code of Conduct. *YouTube.com.* February 1, http://youtu.be/-063clxiB8I (accessed August 15, 2011).

Church of Scientology. 2008c. Message to Scientology. *YouTube.com.* January 21, http://youtu.be/JCbKv9yiLiQ (accessed August 15, 2011).

Church of Scientology. 2008d. Reclamation: Phase Three. *YouTube.com.* August 1, http://youtu.be/VPoIGXJJmnM (accessed August 15, 2011).

Ciderhelm. 2010. Tankspot Guide to Icecrown Sindragosa. *Tankspot.com.* February 3, http://www.tankspot.com/article.php?id=369243&title= Icecrown_Sindragosa (accessed August 25, 2011).

Cohen, N. 2010. Web Attackers Find a Cause in WikiLeaks. *The New York Times.* December 9, http://www.nytimes.com/2010/12/10/world/10wiki.html (accessed July 17, 2011).

Coleman, G. 2011. Anonymous: From the Lulz to Collective Action. *The new everyday.* April 6, http://mediacommons.futureofthebook.org/tne/pieces/ anonymous-lulz-collective-action (accessed September 15, 2012).

Coleman, G. 2012a. Beacons of Freedom: The Changing Face of Anonymous. *Index on Censorship.* http://www.indexoncensorship.org/2012/12/beacons-freedom-hacking-anonymous/ (accessed August 30, 2013).

Coleman, G. 2012b. *Coding Freedom.* Princeton, NJ: Princeton University Press.

Coleman, G. 2012c. Our Weirdness Is Free, The Logic of Anonymous—Online Army, Agent of Chaos, and Seeker of Justice. *Triple Canopy.* January, http:// canopycanopycanopy.com/15/our_weirdness_is_free (accessed September 15, 2012).

Coleman, G. 2012d. Phreaks, Hackers, and Trolls and the Politics of Transgression and Spectacle. In Michael Mandiberg (Ed.), *The Social Media Reader.* New York: New York University Press, 99–19.

Collier, D. 1993. The Comparative Method. In Finifter, A. (Ed.), *Political Science: The State of the Discipline II.* Washington, DC: American Political Science Association, 105–119.

Collier, D., Mahoney, J., & Seawright, J. 2004. Claiming Too Much: Warnings about Selection Bias. In Brady, H. & Collier, D. (Eds.), *Rethinking Social Inquiry: Diverse Tools, Shared Standards.* Oxford: Rowman & Littlefield, 85–102.

Collier, R. & Collier, D. 1991. *Shaping the Political Arena: Critical Junctures, the Labor Movement, and Regime Dynamics in Latin America.* Princeton, NJ: Princeton University Press.

Corneliussen, H. & Walker Rettberg, J. (Eds.) 2008. *Digital Culture, Play, and Identity: A World of Warcraft Reader.* Cambridge: MIT Press.

Cosgrove-Mather, B. 2003. Poll: Young Say File Sharing OK. *CBS News.* September 18, http://www.cbsnews.com/stories/2003/09/18/opinion/polls/main573990.shtml (accessed August 15, 2011).

Cover, R. 1983. Foreword: Nomos and Narrative. *Harvard Law Review* 97, 4–68.

Dahlberg, L. 2001. The Internet and Democratic Discourse: Exploring the Prospects of Online Deliberative Forums Extending the Public Sphere. *Information, Communication, & Society* 4(4), 615–33.

Dányi, E. 2006. Xerox Project: Photocopy Machines as a Metaphor for an "Open Society." *Information Society* 22(2), 111–15.

Dash, A. 2011. If Your Website's Full of Assholes, It's Your Fault. Blog. July 20, http://dashes.com/anil/2011/07/if-your-websites-full-of-assholes-its-your-fault.html.

Dearfoxnews. 2007. Dear Fox News. *YouTube.com.* July 29, http://youtu.be/RFjU8bZR19A (accessed July 17, 2011).

Delgado, R. 2004. Law Professors Examine Ethical Controversies of Peer-to-Peer File Sharing. *Stanford Report.* March 17, http://news-service.stanford.edu/news/2004/march17/fileshare-317.html (accessed January 10, 2010).

Depoorter, B. & Vanneste, S. 2005. Norms and Enforcement: The Case against Copyright Litigation. *Oregon Law Review* 84(4): 1127–80.

De Voegt, K. 2013. PP Croatia Reaches 21% in City District, Winning Two out of Nine Board Seats. *Pirate Times.* May 22, http://piratetimes.net/croatia-election-success/ (accessed July 10, 2013).

Dibbell, J. 1993. A Rape in Cyberspace. *Village Voice.* December 23, http://www.juliandibbell.com/texts/bungle_vv.html.

Dickey, M. 2009. Game Design and Learning: A Conjectural Analysis of How Massively Multiple Online Role-Playing Games (MMORPGs) Foster Intrinsic Motivation. *Educational Technology Research and Development* 55(3), 253–73.

DiMarco, H. 2003. The Electronic Cloak: Secret Sexual Deviance in Cybersociety. In Jewkes, Y. (Ed.), *Dot.cons: Crime, Deviance, and Identity on the Internet.* Cullompton: Willan, 53–67.

disposableacc. 2008. Reglas para el 10 de Febrero. *YouTube.com.* February 3, http://youtu.be/_YKAKhRQ5xk (accessed August 15, 2011).

Donath, J. 1998. Identity and Deception in the Virtual Community. In Kollock, P. & Smith, M. (Eds.), *Communities in Cyberspace.* London: Routledge, 29–59.

Ducheneaut, N., Yee, N., Nickell, E., & Moore, R. 2007. The Life and Death of Online Gaming Communities: A Look at Guilds in World of Warcraft. *CHI 2007 Proceedings.* http://www.nickyee.com/pubs/Ducheneaut,%20Yee,%20Nickell,%20Moore%20-%20Chi%202007.pdf (accessed March 5, 2014).

Durkheim, E. 1893. *The Division of Labor in Society*. (W. D. Halls, Trans.). New York:Free Press.

Earl, J. & Kimport, K. 2011. *Digitally Enabled Social Change: Activism in the Internet Age*. Cambridge: MIT Press.

Earl, J. & Schussman, A. 2008. Contesting Cultural Control: Youth Culture and Online Petitioning. In Bennett, W. L. (Ed.), *Civic Life Online: Learning How Digital Media Can Engage Youth*. Cambridge: MIT Press, 71–95.

Eckstein, H. 1975. Case Study and Theory in Political Science. In Greenstein, F. & Polsby, N. (Eds.), *Handbook of Political Science*, vol. 7. Reading, MA: Addison-Wesley, 119–164.

Eisenstadt, S. 1973. *Traditional Patrimonialism and Modern Neopatrominialism*. London: Sage.

Ekman, I. 2006. Police Raid Sparks Piracy Debate in Sweden. *New York Times*. June 4, http://www.nytimes.com/2006/06/04/technology/04iht-pirate05.1879427. html (accessed August 21, 2011).

Elgesem, D. 2002. What Is Special about the Ethical Issues in Online Research. *Ethics and Information Technology* 4(3), 195–203.

Elias, N. 2000. *The Civilizing Process: Sociogenetic and Psychogenetic Investigations*. Rev. ed. Hoboken, NJ: Blackwell.

Elola, J. 2010. EE UU ejecutó un plan para conseguir una ley antidescargas. *El País*. December 3, http://www.elpais.com/articulo/espana/EE/UU/ejecuto/ plan/conseguir/ley/antidescargas/elpepuesp/20101203elpepunac_52/Tes (accessed August 18, 2011).

Erlingsson, G. & Persson, M. 2011. The Swedish Pirate Party and the 2009 European Parliament Election: Protest or Issue Voting? *Politics 31*(3), 121–28.

Ernesto. 2006. BitTorrent: The "One Third of All Internet Traffic" Myth. *Torrent Freak*. September 17, http://torrentfreak.com/bittorrent-the-one-third-of-all-internet-traffic-myth/ (accessed August 25, 2011).

Ernesto. 2007a. Anti-piracy Organization Domain IFPI.com Now Owned by The Pirate Bay. *Torrent Freak*. October 12, http://torrentfreak.com/ ifpi-now-owned-by-the-piratebay-071012/ (accessed August 25, 2011).

Ernesto. 2007b. The Pirate Bay: Sponsored by Wal-Mart. *Torrent Freak*. January 11, http://torrentfreak.com/the-pirate-bay-sponsored-by-wall-mart/ (accessed August 25, 2011).

Ernesto. 2007c. The Pirate Bay About to Relaunch Suprnova.org. Torrent Freak. August 2, http://torrentfreak.com/the-pirate-bay-about-to-relaunch-suprnovaorg/ (accessed August 12, 2011).

Ernesto. 2010a. OiNK Admin Received Nearly 300k in Donations. *Torrent Freak*. January 7, http://torrentfreak.com/oink-admin-received-nearly-300k-in-donations-100107/ (accessed August 25, 2011).

Ernesto. 2010b. Pirate Bay's Founding Group "Piratbyrån" Disbands. *Torrent Freak*. June 23, http://torrentfreak.com/pirate-bays-founding-group-pira tbyran-disbands-100623/ (accessed September 8, 2012).

Ernesto. 2010c. WikiLeaks Cable Shows US Involvement in Swedish Anti-Piracy Efforts. *TorrentFreak*. December 8, http://torrentfreak.com/wikileaks-cable-shows-us-involvement-in-swedish-anti-piracy-efforts-101207/ (accessed August 15, 2011).

Ernesto. 2011. Pirate Party Enters Berlin Parliament after Historic Election Win. *Torrent Freak*. September 18, http://torrentfreak.com/pirate-party-enters-berlin-parliament-after-historical-election-win-110918/ (accessed July 10, 2013).

Ess, C. 2002. Introduction to Special Issue. *Ethics and Information Technology* 4(3), 177–88.

Ess, C. & the AoIR Ethics Working Committee. 2002. Ethical Decision-Making and Internet Research. Approved by AoIR, November 27, www.aoir.org/reports/ethics.pdf.

Ewick, P. & Silbey, S. 1998. *The Common Place of Law: Stories from Everyday Life*. Chicago: University of Chicago Press.

Ewing, A. 2006. Young Voters Back File Sharing. *The Local*. June 6, http://www.thelocal.se/article.php?ID=4014&date=20060608 (accessed January 15, 2010).

Falkvinge, R. 2012. Austrian Pirate Party Wins First Seat, Makes Frontpage News. *Falkvinge & Co. On Info Policy*. April 17, http://falkvinge.net/2012/04/17/austrian-pirate-party-wins-first-seat-makes-frontpage-news/ (accessed July 10, 2013).

Fiveash, K. 2010a. Pirate Bay Co-founder Hopes It Will Die. *The Register*. April 30, http://www.theregister.co.uk/2010/04/30/pirate_bay_brokep_interview/ (accessed August 25, 2011).

Fiveash, K. 2010b. Swedish Pirate Party Membership Numbers Sink. *The Register*. April 20, http://www.theregister.co.uk/2010/04/20/pirate_bay_trial_one_year_on/ (accessed August 15, 2011).

Foresman, C. 2010. Pirate Party membership plummets post Pirate Bay verdict. *Ars Technica*. April 20, http://arstechnica.com/tech-policy/2010/04/pirate-party-membership-plummets-post-pirate-bay-verdict/ (accessed August 13, 2011).

Freelon, D. 2011. Talking amongst Themselves. *Information, Communication and Society* 14(2), 198–218.

Freelon, D., Kriplean, T., Morgan, J., Bennett, W. L., & Bourning, A. 2011. Facilitating Encounters with Political Difference: Engaging Voters with the Living Voters Guide. Presented at the Journal of Information Technology & Politics Annual Conference, Seattle.

Froomkin, A. M. 2003. Habermas@discourse.net: Toward a Critical Theory of Cyberspace. *Harvard Law Review* 116(3), 751–873.

Garcia, A., Standlee, A., Bechkoff, J., & Cui, Y. 2009. Ethnographic Approaches to the Internet and Computer-Mediated Communication. *Journal of Contemporary Ethnography* 38(52), 52–84.

Geist, M. 2010. WikiLeaks Copyright Cables: Confirmations Not Revelations. Blog post. December 6, http://www.michaelgeist.ca/content/view/5504/125/ (accessed August 20, 2011).

George, A. & Bennett, A. 2005. *Case Studies and Theory Development in the Social Sciences.* Cambridge: MIT Press.

German Pirate Party. Mandate. http://wiki.piratenpartei.de/Mandate (accessed September 10, 2013).

Gerring, J. 2004. What Is a Case Study and What Is It Good For? *American Political Science Review 98*(2), 341–54.

Goldstein, J. 1993. *Ideas, Interests, and American Trade Policies.* Ithaca, NY: Cornell University Press.

Gong, A. 2011. An Automated Snowball Census of the Political Web. Presented at the Journal of Information Technology & Politics Annual Conference, Seattle.

Gray, K. L. 2012. Deviant Bodies, Stigmatized Identities, and Racist Acts: Examining the Experiences of African-American Gamers in Xbox Live. *New Review of Hypermedia and Multimedia 18*(4), 261–76.

Gray, M. L. 2009. *Out in the Country: Youth, Media, and Queer Visibility in Rural America.* New York: New York University Press.

Greenberg, A. 2013. Meet the Dread Pirate Roberts, the Man behind Booming Black Market Drug Website Silk Road. *Forbes Magazine.* September 2, http://www.forbes.com/sites/andygreenberg/2013/08/14/meet-the-dread-pirate-roberts-the-man-behind-booming-black-market-drug-website-silk-road/ (accessed September 10, 2013).

Gross, E. 2004. Adolescent Internet Use: What We Expect, What Teens Report. *Applied Developmental Psychology 25*, 633–49.

Grünen-GründerRuschewechseltzurPiratenpartei. 2009. *Bild.de.* August 27, http://www.bild.de/BILD/regional/frankfurt/dpa/2009/08/27/gruenengruender-rusche-wechselt-zur-piratenpartei.html (accessed January 15, 2010).

Habermas, J. 1989. *The Structural Transformation of the Public Sphere.* Cambridge: MIT Press.

Hackers Hit Swedish Police Site. 2006. *BBC News.* June 2, http://news.bbc.co.uk/2/hi/technology/5041848.stm (accessed August 15, 2011).

Hall, P. 1986. *Governing the Economy: The Politics of State Intervention in Britain and France.* New York: Oxford University Press.

Hall, P. & Taylor, R. 1996. Political Science and the Three New Institutionalisms. *Political Studies 40*(4), 936–57.

Herring, S. 1999. Rhetorical Dynamics of Gender Harrassment On-Line. *Information Society 15*, 151–67.

Herring, S. C., Job-Sluder, K., Scheckler, R., & Barab, S. 2002. Searching for Safety Online: Managing "Trolling" in a Feminist Forum. *Information Society 18*(5), 371–83.

Hine, C. (Ed.) 2005. *Virtual Methods*. New York: Bloomsbury Academic.

Holisky, A. 2010. A Look at GM Island and the Player Jail. *WoW Insider*. February 26, http://www.wow.com/2010/02/26/a-look-at-gm-island-and-the-player-jail/ (accessed August 25, 2011).

Howard, P. 2010. *The Digital Origins of Dictatorship and Democracy: Information Technology and Political Islam*. Oxford: Oxford University Press.

Howard, P. & Hussain, M. 2011. The Role of Digital Media. *Journal of Democracy*, 22(3), 35–48.

Huntington, S. 1968. *Political Order in Changing Societies*. New Haven: Yale University Press.

IGN.com. 2010. The Greatest Sites Known to Men. http://corp.ign.com/ (accessed August 2011).

IGN.com. 2011. IGN.com Rules (accessed February 2011).

Ingebritsen, C. 2006. *Scandinavia in World Politics*. Lanham, MD: Rowman & Littlefield.

Internet Hate Machine. *Know Your Meme*. http://knowyourmeme.com/memes/internet-hate-machine (accessed August 25, 2011).

Jardin, X. 2009. Interview with The Pirate Bay's cofounder Peter Sunde at the Open Video Conference. *YouTube.com*. June 7, http://www.mefeedia.com/watch/21558676 (accessed August 25, 2011).

Jones, B. 2007. The Pirate Bay in the Hot Seat. *Torrent Freak*. January 24, http://torrentfreak.com/the-pirate-bay-in-the-hot-seat/ (accessed August 15, 2011).

Jones, B. 2012. First Pirate Party Senator Elected in the Czech Republic. *Torrent Freak*. October 22, http://torrentfreak.com/first-pirate-party-senator-elected-in-the-czech-republic-121022/ (accessed July 10, 2013).

Jones, Q. & Rafaeli, S. 2000. Time to Split, Virtually: "Discourse Architecture" and "Community Building" Create Vibrant Virtual Publics. *Electronic Markets* 10(4), 214–23.

Jourde, C. 2009. The Ethnographic Sensibility: Overlooked Authoritarian Dynamics and Islamic Ambivalences in West Africa. In Schatz, E. (Ed.), *Political Ethnography: What Immersion Contributes to the Study of Power*. Chicago: University of Chicago Press, 201–16.

Julander, O. 2009. Professornvittnade—dåströmmadeblommorna in. *Expressen*. February 26, http://www.expressen.se/Nyheter/1.1480620/professorn-vittnade-da-strommade-blommorna-in (accessed August 15, 2010).

Kafal, Y. 1995. *Minds in Play: Computer Game Design as a Context for Children's Learning*. Hillsdale, NJ: Lawrence Erlbaum Associates.

Kedar, A. World of Whitecraft. *Dark Legacy Comics*. http://www.darklegacycomics.com/190.html (accessed August 20, 2011).

Kier, E. 1999. *Imagining War: French and British Military Doctrines between the Wars*. Princeton, NJ: Princeton University Press.

King, J. 2006. *Steal This Film*. The League of Noble Peers.

Kirkpatrick, D. 2010. *The Facebook Effect: The Inside Story of the Company That Is Connecting the World.* New York: Simon & Schuster.

Knappenberger, B. 2012. *We Are Legion: The Story of the Hacktivists.* Los Angeles, CA: Luminant Media.

Knuttila, L. 2011. User Unknown: 4chan, Anonymity, and Contingency. *First Monday 16*(10), http://firstmonday.org/htbin/cgiwrap/bin/ojs/index.php/fm/article/view/3665/3055.

Kraut, R., Olson, J., Banaji, M., Bruckman, A., Cohen, J., & Couper, M. 2004. Psychological Research Online: Report of Board of Scientific Affairs' Advisory Group on the Conduct of Research on the Internet. *American Psychologist,* February–March, 105–17.

Kudinoff, T. 2006. Nu vänder v och m i piratfrågan. *Expressen.* June 6, http://www.expressen.se/1.367477 (accessed January 15, 2010).

Legal Defense and Monitoring Group. 2001. Protesting: Legal Information. http://www.urban75.org/mayday02/legal.html (accessed August 15, 2011).

Legio9000Brittanica. 2008. /b/ritfags Confirmed for Brawl. *YouTube.com.* January 25, http://youtu.be/U98bio91ygM (accessed August 15, 2011).

Lester, T. 2011. Strong Support for WikiLeaks among Australians. *The Age.* January 6, http://www.theage.com.au/national/strong-support-for-wikileaks-among-australians-20110105-19g8z.html (accessed August 12, 2011).

LetterfromAnon. 2010. A Letter from Anonymous, 9th of December 2010. *YouTube.com.* December 9, http://youtu.be/WpwVfl3m32w (accessed July 17, 2011).

Levine, P. & Lopez, M. H. 2002. Youth Voter Turnout Has Declined, by Any Measure. *The Center for Information & Research on Civic Learning & Engagement Report.* http://www.civicyouth.org/research/products/Measuring_Youth_Voter_Turnout.pdf (accessed August 25, 2011).

Levy, S. 1984. *Hackers: Heroes of the Computer Revolution.* New York: Anchor Press/Doubleday.

Leyden, J. 2009. Music Industry Sites DDoSed after Pirate Bay Verdict. *The Register.* April 20, http://www.theregister.co.uk/2009/04/20/ddos_hacktivism_pirate_bay/ (accessed January 15, 2010).

Lijphart, A. 1971. Comparative Politics and the Comparative Method. *American Political Science Review 65*(3), 682–93.

Linkletter Knapp, I. 2000. Comment: The Software Piracy Battle in Latin America: Should the United States Pursue its Aggressive Bilateral Trade Policy Despite the Multilateral TRIPS Enforcement Framework? *University of Pennsylvania Journal of International Economic Law,* Spring, 21.

Long, C. 2010. In Costa Rica, CAFTA Hits a Snag. *Daily News.* January 15, http://www.ticotimes.net/dailyarchive/2010_01/0115101.cfm (accessed February 2010).

MacKinnon, R. 2012. *Consent of the Networked: The Worldwide Struggle for Internet Freedom.* New York, NY: Basic Books.

Markham, A. & Baym, N. 2008. *Internet Inquiry: Conversations about Method*. New York: Sage.

Martin, D. C. 2002. *A la recherché des OPNI*. Paris: Karthala.

Martinez, M. 2010. Poll: Almost half of Britons feel WikiLeaks sex charges are 'excuse.' *CNN International*. December 14, http://edition.cnn.com/2010/WORLD/europe/12/13/uk.poll.wikileaks/?hpt=Sbin (accessed August 13, 2011).

McCann, M. 1994. *Rights at Work: Pay Equity Reform and the Politics of Legal Mobilization*. Chicago: University of Chicago Press.

McKelvey, F. 2008. The Code and Politics of Drupal and The Pirate Bay: Alternative Horizons of Web 2.0. M.A. thesis, Ryerson University, Toronto.

McKelvey, F. 2012. *Internet Routing Algorithms, Transmission, and Time: Toward a Concept of Transmissive Control*. Doctoral dissertation, Ryerson University/York University, Toronto.

McMillan, R. 2008. Hackers Hit Scientology with Online Attack. *PC World*, http://www.pcworld.com/article/id,141839-c,hackers/article.html (accessed August 20, 2011).

Merriam, S. B. 2001. *Qualitative Research and Case Study Applications in Education*. San Francisco: Jossey-Bass.

Merry, S. E. 1988. Legal Pluralism. *Law & Society Review* 22(5), 869–96.

Meiritz, A. 2012. Suddenly out of Fashion: Support Wanes for Germany's Upstart Pirates. *Spiegel Online*. August 24, http://www.spiegel.de/international/germany/pirate-party-in-germany-loses-popularity-a mid-growing-problems-a-851864.html (accessed July 10, 2013).

Migdal, J. S. 1988. *Strong Societies and Weak States: State-Society Relations and State Capabilities in the Third World*. Princeton, NJ: Princeton University Press.

Migdal, J. S. 2001. *State in Society: Studying How States and Societies Transform and Constitute One Another*. Cambridge: Cambridge University Press.

Migdal, J. S. 2008. *Boundaries and Belonging: States and Societies in the Struggle to Shape Identities and Local Practices*. Cambridge: Cambridge University Press.

Moore, R. & McMullan, E. C. 2004. Perceptions of Peer-to-Peer File Sharing among University Students. *Journal of Criminal Justice and Popular Culture* 11(1), 1–19.

Morozov, E. 2010a. In Defense of DDoS: Denial-of-Service Attacks Are Just Another form of Civil Disobedience. *Slate*. December 13, http://www.slate.com/articles/technology/technology/2010/12/in_defense_of_ddos.html (accessed September 15, 2012).

Morozov, E. 2010b. *The Net Delusion: The Dark Side of Internet Freedom*. New York: Public Affairs.

Mortensen, T. E. 2006. WoW Is the New MUD: Social Gaming from Text to Video. *Games and Culture* 1(4), 397–413.

Munck, G. L. 2004. Tools for Qualitative Research. In Brady, H. & Collier, D. (Eds.), *Rethinking Social Inquiry: Diverse Tools, Shared Standards.* Oxford: Rowman & Littlefield, 105–22.

Munson, S. 2012. Exposure to Political Diversity Online. Doctoral dissertation, University of Michigan, Ann Arbor.

Munson, S. & Resnick, P. 2011. The Prevalence of Political Discourse in Non-political Blogs. Fifth International Association for the Advancement of Artificial Intelligence Conference on Weblogs and Social Media.

Nahon, K. & Hemsley, J. 2011. Political Blogs and Content: Homophily in the Guise of Cross-Linking. http://ekarine.org/publications/ (accessed August 15, 2011).

Neff, G. & Stark, D. 2004. Permanently Beta: Responsive Organization in the Internet Era. In Howard, P. & Jones, S. (Eds.), *Society Online: The Internet in Context.* Thousand Oaks, CA: Sage, 173–88.

Nielsen, L. B. 2004. *License to Harass: Law, Hierarchy, and Offensive Public Speech.* Princeton, NJ: Princeton University Press.

Nordenfur, A. 2012. Alex Arnold Becomes the First Elected Pirate Mayor! *Pirate Times.* September 24, http://piratetimes.net/alex-arnold-becomes-the-first-elected-pirate-mayor/ (accessed July 10, 2013).

Norton, Q. 2011a. Anonymous 101: Introduction to the Lulz. *Wired Magazine.* November 8, http://www.wired.com/threatlevel/2011/11/anonymous-101/ (accessed September 15, 2012).

Norton, Q. 2011b. Anonymous 101 Part Deux: Morals Triumph over Lulz. *Wired Magazine.* December 30, http://www.wired.com/threatlevel/2011/12/anonymous-101-part-deux/ (accessed September 15, 2012).

Norton, Q. 2012a. 2011: The Year Anonymous Took on Cops, Dictators, and Existential Dread. *Wired Magazine.* January 11, http://www.wired.com/threatlevel/2012/01/anonymous-dicators-existential-dread/ (accessed September 15, 2012).

Norton, Q. 2012b. How Anonymous Picks Targets, Launches Attacks, and Takes Powerful Organizations Down. *Wired Magazine.* July 3, http://www.wired.com/threatlevel/2012/07/ff_anonymous/all/ (accessed September 15, 2012).

O'Connor, A. 2010. Amazon Removes WikiLeaks from Servers. *New York Times.* December 2, http://www.nytimes.com/2010/12/02/world/02amazon.html (accessed July 17, 2011).

Olson, P. 2012. *We Are Anonymous: Inside the Hacker World of LulzSec, Anonymous, and the Global Cyber Insurgency.* New York: Little, Brown.

Orgad, S. 2005. From Online to Offline and Back: Moving from Online to Offline Relationships with Research Informants. In Hine, C. (Ed.), *Virtual Methods.* New York: Bloomsbury Academic, 51–65.

Pace, L. & Livingston, M. 2005. Protecting Human Subjects in Internet Research. *Electronic Journal of Business Ethics and Organizational Studies 10*(1), 35–41.

Papacharissi, Z. 2005. The Real/Virtual Dichotomy in Online Interaction: A Meta-analysis of Research on New Media Uses and Consequences. *Communication Yearbook 29*, 215–38.

Papacharissi, Z. 2010. *A Private Sphere: Democracy in a Digital Age*. Cambridge: Polity Press.

Parrish, K. 2010. Can World of Warcraft Boost Your Career? *BestofMedia.com*. http://www.tomshardware.com/news/world-of-warcraft-mmo,10926.html (accessed August 25, 2011).

Penny Arcade. 2004. The Internet Fuckwad Theory. http://www.penny-arcade. com/comic/2004/03/19 (accessed August 30, 2013).

Phillips, W. 2011. LOLing at Tragedy: Facebook Trolls, Memorial Pages, and Resistance to Grief Online. *First Monday 16*(12), http://firstmonday.org/ htbin/cgiwrap/bin/ojs/index.php/fm/article/view/3168/3115.

Phillips, W. 2012a. Cats and Penises All the Way Down: Performances of Gender and Sexuality on 4chan /b/. International Communication Association Annual Conference, http://billions-and-billions.com/2012/05/25/cats-and-penises-all-the-way-down-performances-of-gender-and-sexuality-on-4chanb-ica-2012-presentation/ (accessed September 10, 2012).

Phillips, W. 2012b. The House That Fox Built: Anonymous, Spectacle, and Cycles of Amplification. *Television & New Media*. Published online before print. August 30, http://tvn.sagepub.com/content/early/2012/08/27/1527476412 452799.abstract.

Phillips, W. 2013. A Brief History of Trolls. *Daily Dot*. http://www.dailydot.com/ opinion/phillips-brief-history-of-trolls/ (accessed July 15, 2013).

Pleming, S. 2009. U.S. State Department Speaks to Twitter over Iran. *Reuters*. June 16, http://www.reuters.com/article/2009/06/16/us-iran-election-twitter-usa-idUSWBT01137420090616 (accessed August 25, 2011).

Poole, C. 2011. Keynote Speech, SXSW. March 13. Accessed on YouTube. Audio available as of September 2012, http://schedule.sxsw.com/2011/events/ event_IAP000001.

Poole, C. 2012a. Beyond One Billion. 4chan.org News. August 6, http:// www.4chan.org/news?all#106 (accessed August 7, 2012).

Poole, C. 2012b. If Only It Grew on Trees. 4chan.org News. September 18, http:// www.4chan.org/news?all#109 (accessed September 19, 2012).

Poole, C. 2013. Full House 4chan.org News. September 18: https://www.4chan. org/news?all#114 (accessed September 20, 2013).

Postigo, H. 2012. *The Digital Rights Movement: The Role of Technology in Subverting Digital Copyright*. Cambridge: MIT Press.

Powell, W. & DiMaggio, P. (Eds.) 1991. *The New Institutionalism in Organizational Analysis*. Chicago: University of Chicago Press.

Preece, J. 2001. Sociability and Usability in Online Communities: Determining and Measuring Success. *Behaviour & Information Technology 20*(5), 347–56.

Preece, J. & Maloney-Krichmar D. 2003. Online Communities. In Jacko, J. & Sears, A. (Eds.), *The Human-Computer Interaction Handbook*. Mahwah, NJ: Lawrence Erlbaum, 596–620.

Przeworski, A. 2010. *Democracy and the Limits of Self-Government*. New York: Cambridge University Press.

Purcell, K. 2010. Teens and the Internet: The Future of Digital Diversity. Presented at the Fred Rogers Center's Fred Forward Conference. March 23, http://pewinternet.org/Presentations/2010/Mar/Fred-Forward.aspx (accessed August 15, 2011).

Putnam, R. 2000. *Bowling Alone: The Collapse and Revival of American Community*. New York: Simon & Schuster.

Ragin, C. 2004. Turning the Tables: How Case-Oriented Research Challenges Variable-Oriented Research. In Brady, H. & Collier, D. (Eds.), *Rethinking Social Inquiry: Diverse Tools, Shared Standards*. Oxford: Rowman & Littlefield, 123–38.

Reagle, J. 2013. Free as in Sexist? Free Culture and the Gender Gap. *First Monday* 18(1), http://firstmonday.org/ojs/index.php/fm/article/view/4291/3381.

Reeves, B., Malone, T. W., & O'Driscoll, T. 2008. Leadership's Online Labs. *Harvard Business Review*. http://hbr.org/2008/05/leaderships-online-labs/ar/1 (accessed August 25, 2011).

Reid, E. 1996. Informed Consent in the Study of Online Communities: A Reflection on the Effects of Computer-Mediated Social Research. *Information Society* 12(2), 169–74.

Rheingold, H. 1993. *The Virtual Community: Homesteading on the Electronic Frontier*. Reading, MA: Addison-Wesley.

RIAA. 2010a. For Students Doing Reports. http://www.riaa.com/faq.php (accessed January 10, 2010).

RIAA. 2010b. Who Music Theft Hurts. http://www.riaa.com/physicalpiracy.php (accessed January 10, 2010).

Roberts, Foehr, & Rideout. 2005. Generation M: Media in the Lives of 8–18 Year-Olds. A Kaiser Family Foundation Study.

Romig, R. 2012. The First Church of Pirate Bay. *New Yorker*. January 12, http://www.newyorker.com/online/blogs/culture/2012/01/the-missionary-church-of-kopimism.html (accessed August 9, 2013).

Rutter, J., & Smith, G. 2005. Ethnographic Presence in a Nebulous Setting. In Hine, C. (Ed.), *Virtual Methods*. New York: Bloomsbury Academic, 81–92.

Sabbagh, D. 2008. Average Teenager's iPod Has 800 Illegal Music Tracks. *Times Online*. June 16, http://technology.timesonline.co.uk/tol/news/tech_and_web/personal_tech/article4144585.ece (accessed January 10, 2010).

Salomon, M. & Soudoplatoff, S. (Eds.) 2010. Virtual Economies, Virtual Goods and Service Delivery in Virtual Worlds. *Journal of Virtual Worlds Research* 2(4), 4–16.

Samuel, A. 2004. Hacktivism and the Future of Political Participation. Doctoral dissertation, Harvard University.

Sanders, T. 2005. Researching the Online Sex Work Community. In Hine, C. (Ed.), *Virtual Methods*. New York: Bloomsbury Academic, 67–79.

Sartori, G. 1970. Concept Misformation in Comparative Politics. *American Political Science Review 64*(4), 1033–53.

Sauter, M. 2012. Guy Fawkes Mask-ology. *HiLobrow.* April 30, http://hilobrow. com/2012/04/30/mask/ (accessed August 12, 2013).

Sauter, M. 2013. Distributed Denial of Service Actions and the Challenge of Civil Disobedience on the Internet. M.A. thesis, MIT, Cambridge.

Schaap, F. 2002. *The Words That Took Us There: Ethnography in Virtual Reality.* Amsterdam: Askant Academic Publishers.

Schatz, E. (Ed.) 2009. *Political Ethnography: What Immersion Contributes to the Study of Power.* Chicago: University of Chicago Press.

Scheingold, S. 1974. *The Politics of Rights: Lawyers, Public Policy, and Political Change.* New Haven: Yale University Press.

Schiesel, S. 2008. Gary Gygax, Game Pioneer, Dies at 69. *New York Times.* March 5.

Schramm, M. 2009. Nielsen Says WoW Still Tops the List. *WoW Insider.* January 1, http://www.wow.com/tag/average-playtime/ (accessed August 15, 2011).

Seely Brown, J. & Thomas, D. 2006. You Play World of Warcraft? You're Hired! *Wired Magazine 14*(4), http://www.wired.com/wired/archive/14.04/learn. html (accessed August 25, 2011).

Simcoe, L. 2012. The Internet Is Serious Business: 4chan's /b/ Board and the Lulz as Alternative Political Discourse on the Internet. M.A. thesis, Ryerson University/York University, Toronto.

Simpson, B. 2005. Identity Manipulation in Cyberspace as a Leisure Option: Play and the Exploration of Self. *Information & Communications Technology Law 14*(2), 115–31.

Singel, R. 2008. Internet Mysteries: How Much File Sharing Traffic Travels the Net? *Threat Level: Wired Magazine.* May 5, http://www.wired.com/threat-level/2008/05/how-much-file-s/ (accessed January 15, 2010).

Singel, R. 2011. Twitter's Response to WikiLeaks Subpoena Should Be the Industry Standard. *Wired.* January 10, http://www.wired.com/threatlevel/2011/01/twitter/ (accessed July 10, 2013).

Solutions Research Group 2006. Movie File-Sharing Booming: Study. January 24, http://www.srgnet.com/pdf/Movie%20File-Sharing%20Booming%20Release%20Jan%2024%2007%20Final.pdf (accessed August 15, 2011).

Star, S. L. & Griesemer, J. R. 1989. Institutional Ecology, "Translations" and Boundary Objects: Amateurs and Professionals in Berkeley's Museum of Vertebrate Zoology, 1907–39. *Social Studies of Science 19*(3), 387–420.

Steadman, I. 2013. Iceland's Pirate Party Scrapes in at National Elections. *Wired.co.uk.* April 29, http://www.wired.co.uk/news/archive/2013-04-29/pirate-party-victory (accessed July 10, 2013).

Success at the German Parliamentary Elections. 2009. Pirate Party International News Release. October 1, http://www.pp-international.net/node/455 (accessed January 15, 2010).

Suler, J. 2004. The Online Disinhibition Effect. *CyberPsychology & Behavior* 7(3), 321–26.

Sunde, P. K. 2009a. Fail in NL. Blog. October 8, http://blog.brokep. com/2009/10/08/fail-in-nl/ (accessed January 15, 2010).

Sunde, P. K. 2009b. Follow-up in BREINfail. Blog. October 10, http://blog.brokep. com/2009/10/10/follow-up-in-breinfail/ (accessed January 15, 2010.

Svensson, M. & Larsson, S. 2009. Social Norms and Intellectual Property: Online Norms and European Legal Development. Lund University.

Svensson, M., Larsson, S. & de Kaminski, M. 2014. The Research Bay—Studying the Global File Sharing Community. In Gallagher, W. & Halbert, D. (Eds.), *Law and Society Perspectives on Intellectual Property Law*. http://www.thesurveybay.com/about.php.

Swedes Demonstrate in Support of Pirate Bay. 2009. *The Local*. April 19, http:// www.thelocal.se/18954/20090419/ (accessed August 25, 2011).

Swedish Pirate Party. 2009. Internet kokar, Piratpartiet har nu fler medlemmar an FP. April 17, http://www.piratpartiet.se/nyheter/internet_kokar_piratpartiet_har_nu_fler_medlemmar_an_fp (accessed August 15, 2011).

Tarrow, S. 1998. *Power in Movement: Social Movements and Contentious Politics*. Cambridge: Cambridge University Press.

Terdiman, D. 2006a. The Business Lessons of 'World of Warcraft. *CNET News*. March 12, http://news.cnet.com/8301-10784_3-6048770-7.html (accessed August 25, 2011).

Terdiman, D. 2006b. Online Game Warns Gay-Lesbian Guild. *CNET News*. January 31, http://news.cnet.com/2100-1043_3-6033112.html (accessed August 25, 2011).

Theocharis, Y. 2013. The Wealth of (Occupation) Networks? Communication Patterns and Information Distribution in a Twitter Protest Network. *Journal of Information Technology & Politics* 10(1), 35–56.

TheOddOne2. 2009. Pirate Bay Trial w/ Eng Subs (SVT1 Kulurmyheterna). *YouTube. com*. March 18, http://youtu.be/qAcpZ4Js1Vo (accessed August 15, 2011).

The Pirate Bay. 2007a. TPB Files Charges against Media Companies. Blog. June 21, http://thepiratebay.org/blog/86 (accessed August 20, 2011).

The Pirate Bay. 2007b. Time for Some Statistics. Blog. January 27, http://thepiratebay.org/blog/55 (accessed August 25, 2011).

The Pirate Bay. 2008a. Two Years and Still Going. Blog. May 5, http://thepiratebay. org/blog/111 (accessed August 20, 2011).

The Pirate Bay. 2009a. Peter Sunde Sues Mr. Kuk. Blog. July 23, http://thepiratebay.org/blog/168 (accessed August 20, 2011).

The Pirate Bay. 2009b. TPB Might Change Owner. Blog. June 6, http://thepiratebay.org/blog/164 (accessed August 25, 2011).

The Pirate Bay. 2009c. User Deletion. Blog. June 30, http://thepiratebay.org/ blog/165 (accessed August 25, 2011).

Thomas, J. 1996. A Debate about the Ethics of Fair Practices for Collecting Social Science Data in Cyberspace. *Information Society* 12(2), 107–18.

Torsson, P. & Fleischer, R. 2005. Piratbyrån's Speech. Speech Given at Choast Communication Congress. http://piratbyran.org/index.php?view=articles&id=107 (accessed January 10, 2010).

Tufekci, Z. & Wilson, C. 2012. Social Media and the Decision to Participate in Political Protest: Observations from Tahrir Square. *Journal of Communication* 62(2), 363–79.

United Nations Interregional Crime and Justice Research Institute. *Issues and Explanations: Terrorism and the Internet.* http://www.unicri.it/special_topics/cyber_threats/cyber_crime/explanations/terrorism/ (accessed September 25, 2013).

United States of Australia: How to Troll. *Encyclopedia Dramatica.* http://encyclopediadramatica.ch/Australia (accessed July 30, 2011).

US Lobbied NZ over Copyright Laws—WikiLeaks Cables. 2011. *TVNZ.* May 2, http://tvnz.co.nz/technology-news/us-lobbied-nz-over-copyright-laws-wikileaks-cables-4149178 (accessed August 18, 2011).

Wachowski, E. 2007. Blizzard Disbands Extreme Erotic Roleplaying Guild. *WoW Insider.* September 17, http://www.wow.com/2007/09/17/blizzard-disbands-extreme-erotic-roleplaying-guild/ (accessed August 25, 2011).

Waskul, D. 1996. Considering the Electronic Participant: Some Polemical Observations on the Ethics of On-Line Research. *Information Society* 12(2), 129–40.

WhyWeProtest. 2009a. Anonymous Celebrates One Year of Protests. February 9, http://www.whyweprotest.net/en/pressreleases/february-9th2-2009/ (accessed August 15, 2011).

WhyWeProtest. 2008. Several High Level Managers within the Church of Scientology Are Currently Working in the United Kingdom Illegally. August 8, http://www.whyweprotest.net/en/pressreleases/august-8th/ (accessed August 15, 2011).

WhyWeProtest. 2009b. Who Is Anonymous? *WhyWeProtest.net.* http://www.whyweprotest.net/en/ (accessed November 2, 2009).

Wilson, D. 2010. US Pressure Backfires as Site Blocking Is Voted Down in Spain. *ZeroPaid.* December 21, http://www.zeropaid.com/news/91654/us-pressure-backfires-as-site-blocking-is-voted-down-in-spain/ (accessed August 18, 2011).

Winner, L. 1980. Do Artifacts Have Politics? *Daedalus* 109, 121–36.

Wisel, K., Hamman, B., Kjerstin, T. 2006. Moderation, Response Rate, and Message Interactivity: Features of Online Communities and Their Effects on Intent to Participate. *Journal of Computer Mediated Communication* 12(1), 24–41.

Wojcieszak, M. & Mutz, D. 2009. Online Groups and Political Discourse: Do Online Discussion Spaces Facilitate Exposure to Political Disagreement? *Journal of Communication* 59(1), 40–56.

Woodcock, B. MMOG Active Subscriptions, 200,000+. *MMOGCHART.com.* http://www.mmogchart.com/Chart1.html (accessed August 25, 2011).

xenutv1. 2008. Scientology: Wise Beard Man Responds to Anonymous—Part 1. *YouTube.com.* January 28, http://youtu.be/3A3WnmcRbTQ (accessed August 15, 2011).

Yee, N. 2003. The Demographics of Groups and Group Leadership. *The Daedalus Project.* September 3, http://www.nickyee.com/daedalus/archives/000553.php (accessed August 25, 2011).

Yee, N. 2005a. Motivations: The Bigger Picture. *The Daedalus Project.* March 13, http://www.nickyee.com/daedalus/archives/001299.php (accessed August 25, 2011).

Yee, N. 2005b. Playing with Someone. *The Daedalus Project.* October 17, http://www.nickyee.com/daedalus/archives/001468.php (accessed August 25, 2011).

Yee, N. 2005c. WoW Basic Demographics. *The Daedalus Project.* July 28, http://www.nickyee.com/daedalus/archives/001365.php (accessed August 25, 2011).

Yee, N. 2005d. Who Introduced You to the Game. *The Daedalus Project.* May 10, http://www.nickyee.com/daedalus/archives/001335.php (accessed August 25, 2011).

Yee, N. 2007a. Making Friends. *The Daedalus Project.* October 14, http://www.nickyee.com/daedalus/archives/001586.php (accessed August 25, 2011).

Yee, N. 2007b. Status Reversal. *The Daedalus Project.* October 15, http://www.nickyee.com/daedalus/archives/001585.php (accessed August 25, 2011).

Yee, N. 2009. Content Types. *The Daedalus Project.* March 1, http://www.nickyee.com/daedalus/archives/001645.php (accessed August 25, 2011).

Zetter, K. 2011. WikiLeaks Donations Topped $1.9 million in 2010. *Wired Magazine: Threat Level.* April 26, http://www.wired.com/threatlevel/2011/04/wau-holland-report/ (accessed August 15, 2011).

Zhuo, J. 2010. Where Anonymity Breeds Contempt. *New York Times.* November 29, http://www.nytimes.com/2010/11/30/opinion/30zhuo.html.

Zuckerman, E. 2007. The Connection between Cute Cats and Web Censorship. Blog: . . . My Heart's in Accra. July 16, http://www.ethanzuckerman.com/blog/2007/07/16/the-connection-between-cute-cats-and-web-censorship/.

Zuckerman, E. 2008. The Cute Cat Theory Talk at ETech. Blog: . . . My Heart's in Accra. March 8, http://www.ethanzuckerman.com/blog/2008/03/08/the-cute-cat-theory-talk-at-etech/.

Index